Positively Beam...ing

A collection of newspaper columns

By Jim Beam

Reprinted with permission
of the *American Press*
P.O. Box 2893
Lake Charles, La. 70602

Published 2003

Cover design by Bobbijo Vittorio
American Press

Book editing by Donna Price
American Press

For information contact
Jim Beam
American Press
337-494-4025

ISBN 0-9743566-0-3

Dedication

To the loving family that inspired so much of my work, the people I have met along life's way who left a lasting impression and the Thomas B. Shearman Sr. family that gave me the opportunity and the freedom to write about those things that I felt are important in our lives.

Contents

Chapter 1
One Man's Family

New twist to old enjoyment   3
Dad is waiting for next season   5
When things go wrong   8
Dad remembers the 21 years   10
It's a time for reflection   13
You can get lost in shuffle   16
Grandpa is in love again   19
It was a day she won't forget   22
Grandpa teaches shoe tying   25
Someone else did the talking   28
American families alive, well   31
This Father's Day was special   34
Andrew newest member of clan   37
Mothers give lives meaning   40
Most people called him Charlie   43
We need someone to love us   46
Thank God for grandchildren   49
Trucker challenges his uncle   52
Family ties enrich our lives   55
Jessica celebrates milestone   58
Things we cherish never change   61

Chapter 2
You Don't Forget Them

They're just outside the door   67
Will Rogers' wit is ageless   69
Apathy has consequences   71
Flooding had its good sides   74
Lunchtime won't be same   77
Dumars experience says it all   80
New mayor sees bright future   84
Grizzard covering a new beat   87
Smitty at home in his yard   90
Brinkley doesn't pull punches   93
Rex saw lighter side of news   97
Brooms were his calling card   101
Don't look for Eddie behind bar   105
Ernie Pyle was our man at front   108
GI Joe earns 20th century title   111
Mr. Glenn patriarch at John's   114
Stelly leaving legacy   117

Chapter 3
A Personal Journey

Going after the big ones   123
Where did wallet go?   125
When spirit moves you, go   127
"Experts" hold up progress   129
Take it one day at time   131
We are what we come from   134
Guess who came to lunch   137
Memories should be cherished   140

It began with late paper   144
How are you cutting grass?   147
Jim Beams party with Booker   150
Is my body wearing out?   153
Is it aging or changing times?   156
New year is end, beginning   159
I'm a legitimate senior citizen   162
Retirement isn't end of work   165
Case of mistaken identity   168
Accident becomes personal thing   171
You get attached after 31 years   174
Coffee, friends great blend   177

Chapter 4
Those Who Govern

Treen must take charge   183
Ex-King Edwin holds court   186
Louisiana politics fascinating   189
Huey Long stops in Lafayette   193
Assassination still in news   197
Roemer bowed out with class   201
Huey has 100th birthday   205
Take another look at '91 race   208
Politics are our bread, butter   212
Foster turning state around   215
Friends remember Uncle Earl   218
Johnson impeached first   221
Impeachment isn't fun, games   224
"Big John" learned from pros   227
Carl Weiss picks up support   230
Ron survives political process   233
Conviction scars Edwards   236
EWE has trouble with truth   239

Chapter 5
Memories of Another Time

JFK anniversary still painful	245
Rejoice with East Germans	248
D-Day only part of story	251
It was proud day for Press	254
Old Ironsides in LC in '32	257
First story said Titanic was OK	260
What would we have done?	263
1952 election changed parish	266
What are lessons of Sept. 11?	269
City hit by two major storms	272

Chapter 6
Pets are People, Too

Move over, dad, Levi's coming	279
It's not really man's world	281
It shouldn't happen to dog	284
Our dogs are getting older	287
Levi said he wasn't ready	290
Levi leaves fond memories	293
Lucy everyone's best friend	296

Chapter 7
Rounding Up the Rest

Vending machines are boss   301
Ritz comes tumbling down   303
Only the memories remain   305
"Rose by any other name"   308
Speaking of best-laid plans   311
Sometimes deck is stacked   314
What happened to comics?   317
Who said country isn't cool?   320
It's an "Achy Breaky" summer   323
Playoff game was rerun of '51   326
Muller's gone, not forgotten   330
McNeese enriches many lives   333
Lake Charles needs links to past   336
5,500 left their imprint   339
Familiar item back on menu   342
Astrodome was our place   345
Saints keep dream season alive   348

Introduction

Each of us has an opportunity on occasion to talk about something that touched our lives at some time in the past. Maybe the experience happened yesterday or decades ago. Whatever the case, it left an impression that we want to share with others.

I have been sharing my personal and professional experiences and political opinions with newspaper readers for nearly 30 years through a personal column I write for the American Press of Lake Charles. Its early title was "People and Politics," but the columns have covered a multitude of topics through the years.

At the urging of friends and newspaper colleagues, I have chosen more than 100 of those personal columns dating back to 1966 and published them in this book.

Members of my family were the inspiration for the columns in the first chapter, and those have elicited the most favorable comments from readers. That isn't surprising since so many people know what it's like to rear and love children and then relive those experiences through our grandchildren.

I have come across a number of people in my line of work that left a lasting impression, and they are the basis for the chapter titled, "You Don't Forget Them." In addition to local folks, there are also people of national stature like writer Lewis Grizzard, newsman David Brinkley, war correspondent Ernie Pyle and humorist Will Rogers who will always be remembered.

Some of my personal experiences are recounted in the third chapter which contains columns about aging, mowing the lawn, seeing my double and trying to dance with a movie star. Anyone who has also retired will identify with that experience, and see what it's like to be "lonely in the bleachers."

A book of this kind wouldn't be complete without a chapter about some of the colorful politicians like Huey and Earl Long who helped create a political climate in Louisiana that is unique and colorful. I have written numerous columns about former Gov. Edwin W. Edwards, and some of them are included here. Edwards, who is currently serving a prison term for earlier misdeeds, was a major political player while in and out of office.

Memorable national and international events like D-Day, the assassination of John F. Kennedy and a presidential visit often had a local flavor, and they are the subjects of a chapter titled, "Memories of Another Time." You will also see what it was like when 121 persons named Jim Beam showed up at a reunion where the famous Kentucky whiskey is distilled.

Pets play important roles in our lives, and I have lived with more than my fair share of man's best friends. Families with pets will find our experiences much like theirs, and they will also know what it is like when we lose a pet. Those experiences are the basis for Chapter 6.

Finally, there are those columns that didn't seem to fit anywhere else, but they also tell a lot about people and events and are worth reading again. Like the time our newspaper left out the comics page, or a familiar landmark closed its doors or that time when over 5,000 citizens left their imprint on the community.

I hope you enjoy these columns. They are a small part of the total collection that numbers in the hundreds, but they touch on many important aspects of the personal and political life in our community, state and nation. You don't have a plot to worry about, and there is no reason to rush through the book. Pick your subjects and read at your leisure.

Jim Beam

Foreword

"So what's Jim Beam really like?"

You hear that question a lot when you work for the American Press. This book offers some of the answers.

For decades, Jim Beam has talked in the newspaper about his life, his family, his city and his state. His columns have made him the most asked-about person ever affiliated with the American Press newsroom.

For the record: Jim Beam is a husband, father and newsman. He keeps an ear carefully tuned to his family and his readership. He savages politicians but brags on his grandchildren. He shops with careful thrift but makes fun of himself in Gridiron shows. He rails against foul play in government but faithfully endures the Saints each season.

Better known about him, however, is that his columns for the American Press are a personal and public lightning rod.

Jim Beam writes columns in ways where it's hard not to have an opinion about them. His columns evoke and provoke. He likes it that way.

His simple, conversational style prompts readers to continue the conversation. People who've never met him feel they know him, and they want to put in their two cents. They express those thoughts in letters to the newspaper and in impromptu chats at the supermarket. They swear by, and swear at, what Jim Beam has to say. Perhaps you're one of those people.

All of those columns won't fit in a single book. What follows is a sampling of them. Just as readers have long expressed their own opinions about Jim Beam columns, colleagues offered unsolicited advice on which pieces he needed to put in this book. He missed a few good ones, but that's just one man's opinion.

Read these columns collectively, and you'll relive the past few decades in Southwest Louisiana. You'll also learn about him, and what he's like — because in the end, the best words about Jim Beam are his own.

When you're done reading, be sure to tell him exactly what you think.

Brett Downer
Editor
American Press
May 9, 2003

Chapter 1

One Man's Family

New twist to old enjoyment

It's really quite an experience to see the "greatest show," but when you see it in what might be the "greatest place on earth" that's really livin'.

The show I'm speaking of is the Ringling Bros. and Barnum and Bailey Circus. The place is the Astrodome in Houston, Texas.

A colleague explained it best as he sat in one of the Dome's cushioned seats, sipping a refresher among the cool breezes:

"This is the American way."

If you've ever taken six hands full of youngsters to the Big Top or any other circus locale you'll understand his statement. I've never taken that many, but my youngest is just as active as any dozen toddlers.

We did have a large group when we invaded Houston Thursday night. There were six adults and eight children in our party and that's plenty when you've got to hustle your way through a city like Houston on foot or in a car.

Oh, yes – Chester the Chimp was along. He's my daughter's talking monkey she got for Christmas. It's the string-pulling type pet you don't have to feed bananas. "I brought Chester with us so he could see his relatives," she said.

It took some time to get our 14 tickets and find our seats, but once that hurdle was crossed we sat back in royal splendor, taking in all the wonderful sights and sounds of the circus in the air-conditioned palace.

The clowns were there to spice things for the kiddies and the colorful costumes of the performers were accented against the backdrop of the beautiful Astrodome.

Circuses haven't changed a great deal. In addition to the clowns, they still have performing monkeys, horses, bears, tigers, elephants and other assorted members of the animal family. A new innovation was a bird act that delighted the fancies of the fans.

Everyone will be happy to know they still have the familiar three rings. The only difference is that in the Dome the rings are in a circle with the center ring near home plate.

I had a difficult time watching the trained animal acts. My youngest was preoccupied with the idea of popcorn. I had him pretty well subdued until some loud-mouthed vendor starting singing out his wares.

Once I gave in, I knew we were sunk. That first box of popcorn led to cold drinks and other assorted goodies. I began to wonder if perhaps that little rascal of mine had come all the way to Houston just to munch on popcorn and soda pop.

When I was about to throw up my hands in defeat, on came the aerialists. Say what they will, but the flying artists still provide the circus with thrills and fill the air with magical wonder.

The couple on the swinging poles over 280 feet in the air went through their paces with such daring and deliberation my son almost forgot he clutched a crumpled bag of popcorn. His mouth was wide open as he took in the thrills. And when the motorcyclist rode out on a wire even higher with two beauties on a frame below his cycle, we all sat in stunned delight.

Many other acts were truly entertaining. And it was all climaxed with the circus on parade and the human cannonball, which was fired across the turf to a waiting net.

Yes, a great circus in a great place is really something.

One misses the sideshows, however. The fat lady, the strong man, the fire-eater and the dancing beauties from Tahiti just seem to add that little extra when one thinks of the circus.

And, believe it or not, you don't really feel at home without that certain smell you get amid the straw floor under the heat of the Big Top.

June 19, 1966

Dad is waiting for next season

Take the word of a novice; kid baseball is everything you've always heard it was and more.

My son played for the first time this year, starting in the Pee Wee League.

Based on my athletic abilities, the fact that he even made the team was nothing short of miraculous.

Baseball was never my game. In fact, neither was football, basketball, tennis, golf or any other sport. After failing miserably on the athletic field, I finally found my place — as a cheerleader.

I learned early that kid baseball requires three essentials — money, folding chairs and stamina.

Money requests dribble in all season. They cover such items as uniforms, photographs, trophies, yearbooks and parties. Whoever planned these things had an eye for business. The amounts requested are never too large at one time so you keep on giving and giving.

Pee Wee players haven't reached the big time, so you have to bring your own chair. There are no bleachers until you graduate to a bigger league, and you'll always have use for those aluminum, plastic strip contraptions.

Your kid could probably manage to play without money or chairs, but stamina is something parents just have to have. It's the only thing that will get you through the whole season.

The season started out rather calmly, I thought. Parents showed some enthusiasm, but it didn't get out of hand. It was only noticed when a father would tell his son to play a little to the left seconds after the coach told him to move to the right.

Perhaps the parents in my group never got out of hand because we never came close to the race for the pennant. We weren't even close to a winning season.

However, as the season wore on I began to understand those stories I've read about kid baseball.

The first big rhubarb came when one of the parents in my group volunteered to umpire. We were playing a No. 1 team, and one of our parents touched a ball on the sidelines as it rolled out of the field of play.

Immediately, the brave ump waved in a member of our team, ruling he was entitled to a base on the interference. The opposition was ahead 7-0, and you'd have thought they wouldn't mind giving us one measly run.

The opposition mothers let out a howl. Their coach pulled out the rulebook and badgering continued back and forth. Finally the umpire said he didn't care what the rulebook said the run was scored.

I noticed after that he was never hanging around close to where he could be drafted to umpire. I soon learned it was safer to battle the Viet Cong in the jungles than to umpire kid baseball. You'll never catch me behind the plate — I love life too much.

Tension mounted with each passing game. My wife gradually went to pieces.

Each time my son got up to bat she couldn't bear to look. It was particularly bad when he was the third out in the last inning.

I soon knew the game had gotten the best of her when I heard her say she hoped the pitcher would hit our son so he could get on base. "I don't want him to get hit too hard," she lovingly added.

My calm nature made it possible for me to make it to the next to the last game before I blew my top. And even then, I waited until I got home to let off steam.

The coach asked my youngster, who, in my opinion, did an outstanding job as catcher, if he was tired of playing after the third inning. He said he was and was replaced. The substitute kid threw wild and two runs scored.

"I knew it," I mulled to myself. He should never have taken my son out. But when I learned he volunteered to be relieved, I didn't know whom to get mad at.

Actually, the season was a great experience, all things considered. I saw 8- and 9-year-olds who didn't know the first thing about baseball become fairly proficient at the game. If you know anything about youngsters that age, you know it takes managers and coaches with a barrel of patience just to keep track of 15 wild tykes.

Seeing your flesh and blood taking part in such activities also arouses new interest in the game. As someone said, you start driving around looking for a game in progress.

Pee Wee players get to see action in every game. I have heard of youngsters in more advanced leagues who train all season and never play. That's when kid baseball ceases to be fun for spectator and player alike.

It's not that way in Pee Wee, and I can hardly wait for next season to see those little rascals in action, excitable mothers and all.

July 25, 1971

When things go wrong

"Look, I don't want to hear about anything else around here that is broken or that doesn't work."

That's the law I laid down Thursday evening when my son informed me a new side view mirror on our foreign import was rattling.

His remarks happened to come at a time when a long string of little things going wrong were about to drive me up a wall.

I purchased a new mirror that afternoon for almost $12. The mounting screw broke off as I was tightening the nut. Somehow, the mirror was still firmly mounted, but it vibrated when the car was running.

"Don't tell me about it," I told him. "Besides, it's not rattling, it's vibrating."

Sunday, a week ago, I stayed home from church to flush out a drain line from the lavatory in the bathroom. It was my second attempt at cleaning the line. It's draining, but with my luck I expect it to get sluggish any day now.

The week before I spent $21 to get the heating and air-conditioning fan in the attic to stop running.

It cost $25 to repair a hole in the sheet rock in the ceiling that same week. A Good Samaritan's foot slipped through the ceiling when he was trying to find out why my air conditioning wasn't working.

Remember the trunk in my big car that was leaking before vacation time last summer? It's still at it, and I look for the bottom of the car to fall out eventually. The heater doesn't warm up in the mornings until I get to work.

A brick in the front wall of the house has been missing for about two years, and my wife won't let me forget it.

My Thanksgiving vacation was spent getting some of the minor problems corrected, but each time I fix something two more things go haywire.

The easiest solution is to call in experts who know what they are doing, but just try to get a craftsman to handle a small job when big-money projects can be found everywhere.

Back to last Thursday. I guess it was one of those bad days.

After laying down the law about everyone keeping malfunctions to themselves, I noticed the new sink faucet was water-spotted. I had installed it during my vacation.

"I wish people would learn to wipe off this faucet so it will look nice a little longer," I told the family gathering.

My daughter wasn't about to let that remark get by.

"It's no fun living here," she said. "We have to wipe off the faucet, cut off the lights, keep the bathroom door closed, pick up our things, keep the newspaper in order, make sure everything in the refrigerator is in the right place and be sure we don't block the driveway."

I gave up and moved into the living room to watch television.

Cold weather had aroused my allergies, which, in turn, have blocked up my ear canals, making it difficult to hear. So I turned up the volume.

My son went to bed at 10, and minutes later he was mumbling something.

I got up from a comfortable position to go into his room to find out what he was muttering about. He's good at going to bed and then trying to carry on a conversation with his door closed.

"Would you mind turning down the volume?" he asked.

That was the crowning blow. I felt like a man without a country.

I gave some thought to leaving home, but I was already in my pajamas and didn't feel like getting dressed.

Dec. 11, 1977

Dad remembers the 21 years

It was November 1957 when I loaded up all my Army collections after two years' active duty, stashed my two-week-old daughter in her bassinet in the back seat of our car and left Columbus, Ga., for home.

Now, over 21 years later, her bedroom is empty, daddy's lonely and the groom has whisked her off to places unknown.

That's about the size of things this morning following my daughter's wedding last night, which culminated the most intensive planning campaign since the invasion of Normandy during World War II.

People were asking me two weeks before the wedding if I was getting nervous. There had been so much activity around the house that I hadn't really given the wedding much serious thought.

Then last Sunday night as I lay awake in a restless mood, I thought about that time we loaded up the car in Columbus and reflected on how much had transpired from that time until Saturday night. Suddenly, daddy felt his first real pangs of loneliness.

Mothers and fathers everywhere know the feeling. Those demanding early years, the little friends — some of them now grown and gone and the others who still keep in touch — the first days of school, that first date and the first big dance, the serious and not-so-serious courtships, high school graduation and the college years.

There were crises all along the way, but somehow each new problem found a solution.

I suppose every father thinks about those things when his little girl is leaving home. And you remember the times you were out of town and mother called and said, "Jamie said she wished you were here because you'd know what to do."

That's the kind of pride that's priceless.

Marriage, of course, was a whole new ball game. The rest were preliminaries. This was the real thing.

You hope he's the right guy, but there's not a lot you can do if he isn't. When you think about some of those early courtships, you know this fellow has a lot of pluses going for him.

He doesn't park his car in the driveway behind yours. And although he's been living away from home and gotten a little sloppy, you can see there is some class and a wholesome upbringing behind that sometimes-rough exterior.

He's like most fellows his age. There isn't much they think they don't know and they don't hesitate to try to impress you about how smart they are. You know he's really green about much of life, but understand that only time will cure his overconfidence.

He's got a sixth sense about knowing when supper's ready. In fact, sometimes I wonder if I agreed to the marriage thinking it was the only way to get that guy away from the dining room table.

I suppose the real clincher, though, was the kindness and love he shows for daddy's little girl. She's a long way from being an angel and can be awfully trying at times. And he's shown a lot more patience than dad has in similar circumstances.

He never formally asked my permission, but I guess that's old-fashioned these days. Apparently he figured it was OK since I didn't lodge any official protest.

When I saw the magnitude of the event, we canceled plans to remodel the bathroom. No vacation, either. When you have only one daughter, I suppose you can afford to make a few sacrifices.

With the help of friends and the groom's family, the massive undertaking went off without a hitch.

I wasn't too involved with the material pursuits, except for trying on a tuxedo and driving a nail in the wall to hang up the dress.

Mostly, I guess you could say I was the field general. When a problem proved insurmountable, ole dad came up with the right answers.

I also offered a lot of fatherly advice along the way that money can't buy. And I found out I couldn't give a lot of it away.

Friends and acquaintances quickly dispelled any misgivings I had about losing my daughter.

"Think of it as getting another closet," said a co-worker.

And there was the old saw about "not losing a daughter, but gaining a son."

Finally, someone at work told me, to my dismay, that any visions I had of that guy not ever showing up for a meal was wishing thinking.

Oh, well, you win some and you lose some.

Aug. 12, 1979

It's a time for reflection

Talk about a terrible way to begin a new year. My yardman is moving to Lafayette.

Oh, I know what most folks will say: "That's no big deal. Just get another yardman. There are plenty of them around."

That may be true, but the one I have is mighty special. He's been with us for 22 years now.

No, he hasn't been cutting grass and trimming hedges, bushes and sidewalks for 22 years. In fact, in the early years he cost us more than he saved in home chores. But he eventually carried his weight and made his presence felt.

In case you haven't guessed by now, my son the graduate is leaving his homeport for greener pastures in the working world. He's beginning Chapter 2 in life's continuing story.

What's it like to leave home at such a tender young age?

If I remember correctly, it's frightening as hell. I was 22 and married when I left home for the first time. Even so, I was still green as a gourd.

With a college degree in one hand and an Army commission in the other, my wife and I hit the roadways nearly 30 years ago for a military post in Oklahoma.

13

Everything we owned was stashed in the back seat of my dashing, new, two-tone green, 1955 Ford. Seems to me Uncle Sam was paying second lieutenants in the neighborhood of $3,600 yearly in those days, and that included all those great military benefits.

We spent three tough months in those cold Oklahoma hills around Lawton, trying desperately in artillery school to hold on to that lieutenant's commission and avoid the military draft.

An electric blanket was our one great luxury in those lean months. It was the only way to survive the bone-chilling Oklahoma winter.

Then it was on to the barren reaches of Ft. Benning, Ga., a place I had earlier visited for summer camp and which I had hoped never to see again. But it wasn't meant to be. That's where I finished my two-year hitch 18 months later.

Air conditioning was coming into its own, but it was way out of our financial reach. We spent many an evening in those 25-cent, on-post movie theaters to cool down in the summer. Eventually we managed to buy a house full of furniture for $400 and paid it off at about $30 a month. And we added two more luxuries to our electric blanket — a TV set and a floor fan.

My daughter was thoughtful enough to be born two weeks before I completed active duty, giving us a monetary head start when we returned to the Lake Charles area looking for work. Teachers made less than second lieutenants in those days, but living with my in-laws in Sulphur made survival possible.

Our own home became a reality in 1958, but those $86 monthly notes took a big bite out of every paycheck. A part-time sports job at the newspaper helped us make ends meet.

Newspaper work was appealing, so the job became a full-time thing. Mac said the American Press would pay me $110 a week, which he said was more than they had ever paid a starting reporter. That might not sound like much now, but in those days I couldn't have felt prouder of the achievement.

The rest is history, of course, and I thank my lucky stars that I took the right turn in the road. Everything came up roses, and life has been so much better than I could have ever imagined.

I suppose it's only natural for those memories of yesteryear to surface when the last of your offspring leaves the safe confines of home.

Will he have as tough a time as you did in those formative years? Will he make it on his own away from home?

You tell yourself everything will work out. After all, you had the same empty feeling in the pit of your stomach when the only daughter in your life left home with a fellow you hardly knew.

Things have gone well for both of them. You realize your daughter is making a valuable contribution to society teaching first-graders. Your son-in-law, who never quits trying to eat you out of house and home, turned out to be a decent chap after all. And he, too, has a good job.

Even so, there are still some nagging concerns.

My wife and I are like most parents, I suppose. We raise our children as best we know how, sometimes wondering whether we might have leaned too heavily on Dr. Spock when we didn't know where else to turn.

We survived despite the odds, perhaps because we trusted the values we learned as youngsters. Things like truth, honesty, hard work and fair play never go out of style.

You know your own children are better off materially speaking, but you still wonder whether you successfully passed along those values that you can't measure in dollars and cents.

Only time can answer that question, of course. And I suppose we wouldn't be caring parents if we weren't worried about the future of those we brought into this world.

Meanwhile, we'll keep our fingers crossed and pray a lot. And while we're waiting for the answers, it is fitting near the beginning of this new year to wish you and yours and my yardman all the best in 1985.

Dec. 30, 1984

You can get lost in shuffle

Outside of living that long, reaching the age of 55 holds little significance for most folks. And when that birthday comes right after your only daughter has your first grandchild and about the time your only son gets married, you're lucky if anyone even remembers your birthday.

They did, but there wasn't much time for celebrating. Babies don't stand on ceremony, and you can't put weddings on hold.

That's OK, though, because Grandpa has had plenty to crow about in his "double-nickel year."

Veteran grandfathers said their first time was great, and they weren't kidding. But make no mistake about it; being a grandparent is no soft touch. Anytime you're the one and only in the babysitting chain of command, you soon remember what it means to be "too pooped to grandpop."

Conditions did settle into a routine eventually, and it was time to turn to matrimonial pursuits.

Marrying off a son calls for no great strategy on the part of his parents, but they do have responsibilities. And when the groom lives in New Orleans, his fiancée in Lafayette and his parents in Lake Charles, it can get a wee bit complicated.

Planning a rehearsal dinner, for example, might seem trivial to the uninitiated, but don't believe it.

For starters, it's out of town, so where do you have it? Once that's decided, will it be sit-down or buffet and what will you serve? A buffet wins out and that opens up the guest list. So who gets the extra invitations? And when the list, because of long distance and some-times-confused communications, mushrooms past 40, who gets cut?

Those are just some of the gut issues that occupy a month of detailed planning, but you get it done and everyone has a grand old time.

Then comes the big day – a Saturday. Since there was a wedding rehearsal before that Friday night dinner, everything should be perfect for the main event, right?

Well, not quite. The officiating priest wasn't at the rehearsal the night before. But more important, this is no ordinary Saturday afternoon for a Catholic man of the cloth. This is the same day Notre Dame plays Miami with a national title on the line. And the kickoff is scheduled for about 2:25 p.m.

That explains why the priest whisks the groom and his party to the altar at 2 sharp, even before the mothers of the bride and groom have a chance to be seated. He wastes no words once they get there, either. One song is cut, the groom doesn't get to kiss the bride at the altar and the newlyweds get halfway out the church before the organist strikes up the finale. Seconds later, the priest vanishes.

Everything worked out OK, though. Since they had not attended the rehearsal, most of the guests weren't aware of any minor glitches in the beautiful ceremony. And although it was brief, the knot is tied just as tight.

The priest had a great day, too. Notre dame upset Miami, 31-30.

After two major happenings in a lifetime are squeezed into a three-month span, it seems appropriate to reflect on the years and events that have come and gone.

One thing is immediate and definite. Your former Little Leaguer is a full-fledged adult now, and someone else is playing a major role in his life. She's a lovely young lady from a large and friendly family, which gives you new in-law connections in Lafayette.

It isn't the only change you've noticed. The toddler who grew up on a steady diet of Dallas Cowboy football from the day he was born has been converted to a New Orleans Saints fan. However, considering the year Dallas is having and his new home base, it wasn't unexpected.

That youngster and I have covered a lot of miles together since 1962, and it's been a pleasure trip all the way.

Friends are a major influence on anyone's life, and he's had more than his fair share. You knew he was headed in the right direction because he was always traveling in good company.

His friends, by the way, are typical of the kind of young people who can work wonders for this state if given half a chance. And that's why Louisiana needs to embrace tax reform and other progressive programs that can open up that opportunity and keep some of these talents at home.

While reflecting on the past you also wonder how, in an age of one-parent families and broken homes, everything managed to somehow fall into place.

Dr. Spock was an invaluable source of knowledge in those formative years, but even his wisdom isn't sufficient to overcome all the hurdles.

Perhaps personal experiences while growing up in post-Depression years helped formulate those unwritten rules that are passed along to the next generation. Things like taking responsibility for personal actions, respecting parents and elders, practicing the work ethic, going to church and contributing more than your fair share for the good of the whole.

Could it be that children turn out better than we could have hoped because they counted for something while growing up?

Maybe the foster mother from Chalmette whose adopted teen-ager is now a troubled runaway offered a clue in that respect.

"What most people don't understand is that birth to one year is a critical time for children," said Mrs. Dolores Bertucci.

"If not loved, nurtured, stroked, they lose the ability to bond. You can't go to age 2 and try to put that back."

It's certainly food for thought, particularly at a time when you are turning your attention to an ever-expanding family.

So what if your 55th birthday got lost in this year's shuffle? The other major events were worth it. Besides, consider the other pluses. You're better looking and in better shape than country music star Willie Nelson, who is also 55, and in some circles you've finally qualified for senior citizen status.

Yes, 1988 has definitely been a vintage year.

Nov. 6, 1988

Grandpa is in love again

When was the last time you felt a single blade of grass, or touched the leaf of a shrub, or rubbed the coarse bark of a pine tree?

If it's been a long time, you haven't enjoyed one of life's most enriching experiences — sharing with a new granddaughter the marvels of all those things that are new to her in this world.

Those who have been lucky enough to know what it's like will tell you words cannot adequately express the sheer joy and fulfillment that comes with being a grandparent for the first time.

Most of us know what it's like to fall in love and marry. We can also appreciate that second major plateau in life when we experience the love and satisfaction that comes with raising a family. But being a grandparent for the first time is different.

Perhaps it's because we spend so much of our early lifetime struggling to get ahead financially and vocationally we don't have time to "smell the roses." That changes, as we grow older and more secure. And when a grandchild comes along we learn to enjoy the many special pleasures that have always been there but which we haven't stopped to fully appreciate.

Life has suddenly taken on new meaning and purpose. You look forward to the time you can spend with one of God's latest creations.

When she crawls over to your feet, sits on her knees, tugs on your trousers and raises her arms so you'll scoop her up, you're in seventh heaven.

And when she refuses to leave your arms for "Grammy," you almost burst with pride and self-satisfaction.

She isn't talking yet, but she converses with you just the same. It may sound like strange noises or hissing to others, but you know she's expressing wonderment or satisfaction at something she's seeing for the first time. And that includes almost everything she sees.

That bottom lip also sticks out when she's excited, and it always makes you laugh.

You've seen the same kind of joy on her father's face anytime he enters an electronics showroom. That's when you know genes definitely have a lot to do with man's development.

If your granddaughter points to the back door, you know she wants to go outside and examine those blades of grass, leaves on the shrubbery and bark on the trees.

You witness her added amazement when she notices a dog next door that looks different from the three she's been around since the day she was born.

Singing birds also catch her eyes and ears. She is fast becoming attuned to the beauties and sounds of nature.

She walks along the backyard fence — the experts call it cruising —gaining confidence in her ability to get around on her own.

Those first short, abbreviated footsteps consume every ounce of strength she can muster. You want to lend a hand, but you know this is something she has to handle on her own.

Her attempts to stand up after falling down have her grandmother laughing because she's backing up more than raising up, but eventually she is standing again.

As one of those entertaining Thursday or Sunday afternoons draws to a close, you look forward to the next time you can spend together.

You've always enjoyed those Thursdays off with your daughter and those free Sundays with the entire family. But the anticipation is even greater now because a new, developing granddaughter has made those special moments even richer.

Lunch and grocery shopping on those days off are a little more strenuous than they used to be. There's a youngster to entertain, and if she's tired or hungry it isn't so easy. Getting her in and out of that car seat also takes its toll.

Even so, you wouldn't trade any of it for anything in the world – aching back and all.

Like most toddlers, she doesn't like to take naps. Her mother sometimes has to put her in the baby bed and let her cry.

No one knows how tough that can be on grandfathers unless they've gone through the trying experience.

However, when the crying doesn't stop, guess who gets to go into the bedroom and become the hero to the rescue?

No effort is spared to keep her happy and contented. She has more than enough toys, but likes taboo things. Like the dog's artificial bones and those tennis balls he chews on all the time.

She has her own portion of the kitchen cabinet which is filled with plastic and other unbreakable cookware, but the dog's water bowl is always much more fun.

The television set and the brickwork around the fireplace are her two big "no no's," and it's a constant fight to keep her away from both.

Is she spoiled? You bet she is, and it's probably going to get worse.

That makes it tough on mom and dad, of course, who are making every effort to instill those values that will give their daughter the training, stability and sense of purpose we all need to survive.

But those of us who are new at the game didn't make the rules for grandparents. We just try to live by them.

Besides, what's a grandfather to do? When that nearly 1-year-old puts her arms around your neck or makes that inexperienced effort to plant a big kiss on your forehead or cheek, you're at her mercy.

You don't get exasperated with her often, but when you do on those rare occasions that's usually about the time mom and dad are ready to head for home.

Maybe that's the secret of this love affair grandparents have with their grandchildren. They get to skip most of the hard parts, like the dirty diapers, the sleepless nights, the constant need to be on guard for the child's welfare and safety and the expense of keeping them in shoes and clothes and all those other essentials.

Yes, that could be it. But so what? We served our time, and now it's OK to be on the receiving and enjoyable end for a change.

Those friends and colleagues who said being a grandparent was a unique and rewarding experience certainly know of what they speak. It's more satisfying than anyone can imagine.

Loving and being loved the third time around has to be one of God's greatest gifts.

July 23, 1989

It was a day she won't forget

Working in a convenience store can be tough duty, but it has its rewards. Just ask Eloise Bosarge. She manages the Chevron Food Mart at Lake and McNeese streets.

I spend time with Eloise on most of my days off, and we enjoy the visits.

"When you don't come, it ruins my day," she says.

I made a point to be there last week because it was going to be a special day for her. However, Eloise was the only one who didn't know about it ahead of time.

Sit inside a convenience store for a while and you understand how those outlets got their name. Whether it's gasoline, cigarettes, coffee or a soft drink, you're in and out in minutes and on your way.

My daughter and granddaughter have been with me on many of my Thursday morning coffee breaks at Eloise's place. However, Jamie's teaching part-time now, and Jessica is in kindergarten. So I'm on my own until a holiday comes along.

Frank Wilkinson, one of the regulars, is there most Thursdays. He's usually sipping coffee while sitting by the front window at a table for four. We talk some politics, but it's mostly conversation about less serious subjects.

If Frank isn't there, he and his wife have probably run off to Gulfport in their motor home to do a little gambling. Or they may be visiting family members somewhere in Texas or Louisiana.

Miss Eloise, which is what Frank and many of the customers call her, joins us for fellowship and coffee.

Customers come and go, and Eloise greets most of them by name. When Stacie, her co-worker, isn't there handling the sales, Eloise is up and down during our visit.

There's usually a copy of the paper on the table, and sometimes it's opened to Page 3 where my Thursday column runs.

Most of the time Frank will say he started reading that day's column, but he didn't get finished.

"I didn't read it," Eloise says often, complaining that she isn't interested in politics. She prefers reading about family stuff.

Eloise will throw out a customer's name now and then and ask me if I know them. I'm not good at remembering people's names, so most of the time I have to tell her I'm not sure.

"One man who comes in here really doesn't like you," she said one Thursday.

That's the kind of off-hand remark that will make you sit up and take notice.

As she promised, Eloise pointed the fellow out the next time he came in while I was there. I stayed out of easy reach in case he was the physical type. All I got, though, was a serious look.

Eloise introduces me to many of her customers, and they come from all walks of life. She's always pleasant, and they respond in kind to her familiarity.

On one occasion, three house painters were sitting down at the table when I arrived. They were taking a break from a job down the street.

"I wish they'd get up from our table," Eloise said. "They have been coming in here for a few days and staying too long."

Eloise has come up through the school of hard knocks. She has always had demanding jobs. Her day begins at 5:30 a.m. five days a week when she opens the store. Standing up most of the time is hard on her legs and feet, but she rarely complains.

Being born slap dab in the middle of four brothers didn't get her off to a good start. And she talks about how difficult it was to live in the shadow of one brother who was born 11 months earlier.

She married after high school, had two sons and they lived in Morgan City. When the marriage ended, Eloise moved back to Lake Charles.

Work is a necessity since she's on her own now. But she's a survivor and has made the most of some tough times. And she's managed to stay in a good frame of mind by laughing at herself.

A younger brother used to tease Eloise a lot. He would tell her friends not to look her up in the telephone book. "She's been married so many times, her name won't fit on one line," he said.

He told that story more than once, and Eloise never got tired of hearing it.

She's extremely family-conscious, and remembers things about growing up that most of us forget. She recalls things like that older brother crying because he didn't want to start school. When her parents were ill in their later years, Eloise was always there to offer comfort and compassionate care.

Working at convenience stores has given her an opportunity to display her talents for doing a job and doing it well. Her associates, customers and the people she works for are part of her bigger family now, and they've been good to Eloise.

She has received high marks from trained consumers who shop in secret and evaluate the store's performance. And that brings us to last Thursday.

Tom, Eloise's boss and area supervisor for the company, knows I work at the paper. He called me a week ago to ask about a story on Eloise winning one of 10 national Commitment to Service Excellence awards. The presentation was scheduled for 10 a.m. Thursday, and she was going to receive a $1,000 check that goes with the award.

I got there, as usual, about 9:30 a.m. Tom's daughter, who also works in the store, showed up a little later. Then came Billy, one of Eloise's sons, and Jeanette, a sister-in-law. Tom had apparently told everyone but Eloise.

Since we had all been there at the same time on previous occasions, she was none the wiser. But when Tom walked in with the store's two owners, a district manager from Lafayette and two others, she had to figure something was up.

Tom was worried that the $1,000 prize might put her into shock. It didn't, but the award and the check took a few moments to sink in. And then there was a round of applause from the small crowd that had gathered.

It was Eloise Bosarge's time in the spotlight, and there was general agreement by everyone there that it couldn't have happened to a nicer and more deserving person.

In case you didn't already know, or haven't figured it out by now, Eloise is my only sister. And I'm as proud of her and happy for her good fortune as any brother could be.

Sept. 12, 1993

Grandpa teaches shoe tying

The call came in the middle of a hectic Friday morning. Jackie picked up the phone for me as I was walking through the newsroom.

I had already received more than my share of telephone calls, and wondered who had a problem this time around. Then I heard a soft, quiet voice on the other end of the line.

"Grandpa, I tied my shoes all by myself."

The tension evaporated immediately. It was Jessica, the granddaughter who came into my life exactly six years ago today. I was as proud at that moment as any grandparent could ever be, and here's why:

Jessica and I spent Thursday together, as we have done often over the last six years. However, this was a day off that was harder than most. She had tried my patience almost from the time she arrived at my house.

Her mother was preparing for the upcoming school session, so I had Jessica all on my own.

For starters, she didn't want to go anywhere. After a few threats, we overcame that hurdle. And she was fine during our first two stops. However, our supermarket experience was a disaster.

First, she wanted a plum. Then it was a yellow apple. I vetoed a multi-colored Lion King balloon hanging from the ceiling. However, moments later I noticed her climbing up an orange juice display trying to reach one on her own.

We had some words and then some tears, and, as he usually does, grandpa gave in.

When we got to the cookie aisle, she wanted some of those.

Jessica decided to dilly-dally around the cold cut display, so I gave up trying to keep her in tow. It worked.

I could see her, but she couldn't see me. She looked around and noticed I wasn't in sight. It must have been a bit scary; because when she saw me again she stuck close until our shopping trip was over.

Sometime during the day in between those trying moments Jessica asked me to show her how to tie her shoes. She had tried to do it without success.

We sat next to each other on the couch and started from scratch. I noticed she was folding the shoestring with her left hand.

After I tied the strings on her left shoe, I suggested she try using her right hand to make the loop. "Then you can use your left hand to wrap the other end of the string around the loop and pull it through."

It worked, and I praised her quick response. We went on to other things and forgot all about the shoe-tying lesson.

Now you know why that telephone call turned a stressful Friday morning into pure joy. A simple suggestion from Grandpa had helped make a young child feel confident about her ability to cope with one of life's demands.

I found out later she had also called her grandmother about her accomplishment and given Grandpa all the credit.

"I tied my own shoes, Joey," she said. "I was using my left hand and Grandpa told me to use my right hand."

The shoe-tying success story also erased all the bad memories from Thursday.

As grandfathers are prone to do, I wanted to brag about the experience to anyone who would listen. I happened to be on my way to the business office to pick up payroll checks.

It was the wrong place and the wrong time. Two or three of the women there were up in arms over the cost of school supplies for children and grandchildren.

"Would you look at this?" one of them asked as she produced a page full of requested supplies. "It's ridiculous to expect parents to pay for all of these things."

I certainly sympathized with their plight, but their outrage was destroying a great moment I had wanted desperately to share.

I got out of there as quickly as I could.

When I got home Friday afternoon, it was my wife's turn to deflate my pride. "You aren't going to write about that, are you?" she asked. "Everybody's grandchild learns to tie shoes."

Yes, they do, and I understand their great sense of satisfaction when those special moments of achievement come along. I also know that other grandparents can appreciate my experience more than most, so why not share it?

That's exactly what I've been doing for six years. I started my grandfather days as a background player when we left the hospital where Jessica was born. I was the fellow pushing the cart loaded down with flowers, luggage and gifts who looked like part of the hospital maintenance crew.

My role expanded, as she got older. Jessica and I have enjoyed natural wonders like blades of grass, leaves on trees, singing birds and pesky pets. We have been together on regular and special visits to the doctor.

We have gone on weekly shopping trips with her mother and capped them off with lunch together.

I've played games with Jessica that I never won. Each time I was on the verge of winning, she changed the rules.

Her grandmother and I have kept up with our only grandchild's pre-school activities and been a vital part of each birthday observance. We'll be there again today when she celebrates that monumental sixth birthday.

When school starts soon, we move on to another level in her young life.

I didn't realize it back in 1988, but my life changed forever on that eventful Aug. 7. It's been richer and fuller than I could have ever imagined. Who would have thought, for example, that the simple act of helping someone learn to tie a shoelace could mean so much?

I've stored up great memories that will last a lifetime, and look forward to the experiences yet to come.

Today, on Jessica's sixth birthday, I will rejoice like grandparents do on such occasions. We know how rewarding and enriching it is to love and be loved by God's greatest gifts — our grandchildren.

Aug. 7, 1994

Someone else did the talking

Any time a dozen or more people congregate, I get this uncontrollable urge to make a speech. It's the ham in me, I suppose.

The feeling came over me again Thursday afternoon, but I never got a chance to stand up and say a few words. However, everything worked out for the best.

The occasion was a reception for my wife, who retired last week from her administrative secretary's job at McNeese State University. Family, friends, co-workers and university officials were on hand for the celebration.

It was a captive audience, but I didn't mind playing second fiddle. In fact, I couldn't have improved on anything my wife said. She bowed out with class, thanks to a delightful speech of her own.

Today, however, it's my turn. I'd like to share with you what I would have said Thursday.

I would have told her friends and co-workers how proud my family and I are of Jo Ann. Like so many working women, she's a real professional.

How working women manage to juggle family, work, home, church and civic responsibilities is a continuing miracle.

Jo Ann has worked off and on since we were married in 1954. She brought home the bacon while I finished college at McNeese, and has helped pay the bills since then.

Those early years were tough, even with her additional income. It's difficult to imagine how we could have made it without her help.

Two-income families are almost a necessity these days, so most married couples can identify with our situation.

Thanks to help from our families, Jo Ann was able to be at home when our two children were pre-schoolers. That isn't possible in many families today, but it's nice when it can be done in those formative years.

When Jo Ann went back to work, she was fortunate to get a secretary's job at Lake Charles High School. She could be home when our son and daughter got out of school in the afternoons.

Jo Ann worked for some well-known local educators, people like John Nicosia, Daniel Ieyoub and John Falgout.

Eventually, she moved on to McNeese and spent most of her time there in the Office of Student Services.

Now, there's a beehive of activity. Jeaneal Godwin, a good friend of JoAnn's who also works at McNeese, told me few years ago she couldn't survive in Student Services.

"I'd go crazy in there," she said. "There's too much going on."

Jo Ann not only survived, she thrived. Louis Riviere, who was her boss during most of her 20 years at McNeese, created a working environment that was demanding and challenging, but also rewarding and fulfilling.

Riviere retired last year. If there was ever anyone in the history of the university that deserved the title of Mr. McNeese, he is it. He lived and breathed McNeese, and students and co-workers loved him for it.

It's the people you remember when you leave a place. I know Jo Ann will miss the assistant deans, other secretaries and student workers who became members of her working family. She still hears from many of them who live here and in other places.

Housing directors, the men and woman who supervise dormitories, also became her good friends.

Jo Ann got to know some of the people who have been longtime friends of mine. Kenneth Sweeney, a former vice president at McNeese, was her big boss. Bill Gossett was an assistant dean. Beverly Reina is still secretary to the president.

Johnny Suydam and Charlie Goen probably caught Jo Ann off guard a few times with their jokes and pranks.

I know about a lot of these things because Jo Ann and I have shared our professional lives with one another and benefited from our mutual experiences. I have occasionally sought her advice on complex matters and she has sought mine.

Jo Ann will have fond memories of morning coffee in the Student Services break room. Those had to be lively sessions with some of the folks I've already mentioned.

I was invited, but never made one. There's no telling how many scoops I missed because of it.

Others Jo Ann will remember include Buster Keaton, Joe Moore, John Smith, Jimmy Pitre, Desmond Jones and Philo Brasher. I've probably left someone out, but Jo Ann won't forget who they are.

When you end 20 years in one place as Jo Ann did Friday, it's nice to get together with those folks and others who enriched the experience. McNeese does retirement up right, usually with a dinner with co-workers and a reception for a larger and more diverse group.

Jo Ann and I attended McNeese, and have always felt a special closeness to the university. Her years there as an employee have cemented those ties.

A lot of people asked me what Jo Ann is going to do with all that free time, but I'm not sure. She loves Court TV, so I suppose the O.J. Simpson trial will be on her schedule.

I don't think she'll get hooked on the soaps, Oprah or Phil Donahue, but I'm keeping my fingers crossed.

Naps will definitely be the order of the day.

I may get an extra evening meal or two every week, but I know she won't be ironing my shirts. And since she hasn't learned to sew by now, that's also out of the question.

She's talking about taking a few trips, but nothing definite. She also plans to do some volunteer and church work.

The rest I suppose she'll play by ear. I'll keep you posted.

Thanks for letting me share some personal thoughts about Jo Ann's years at McNeese. My family and I are extremely proud of her record, which is a tribute to working women everywhere.

When my turn comes to hang it up, I hope I can handle the situation as well as she did. I might even get to make a speech.

Jan. 29, 1995

American families alive, well

What better time to talk about the American family than Christmas Eve?

We hear a lot these days about the decline in family values, and there is cause for concern. However, there is also much about family life to celebrate, and I'm one of those who has more reasons to be thankful than he deserves.

Gift giving is a way of telling others how much they mean in our lives, but some of us never quite measure up to the determination that Christmas shopping requires. So maybe the members of my family will let me take this means of telling them how important they are in my life.

This year, I even forgot to make them a wish list for a fellow who's awfully hard to please. When I thought about the missing list Thursday, my wife had a quick response.

"It's too late now," she said. "You better hope you like what you get."

Jo Ann is the solid rock around which much of our family life centers. She's been a major influence in the lives of our son and daughter, who also know how to appreciate this festive season.

One of Jo Ann's projects this year was a family portrait for a picture Christmas card. Getting seven people together for an appointment of that nature takes plenty of coordination and planning, but that's her strong suit.

When the photographer lined us up with our granddaughter on my left side, Jessica stuck her arm through mine. It was her security grip, but it meant much more than that to me.

That grasp of my arm said grandpa was someone she could trust and hold on to — someone who made her feel secure. There isn't a grandfather anywhere who would trade that feeling for anything in the world.

Some of our friends who received those picture Christmas cards told us how nice the family looked together, and they noticed those locked arms.

If Jo Ann hadn't set the whole thing up, the moment would have been lost forever.

Another sign that things must be going right in my family surfaced Wednesday evening. It's our night at our favorite cafeteria, but there was also a McNeese Cowboy basketball game at Burton Coliseum.

Gary asked if I wanted to join him for the game after our meal. It's special in my book when a son-in-law thinks enough of his father-in-law to share an evening with him.

Getting in and out of the coliseum parking lot was a nightmare, but we had a great time.

Then there was the cold weather problem last week. My daughter and I weren't able to take our usual afternoon walk at the McNeese track, and the MSU recreation center was closed.

As the week dragged on, I realized how much I missed that special time Jamie and I share together three or four times a week.

My son and daughter-in-law lived with us part of this year while they were building a house. They moved into their new home in October, but we had nine enjoyable months together. You expect there might be some tense moments living that close, but they never materialized.

We had some great discussions, too. Bryan works in local government, so he had a different perspective of the political landscape than a newspaperman. His boss, a longtime acquaintance of mine, jokingly told him a year ago, "You're going to work for the enemy."

Grocery coupons and eating are two of the bonds that tie my daughter-in-law and me together. Edith is a great cook and a sensitive, caring person, and we've been good friends from the start.

Thanks to my wife's church-every-Sunday, Baptist upbringing, the members of my family have become good Methodists. I haven't quite measured up to the rest. So if Jo Ann hadn't set the example these many years, we might all be lost.

A fellow church member mentioned one Sunday morning how lucky we were to have our entire family there at the same time. Bryan came back to Lake Charles after leaving here a single man 10 years ago, and we couldn't be happier that he's back.

Most of you have read about my granddaughter, who is the newest love in my life. Only another grandparent could explain or understand why I sometimes do things for Jessica I wouldn't think of doing for anyone else.

Like most youngsters her age, she has no inhibitions.

After glancing at my hearing aids the other day, she said, "Grandpa, you know you can buy hearing aids that fit in your ear so you can't see them."

Apparently she isn't happy about the way my hearing aids look. I got her message, but explained that at 600 bucks a throw it isn't easy to change just for the look of things.

Then there was the time she looked closely at my head

"Grandpa, you don't have much hair, but you do have some," she said. "I saw a man the other day who didn't have any. You just don't have any bangs."

It's difficult to explain, but it doesn't hurt a bit when the slings and arrows come from your granddaughter. Maybe that's because she's the latest tie that helps bind our family together.

Forgive me for getting personal today, but I wanted in some small way to let the members of my family know how they have enriched my life.

There are other fathers and grandfathers out there who feel just as proud of the people in their lives. I know that's true because I see their families down the street, around the corner, across town and in places far away.

For one reason or another, the makeup of American families has changed a lot over the years. There are more single-parent families in this country than ever before, but they are families just the same.

We should stop occasionally and reflect on the important role that families play in our lives, and the holiday season is a good time to do it.

Merry Christmas to your family.

Dec. 24, 1995

This Father's Day was special

What do you suppose it says about our personal lives when we get excited about receiving a hardware store gift certificate for Father's Day? Or how about a new electric carving knife?

If dull comes to mind, you're probably right on target.

The sexiest gift I received last Sunday was a new pair of pajamas from my granddaughter. Jessica is doing her part to keep Grandpa thinking young and stylish. She's also trying to make me a dog lover, but that's almost impossible.

My wife came through with an album of contemporary music that also helps keep the youthful spirit alive. It's a collection of songs by Bill Morrissey titled, "You'll Never Get To Heaven."

If she hadn't told me she sampled the music before picking out the tape, I might have speculated that her gift selection was motivated by the title.

Although I enjoyed each of my gifts, dull as they might appear, I found this year's Father's Day an extra special occasion for other reasons.

In an age when many American families are in crisis, Jo Ann and I are among the lucky couples that have been blessed in so many ways. I told her the other day I wasn't sure if we were just lucky or had done some things right.

Most of us benefit from the lessons we learn while growing up, from our friendships with others and from our educational, professional and spiritual experiences. If those relationships are solid and rewarding, we pass the richness we enjoy along to our own children and grandchildren.

My children were no different than others. At times, they were just as mischievous, cantankerous and perplexing as most youngsters. Their parents also occasionally embarrassed them.

We were talking the other day about an old Chevrolet I owned. It was one of those classics, but it was painted yellow and black. I wasn't aware of it at the time, but Jamie was horrified when I took her anywhere in that ugly car. She told her mother she wanted me to drop her off at least a block from school.

Boys don't usually worry about such things, but I'm sure Bryan had his moments when he wished the old man wasn't around.

Parents understand those things. After all, we, too, were young once.

We influence our children in many ways, and we hope most of them are positive. I can remember many of the admonitions from my childhood, which still affect my actions so many years later.

I overheard a conversation my daughter was having the other day about good manners and being polite and courteous.

"Whenever Dad opens a door, he steps back and lets me walk inside first," she said. "I'm not used to being treated that way."

I felt awfully proud at that moment, particularly since it wasn't meant for my ears.

My parents insisted that we be responsible for our actions, and that makes you think before you leap. It doesn't mean you always do the right thing, but you know the difference.

We were taught to stand up when a woman enters the room, to open doors for others, to respect our elders and to use good table manners. None of us dared sit down to eat without a shirt on or while wearing a cap.

When you think about those basic rules of behavior, it's like the freedoms all Americans enjoy in the Bill of Rights. We are free to do what we like so long as our freedoms don't infringe on the rights of others.

There's a valuable lesson there for parents and youngsters.

My mom and dad were probably too strict in some ways, and I've tried to avoid repeating their mistakes. However, some parents probably go too far in the opposite direction.

I thought about all of those things last Sunday and counted myself lucky that the family Jo Ann and I nurtured had turned out so well.

We've had our ups and downs, of course. Who hasn't? A few Sundays back, Jo Ann and I were having one of our occasionally spirited arguments when Jamie interrupted.

"If you two are going to fight, we're leaving," she said.

I explained to Jamie that her mother and I had learned to battle it out on the spur of the moment to get our frustrations out in the open and then move on. Besides, I'm convinced no one was leaving before finishing one of Jo Ann's great Sunday meals.

I also had other plans. This was one Father's Day that wasn't going to end for me until I told the members of my family how I felt about each of them.

Many of us who grew up in the post-Depression years have a difficult time expressing our emotions. I have written before about how difficult it was the first time I told my son how much I loved him. However, once you make that first giant leap, the words come easier.

The experiences the members of our family have shared for so many years have been positive and rewarding, and I wanted to tell them so.

I stopped Gary in his tracks. He's my favorite son-in-law (actually, he's the only one I have), and he was chomping at the bit to get back to his home computer.

Then there's Edith, who is the kindest, most caring daughter-in-law a father-in-law could hope for.

I told each of them how proud we were that they had turned out so well and how much it had enriched our lives. We've had some great family times together, and I wanted them to know how much we cherish every enjoyable moment.

Other families have had similar experiences, and I know they can appreciate my sentiments. If you have shared some great times with members of your family and haven't told them so, let them know how you feel.

When you think about the richness of close relationships, you realize your life isn't as dull as that new carving knife or gift certificate might indicate.

June 23, 1996

Andrew newest member of clan

If you follow the comic strip "For Better or Worse," you have some idea of what life is currently like in the extended Beam Family. We have a new member who will fill the eighth chair at our dining room table.

He's Andrew James Beam, and his middle name should explain why Grandpa is especially proud to welcome him into our close-knit family.

Andrew is the son of our son, Bryan, and our daughter-in-law, Edith. Andrew is a longtime dream come true for them, and that makes it easier for both to cope with the demands of raising a newborn.

Even so, it has to be somewhat of a shock for two people who have been living with Franklin planners for much of their adult lives.

I'm sure Edith and Bryan have read up on parenting, and been given a lot of advice on how to raise a child. However, there is nothing like putting all those tips and suggestions into practice. It can sometimes be a trying experience, with lack of sleep at the top of the list.

That's where the "For Better or Worse" comic strip offers some insight into the perils of parenthood.

John and El are the parents in that mythical household, and they have three children — Michael, Elizabeth and April.

Michael has a good friend, Gordon, whose wife, Tracey, has just had a baby.

El is helping the young couple adjust to their new responsibilities.

"Was the hospital staff helpful?" El asked Tracey in Thursday's strip.

"Oh, sure," she answered. "And my mother and Gord's mother, and everyone around us has give us volumes of advice!"

"So, why is it that we still don't know what we're doing?" Tracey asked.

Anyone who has been a parent — or grandparent — for the first time can identify with Tracey and Gord.

Our first grandchild was born almost nine years ago, just when it appeared we might never know what it's like to be grandparents. Now, we get to experience those same joys all over again.

Like El in the comic strip, we've almost forgotten how to hold a new baby and how much work there is to do. However, it doesn't take long to catch up on those rusty skills.

In fact, I danced around with Andrew last week when he got a little fussy.

Jessica always enjoyed a whirl around the floor with Grandpa when she was a toddler, and it felt great to be prancing around like a silly grandfather – again.

Jessica, 8, who has enriched our lives beyond measure, is fascinated with her tiny first cousin. She can't hold him enough, and follows him like his shadow.

Bryan bought a VCR camera and, combined with countless still photographs, there is little about Andrew's beginnings that haven't been captured on film. Seeing Bryan looking for even more photo opportunities the other day, Jo Ann couldn't help but recall a comment Bryan made when Jessica was a baby.

Jamie and Gary, Jessica's mom and dad, were shooting a lot of pictures at the time. Gary's a photographer, and he's been known to shoot more snapshots than necessary about his favorite subjects.

Bryan said back then that Jessica "had to be the most photographed baby in the world."

Now, the shoe is on the other foot.

Thanks to several showers and gifts from friends of the new parents, Andrew is beginning life with a splendid wardrobe. Even so, Edith manages to pick up another new outfit occasionally.

That's a new mother's prerogative, of course.

Between family, friends and acquaintances, there are extra car seats, beds, bouncing chairs and goodness knows what else around should Andrew need anything.

Andrew was baptized last Sunday, and he was probably unaware of how big an event that was in his young life. His other grandparents were here from Lafayette, along with his aunt and uncle, who are his Godparents.

The 12 of us had lunch together, and it turned out to be one of the most enjoyable days in all of our lives.

I will never be able to explain to Bryan and Edith how much it means to me to have a grandson whose middle name is James. It's not an unusual name, of course, but it's mine and I get to share it with Andrew.

Bryan could have seen things differently. When he was born, my mother — and his grandmother — insisted we should give him part of my name. If we didn't, she said he was going to be hurt when he grew up and realized our daughter had been named Jamie and he had been left out in the cold.

That's how Bryan got his middle name — Carroll — and he hasn't been too thrilled about it since. Thank goodness he didn't hold a grudge.

God has been good to my family, and now He has seen fit to bless us again with Andrew. I suppose it's God's way of reminding us how important families are in His overall scheme of things.

Although many of us fail to measure up to His expectations, it's important that we at least try to make the most of the blessings we receive.

Welcome aboard, Andrew. Your chair at the table is waiting.

April 20, 1997

Mothers give lives meaning

It's been over 17 years since my mother died, but I think about her often. What I wouldn't give to be able to once again put my arm around her and let her know what a tremendous influence she has been in my life.

Mothers are often the moral compass in families, and thank God for that. What a miserable mess some of us would be in if we hadn't had their love and guidance, especially in our formative years.

My mother believed two things would sustain us when everything else failed — faith in God and a good education. She saw to it that we got a heavy dose of both.

Carrie was her name, and she stood no more than five feet tall. However, she was a giant in our eyes.

She was one of five girls who grew up in a family of 12 in Cameron Parish. Her father, A.P. Welch Sr., was registrar of voters in Cameron and her grandfather, James Monroe Welch, served in the Louisiana Legislature.

Sometimes I think that's where I got my interest in politics, although my mother shuddered when I used to joke about running for public office.

My mother attended school at USL when it was Southwestern Louisiana Institute (SLI). She planned to become a schoolteacher, but that didn't turn out to be her cup of tea. Even so, she passed along her deep interest in education.

The five youngsters in our family grew up just as the country was coming out of the Great Depression. We never had much, but I can't ever recall thinking we were poor. Maybe that's because so many other folks were in the same boat.

Everyone was expected to share the responsibilities around our house, and we earned our own money at an early age. Pete Fontana was our neighborhood grocer, and each of us took our turn working there. I followed my oldest brother, Charles, at Fontana's and David took his turn after me.

Eloise was the only girl in our family, and she had more than enough at home to keep her busy. Dale came along later, and the rest of us felt as though he had special privileges because he was the baby in the family.

Our mother saw that we attended First Methodist Church downtown on Sundays at an early age. And when University Methodist Church opened its doors south of town, we became charter members.

I remember seeing a picture recently of my mother holding Dale as a toddler during the first services held at University.

If it hadn't been for my mother, chances are the Christian influence would have been missing in our home. My dad was a believer, but my mother was the driving force when it came to attending church.

The same thing was true about our educational experiences. She was always looking for new ways for us to learn. I'll never forget how proud she was of the Lincoln Library she purchased for our benefit. It was just a two-volume reference book, but it was as close to an encyclopedia as we could afford.

I knew how much education meant to my mother, so I decided I would take advantage of every opportunity to excel. It has paid off handsomely in many ways, and I hope she knows somehow how grateful I am for the goals and examples she set.

I've known some other great mothers in my lifetime, and what better occasion than Mother's Day to single them out?

One of my aunts, Wynona Welch, never married, but she was like a mother to us just the same. She and I were close, and she was a big financial help to our family when times were especially hard.

Aunt Nona worked for the Ration Board during World War II and became registrar of voters in Cameron Parish after her father retired. I spent many enjoyable summers at her home next to the courthouse.

When I met Jo Ann back in the early 1950s, her mother, Myrtle Drachenberg, and I hit it off right away. We lived with Jo Ann's folks before and after my tour in the U.S. Army, and it was awfully nice to have a second family and another mother.

Jo Ann, like her mother and mine, has more than measured up to her maternal responsibilities. She, too, has set a moral tone for our son and daughter, and they are better people because of it.

Our daughter, Jamie, became a mother almost nine years ago, and it opened up a new role for the two of us as grandparents. You have to be a grandparent, of course, to know how that experience can change your life for the better.

Watching Jamie work with Jessica at home and as a room mother at school, I now have a better idea of the struggles Jo Ann was going through with our two youngsters. I was preoccupied with work at the time, and not aware of the awesome responsibilities she faced at home.

Edith, our daughter-in-law, became a new mother recently, so her challenges are just beginning. Like other mothers, however, I'm sure she will measure up to the task and Andrew will be a better man because of it.

Each of you can recount similar experiences in your lifetime, and realize why mothers deserve the special recognition they receive today and much, much more.

We have family pictures hanging up in the hall of our home, and there is one of my mother and dad that always catches my eye. They are sitting on a couch in the home where we spent most of our teen-age years, and both have big smiles on their faces.

My mother went through some difficult times when we were youngsters, but her later years were happy times. That's the mother I'm going to remember today and the one I won't forget as long as I live.

Meanwhile, I'm going to celebrate Mother's Day with the three mothers in my family — the mother of my children and the mothers of my two grandchildren.

If you're lucky enough to see your mother today, give her a great big hug. Tell her how much you love her and let her know how important she has been in your life.

It's an opportunity no one should pass up.

May 11, 1997

Most people called him Charlie

Charlie was his name, and he was representative of a generation of fathers who came up the hard way.

I knew him better than most. He was Charlie Beam, my dad. However, that's not as important on this Father's Day as recounting the odds he and others like him overcame during one of this country's most trying times — the Depression years.

I called him Dad or Pop, but everyone else called him Charlie, so that's how it will be today.

There are still people around who remember Charlie when he had a bread route in Cameron Parish in the late 1930s. They marveled at the fact that he was able to carry a full armload of bread while walking with a crutch.

A victim of polio at age 6, Charlie was destined to live the remainder of his life with a practically useless right leg. However, he never let his handicap stop him from doing whatever he made up his mind to accomplish and he never traded on his disability.

Charlie told us about the time he was standing on a street corner in Shreveport and a panhandler walked up and said, "This is my corner, Move along, pal."

"I'm not begging," Charlie said. "I'm waiting for a bus."

It was interesting to watch Charlie drive an automobile in those early years because there was no such thing as automatic drive. He would lift his bad leg to rest it on the accelerator and keep his good leg near the brake in the event he needed to stop quickly.

Charlie married Carrie Welch, a native of Cameron, and that was another reason the people there knew him so well. There were five children in the Beam family — four sons and one daughter.

We never gave a second thought to our father's disability. In fact, we didn't see him any differently than other fathers we knew.

The Depression days were tougher than most folks can imagine, and jobs were practically non-existent. Charlie said he and some friends were so desperate on one occasion, they jumped in a car and headed to Akron, Ohio, in hopes of landing jobs at a tire manufacturing plant. He said it was a wasted trip.

The Works Progress Administration (WPA) had some construction work going on at what became McNeese State University, and Charlie said he had a job there for a while.

During World War II, Charlie went into the tire vulcanizing business. It was a process by which tires were retreaded to give them longer life.

He also operated a service station at the corner where OB's Deli and Pub is located on Ryan Street. That's also where I pumped gasoline for the first time.

Charlie wasn't too happy when I failed to replace the gas cap on the first car I serviced. The customer came back to complain, and I took a good tongue-lashing.

Charlie had learned to keep books at Vincent Business College and the training served him well in later life. He had other jobs during his lifetime, which included selling cars, dispatching taxicabs and bookkeeping.

He retired from Evangeline Iron Works after keeping the books there for a number of years.

We knew what it was like to carry our own weight, and we knew whatever Charlie said was gospel. We may not have liked, it, but we seldom argued when he laid down the rules.

We couldn't, for example, sit at the dinner table with a hat or cap or without a shirt. Table manners were a high priority. We also got up when anyone entered the room and gave up our chair and opened doors for women.

There was little that Charlie didn't know how to do. And like many fathers, he passed along those skills to each of his children. He knew how to repair automobiles, do plumbing, carpentry and yard work and paint.

Working with our father was difficult at times, but most folks will tell you their dads were no different. Charlie never thought we did things as well as he did. However, he was a great teacher.

When Charlie wanted help, he never asked. It was understood you had better get there as soon as you could after he called. We mumbled and grumbled about his unflinching demands, but anything we might be involved in had to wait.

My son found out what a tough taskmaster he could be. Charlie asked him to cut his grass with his riding mower, and was impatient when Bryan didn't show up right away.

"Tell him I don't have any headlights on that mower," Charlie said.

On one occasion, Bryan helped his grandfather paint a bathroom. It was obvious the experience was extremely taxing.

"I don't want to work with Grandpa anymore," he said when the day ended.

After my mother died, Charlie became an avid TV watcher. He was a big fan of the Dallas Cowboys during their Tom Landry era. We knew idle conversations on Sunday afternoons were taboo when the Cowboys were playing.

Charlie was a cigarette smoker for many years, and that eventually took its toll. He suffered from emphysema in later years, and that made breathing a real chore. He also had to deal with congestive heart failure, which eventually proved his undoing.

My wife does volunteer work at a local hospital one day a week and she has run into two or three patients there who tell her they remember Charlie from his bread-toting days in Cameron Parish.

Whenever I hear that now-familiar story about how a crippled fellow could cope so well with an armload of bread, I think about a rock of a man who had no handicap in our eyes.

Charlie Beam was a great inspiration in my life, and apparently in the lives of others.

Like millions of Americans, I'll be thinking about Dad today as we salute fathers everywhere.

June 15, 1997

We need someone to love us

I knew Andrew James Beam had class the first time I saw him shortly after he was born last March. Now, it's been confirmed. He thinks his grandpa is a prince of a fellow.

Our granddaughter, Jessica Meek, and I have also enjoyed a special relationship since she came into this world more than nine years ago.

What's the big deal? you ask. Don't most grandchildren love their grandparents?

Yes, they do, but grandparents who aren't political columnists might not appreciate the need for such unconditional acceptance.

Political columnists are rarely popular because of the nature of what we do. I am occasionally reminded of that fact of newspaper life when an errant public figure vents his wrath at a public forum. I also get feedback in other ways.

Jerry Wise, a friend who publishes newspapers in DeQuincy and Cameron, said he often runs into people who tell him Jim Beam must be one mean dude.

Wise said he tells them I'm actually a decent sort, but I'm sure many of them aren't buying his defense.

I've developed a pretty thick hide over the last 37 years, but each of us still needs unqualified acceptance from some quarters to retain a sense of stability in our lives.

My wife and the other adults in my family have always been solid supporters, and I wouldn't trade that for anything in the world. However, it's especially gratifying when a child visibly expresses how he or she feels.

Andrew, for example, gives me a hearty wave whenever he comes through the door. Once he's in grandpa's arms, he hangs on for dear life, and that gives me a special lift.

Jessica has a number of other interests — friends, dolls, and her dog and computer games. However, she was like Andrew at his age and still has strong feelings for her grandpa. She will always be a major love of my life, and that will keep me dancing to her tunes for as long as I live.

Then, there's Lucy, my wife's dog. She likes me, too.

I'm not a dog fancier, and that's why it's difficult for Jo Ann to understand why Lucy gets so excited when I come home in the afternoons. Sometimes she (the dog) even runs around in circles.

Lucy knows she isn't supposed to jump on me or on the couch when I'm around, but that doesn't dampen her enthusiasm.

When I'm gone, Jo Ann lets Lucy do pretty much anything she wants to do. Lucy loves to chew up paper, tree leaves and pine cones and spread the remains all over the living and dining room.

Why Jo Ann is surprised when Lucy nags her while she's trying to work her crossword puzzle or enjoy a snack puzzles me. What else should she expect from a dog she has spoiled rotten?

Jo Ann said one afternoon she couldn't understand why Andrew and Lucy got so excited when I was around. I told her it was obvious that my grandchildren and her dog know character when they see it.

She got a big laugh out of that one, but I still think it has merit.

As for my political writing career, I've been fortunate over the last 37 years to have support from more than family. Many of you out there have been in my corner as I've tried to keep you informed and analyzed the political developments which affect our daily lives.

To enjoy that kind of loyalty from family, friends, professional colleagues and readers has been a rewarding experience for which I am especially grateful.

Christmas day is also an appropriate occasion to say a special thanks to a supportive family that has strong ties.

Monday night, it was Gary's birthday and we celebrated as we do on every such occasion by eating out as a family. Gary is my son-in-law and we give him a hard time every year about his birthday being so close to Christmas.

After our meal, we gathered at the Meeks' home to open Gary's birthday presents and watch Andrew and his unique way of crawling from one place to another. He's also starting to pull himself up.

Jessica was videotaping the Monday night action, just as Jamie, her mother, and Gary did when she was that age. Jessica loves Andrew, and it's so great to see them enjoying one another.

Bryan and Edith, my son and daughter-in-law, have been counting their blessings since Andrew's birth, and he has brought new joy to all our lives.

When our evening was over, I realized how pleasurable it was to love and laugh together as we have done so many times before.

I know that their children and grandchildren cherish most grandfathers, but each of us can indulge ourselves a little by believing our circumstances are unique.

My best wishes to you on this Christmas day. Those of us who live in this area have been blessed in many ways, and what better time than Christmas to thank God for the birth of His son and for the many blessings He has bestowed on each of us.

Dec. 25, 1997

Thank God for grandchildren

Grandparents are some of the luckiest people in the world. We get to enjoy our children, then our grandchildren and — sometimes — our great-grandchildren.

Only a grandparent can appreciate what a great joy it is to have a grandchild run up to them with a huge smile and a "happy-to-see-you" look on his or her face. It's the kind of greeting I always get from Andrew James Beam, my grandson who turned 2 Wednesday. He calls me "Paw."

Have you noticed that most grandchildren call you what they want rather than what you or their parents might prefer?

Andrew calls his grandmother "Jo." Jessica Meek, our 10-year-old granddaughter, calls me "Grandpa" and her grandmother "Joey." And that's all right with both of us.

Jessica, by the way, still knows how to turn "Grandpa" into putty with her feminine charms or a tremendous bear hug.

If you're a grandparent, you know there isn't much you wouldn't do for your grandchildren. Our children — on whom we kept tighter reins — have to wonder what brought about that change in our lives, especially at a time when they are trying to hold the line.

I suppose we view life differently as grandparents because we're looking at things from a different perspective. When our own children were young, we spent a lot of time trying to avoid mistakes as we tried to mold them into happy and productive people. In the course of trying to make all the right moves, we sometimes missed some of the joyful moments.

Now, the serious child rearing is in the hands of our children, and grandparents are more than happy to watch developments from the sidelines. Well, most of the time, that is.

We still worry about our grandchildren when they are sick, or on the road, or going through some experience for the first time. We don't want them to have to face too many tough roadblocks as they mature.

I know our children and their spouses would appreciate a little less advice on occasion, but we seldom let them enjoy that luxury.

I am always amazed at the sacrifices we are willing to make for our grandchildren. I have no problem, for example, giving them the last piece of pie — or the last of anything else I might have.

Perhaps I should explain that statement.

When I was growing up, we were taught never to eat the last piece of pie or the last slice of bread or the last of almost anything else. People often ask me why that was so, and, to tell you the truth, I'm not really sure.

Someone has to eat the last piece, of course, or it will go to waste. In my family, I can remember my dad getting the last slice of something special, so maybe that's why it was hands-off for everyone else.

The same process worked in my family for a while, but a slice of egg custard pie changed all that. No one ate that last piece once, and it went bad. Jo Ann had coveted that egg custard pie, and said, "That's it. Never again." She tossed the unwritten rule without a second thought.

I'm not sure Andrew knew exactly what was happening last Saturday when his two sets of grandparents and aunts, uncles and first cousins showed up at his house to celebrate his second birthday a few days early. He was under the weather a bit, but he managed to get into the swing of things and joined the festivities.

Although he got a couple of big gifts, like a three-wheeler, Andrew was content to play with a half-dozen small cars. Isn't that the way it usually happens?

Lily, his 2-year-old first cousin from Lafayette, had a grand time. And Jessica, his local first cousin who has been his best friend since he was born, helped him put those new toys together. She also tried to focus his attention on the events at hand, which was no easy task because of the attraction of those cars.

I'll never forget the day Andrew came home for the first time. Jessica was so excited; she paced back and forth outside his house waiting the happy occasion. And she has continued to love and watch over him since that day.

Our family gathered for its weekly meal Wednesday, and it was another opportunity to celebrate since it was Andrew's actual birth date. We always break routine on birthdays and dine out somewhere special. Andrew's mother said he picked the place, but I'm not so sure about that. After all, he's only 2. However, I didn't press the issue.

The highlight of Andrew's normal Wednesday evenings is to get out of his highchair after he's finished eating and traipse around the dining room at the Piccadilly. All of the friendly folks at the cafeteria have seen Andrew grow up over the last two years, and they always give him a first-class greeting as he makes his way down the serving line.

Whether Andrew is going to experience those "terrible twos" remains to be seen, but up to now he's been one of the happiest youngsters I've ever seen. And he takes long afternoon naps. That suits his grandmother just fine when she's babysitting, because she is convinced daily rest — for her, at least — is good for the soul.

Like Jessica over the last 10 years, Andrew has enriched our lives beyond measure. And maybe that's the greatest of the many gifts grandchildren bring to the people around them.

I've tried to follow the advice of another grandfather who told me once while I was grocery shopping, "Enjoy your grandchildren while they're young, Jim, because they grow up awfully fast."

Isn't that the truth?

March 4, 1999

Trucker challenges his uncle

When your nephew gets on your case, you know you're in deep trouble. Jeff Beam drives 18-wheelers, and he didn't take too kindly to remarks I made in a recent column about the "get-out-of-my-way attitude" of some truckers.

Jeff's mother and stepfather are also truckers, so I'm probably on their hit list as well.

The column in question was about legislation introduced in the current session that is aimed at lowering the truck speed limit from 70 to 60 mph. Jeff, like other truckers, thinks it's dangerous to have different speeds for trucks and other vehicles.

"... Maybe Beam should ride in a truck for a day and see what we put up with dealing with four-wheelers on the road," Jeff said in a letter to the editor last Sunday.

A recent national study agrees with truckers that smaller vehicles are the real menace on the road. Cox Newspapers did a computer analysis of 1997 federal highway safety records.

The study found the most common fatal accident involving a large truck and a car occurs when the car pulls in front of the truck, and the larger vehicle can't slow down in time.

In fatal crashes involving cars and large trucks, the analysis found that investigating police at the accident scene cited car drivers 2,381 times for failure to keep in the proper lane, drowsiness or reckless driving. They cited truck drivers only 679 times.

When drinking was a factor in the fatal crashes, the data showed that 15 percent of the car drivers had an alcohol blood content over the common legal limit of .10 percent. Less than 1 percent of the truck drivers had that much alcohol in their systems.

The General Accounting Office, the investigating arm of Congress, analyzed the same data.

"Car driver errors were cited in 74 percent of the crashes, compared to 35 percent for truck driver errors," said a GAO spokesman (apparently both drivers were cited in some crashes). "This finding lends some support to the hypothesis that, compared to truck drivers, car drivers contributed more to fatal crashes between large trucks and cars."

The Cox analysis concluded, "The numbers suggest that the biggest opportunity to save lives might be teaching car drivers how to stay safe while driving near trucks."

An NBC Nightly News report backed up that finding. It said 18-wheelers have blind spots on three sides that make it difficult for truck drivers to see smaller vehicles. Drivers of smaller vehicles were urged to get around the trucks as quickly as possible.

As you might expect, not everyone agrees with the Cox and GAO findings. The National Highway Traffic Safety Administration said many conclusions at the accident scene are based on the investigating officer's judgment, his observations and discussions with witnesses. It said conclusions "can only be suggestive about why truck crashes occur."

The director of CRASH (Citizens for Reliable and Safe Highways) said truck drivers promote the idea that car drivers are responsible for fatal crashes. She said the car drivers usually are killed, and when police arrive to investigate, "the only one talking is the truck driver."

Those are harsh words, and they give you some idea of the hostility that some drivers of smaller vehicles feel towards truck drivers. One fact stands out from the 1997 studies, regardless of which side you're on. In 1997 crashes involving a large truck, 87 percent of the 5,355 people who died were occupants of the passenger vehicle.

Legislators need to keep that in mind when they decide whether to lower the truck speed limit. If it will help save lives, that's one thing. However, truckers think it will have the opposite effect. Is it possible that reducing the speed limit for all vehicles might be the better solution?

It's food for thought.

My nephew isn't the only one who is upset about something someone else has written. The Times of Shreveport fired off an editorial in response to one in The Advocate of Baton Rouge, which objects to spending state money on improvements to Shreveport's Independence Stadium.

The Times said state money helped finance a $15 million expansion of the Baton Rouge Centroplex events center and a $116 million expansion of the New Orleans Convention Center. The newspaper said state money also figured in the $11.5 million to build the Alexandria Convention Center, the $9 million spent on a convention center and other facilities at Toledo Bend, the $3.85 million for a civic center and covered arena in Beauregard Parish and the $3 million spent to expand the Monroe Civic Center.

It should be noted that hotel-motel sales taxes collected in those areas produced some of those revenues.

"Until these and other local projects stop receiving state money, there is no reason the Independence Stadium project shouldn't draw its share either. In fact, it should if for no other reason than fairness," The Times editorial said.

The newspaper also noted that its city is funding most of the $80 million it will take to build the Shreveport convention center, and Bossier City isn't asking for state money to pay for its $45 million multipurpose arena.

Other cities, including Lake Charles, could be making the same argument as The Times. When it comes to helping local governments, public officials and legislators don't always have equality in mind when they start handing out state dollars.

The moral of this story? Whenever you take a stand on anything, be prepared for flak from someone on the other side. It could even come from a member of the family.

April 1, 1999

Family ties enrich our lives

What better time than Christmas to think about families and what an influential role they play in our lives?

I've had the good fortune to be part of a large family. My mother had seven brothers and four sisters, and my dad had one sister. So I've had an abundance of uncles and aunts.

Those cousins of mine and I who have survived were witnesses a little over a week ago to the end of the generation that preceded us. We said our final goodbyes to our last surviving aunt.

The fact that Dora Cornelia Mudd Welch was still around at 86 was living proof that good things do happen to good people.

Perhaps her daughter, Sharon, best summed up her charitable and giving personality.

"Mamma was a giver, not a taker," Sharon wrote in a tribute to her mother. "She gave love to all, family and friends... People were not black or white, rich or poor, they were just people."

I can still remember the first time I heard Aunt Dora's name many, many years ago. As a child, I spent most of my summers in Cameron, the place of my birth. On one of those occasions, I was on my grandfather's front porch when Uncle Buster (A.P. Welch Jr.) asked his dad for permission to marry the woman who would become Aunt Dora.

My grandfather, Amedy P. Welch Sr., had retired as registrar of voters in Cameron Parish before I was born. He died before my 20th birthday in 1953.

Another aunt, Wynona Welch, became registrar and a lifelong favorite of mine. During hard economic times in my immediate family, it was Aunt Nona who helped clothe and feed my brothers, sister and me.

Uncle C.B. Welch was a carefree member of the family who loved his Saturday nights in Creole at the local dance hall. I can remember pitching a fit at the top of the stairs on one occasion because I couldn't join him on his favorite night out. It never registered with me that I wasn't old enough to tag along.

Most folks kept telling me I looked an awful lot like Uncle L.B. Welch, who was an agriculture official in the parish seat at Cameron. The town was called Leesburg in those days.

Some members of the Welch clan, Uncles Walter, Monroe and Will and another Aunt Dora (Griffith), lived in Port Arthur, Texas. The men worked at the Gulf Refinery there. We didn't see them as often.

Aunt Curry married Bob Doxey, a rural postman in the Grand Chenier area whom I will always remember as a jovial fellow. I never knew Aunt Lucille Welch Nunez, who died in 1920.

Uncle Shine (Russell Welch) and his wife, who lived near the Welch homestead, were victims of Hurricane Audrey in 1957. Aunt Dora Griffith's husband also died in the storm.

Uncle Buster and his family were living in our grandfather's house, and they survived that horrifying storm by tying themselves to a small tree in the yard.

I was in the U.S. Army in 1957 at Ft. Benning, Ga., and remember getting a call in the middle of the night about the devastating hurricane. I left the next morning and eventually witnessed the destruction when residents were allowed back into the area.

A large hole in the ground was all that was left of the two-story Welch home in the Oak Grove community, and other homes on the front ridge were also swept away.

The people of Cameron are a sturdy lot, and they rebuilt and learned a lot from the terrifying and deadly experience.

My Aunt Margaret Herr, from my father's side of the family, lived in Lake Charles. We had close contact with her family as youngsters and at one time I worked with her at Muller's department store.

Later generations of our family haven't maintained the close contacts that existed in those earlier years, but we occasionally renew old ties. Unfortunately, most of those reunions occur when someone dies.

Dale and Eloise, my surviving brother and sister, and I drove down to Aunt Dora's funeral together. We talked about those early years and the many trips we made to Cameron when we were children.

Aunt Dora's daughter talked about that in the tribute to her mother.

"We always had extra kids at our house in the summer, especially the Beam kids," she said.

The relatively short distance to Cameron could become a daylong affair if you hit heavy barge traffic at the Gibbstown Ferry.

Another aspect of life in Cameron that hasn't changed much — too many mosquitoes — was evident when we drove to the Rutherford Cemetery after the service. They were swarming everywhere.

Bothersome as they were, though, my cousin Benny Welch said, "This isn't bad at all."

We went our separate ways after the services at the cemetery and having a bite to eat at Aunt Dora's house. As we drove away, something told me we had just helped write the final chapter about the life and times of one family that was part of what some have called "the greatest generation."

Nevertheless, the future still looks bright and promising. Those of us who belong to a different generation have forged our own strong family ties that will also survive the test of time.

I hope the holiday season gives each of you an opportunity to look back on your family history and appreciate how much it has enriched your lives.

Merry Christmas!

Dec. 24, 2000

Jessica celebrates milestone

My granddaughter is now a teen-ager. However, Aug. 7, 1988, the day Jessica was born, seems like only yesterday. Another grandfather told me once to enjoy grandchildren while they are young because they grow up so fast.

How right he was. Fortunately, we haven't missed many golden moments during Jessica's development over the last 13 years. Because of that, our lives have been enriched beyond measure.

The honoree among our eight-member clan always gets to pick the place for our traditional family birthday meals. On Tuesday evening, Jessica selected a Mexican restaurant. She likes the desserts they give birthday celebrants and enjoyed a few minutes in the spotlight as she was serenaded by the staff.

As you might expect, Jessica has pretty much called the shots over the last 13 years, especially where her dad and her grandfather are concerned. Her mother and grandmother have been the stable influences in her life.

I can still remember the tears of joy Jo Ann shed when she heard the news that Jessica was on the way. It was a moment she had anticipated for 10 years.

Gary and Jamie, Jessica's parents, captured Jo Ann's reaction on tape. It was to be the beginning of countless hours of video centering on Jessica for years to come.

Jamie was able to stay at home during Jessica's formative years, and it has paid numerous dividends. Thanks to that close association, the two of them have become the best of friends.

However, Jessica knows wherein the authority lies. She knows her mother can be a tough taskmaster who won't settle for second best.

Gary has been a good father, too. However, he will always be a kid at heart, and that has been the bond that keeps him and Jessica close. He can be stern, though, when the occasion demands it.

The Meeks have often included Jo Ann and me in their vacation plans, and that has strengthened our ties to Jessica. There isn't much in her life that we haven't shared from the beginning.

Every time she was sick, we were a support system for one another.

I soon learned that there wasn't anything a grandfather wouldn't do for his grandchildren. Anything I had was hers, and if I didn't have it I'd do my best to get it.

Jessica returned the favors a thousand times over with loving hugs for her grandfather that always give me an especially warm feeling all over. There is something magical about those demonstrations of affection that are indescribable.

She's a young woman now and occasionally she has more important things on her mind than giving her grandfather a warm greeting or fond farewell. However, those other times when she gives me one of those bear hugs more than makes up for the slights I might feel.

Jessica has an artistic side, and that will give her a great sense of satisfaction over the years.

Andrew, our first grandson, came into our lives more than four years ago, and Jessica was there for him from the beginning. I can still see her standing out in front of Bryan and Edith's home awaiting Andrew's arrival.

They have become pals, and she's also Andrew's big sister when he needs one.

The church is a major part of our lives, and that has been a good influence on both Jessica and Andrew. Finding eight seats in a row on a church pew is sometimes difficult, but we manage.

Grandpa always gets a warm greeting on Sunday mornings from both his grandchildren. As our associate pastor's wife said recently, "There's nothing like a hug from one of them, is there?"

We also share Sunday meals as a family, and those times are precious.

Although she's just turned 13, Jessica is already looking forward to the driving years. The other day the two of us looked over some spiffy convertibles while we were visiting a new car dealership.

"That's the one I want," she said as she tried out the driver's seat. Later, she wanted to sit in it again. Of course, grandpa was more than willing to oblige.

I'm sure I would try to figure out where to get the money for a car like that when the time comes, but you can bet her mother will have other ideas. She and Jo Ann keep Gary and me straight when we think about giving in to Jessica's every whim.

Looking back over the last 13 years, I can't thank God enough for the blessing he brought into all our lives when Jessica was born. She's not perfect by any stretch of the imagination, but whose grandchild is?

I suppose the best thing about being a grandparent is knowing exactly how other grandparents feel about their grandchildren. Grandchildren are some of the miracles God works in our lives, and we've been blessed with two.

Jessica may be a teen-ager now, but for her grandfather she will always be the little girl who helped him understand what's really important in life — the love of and for a grandchild.

Aug. 12, 2001

Things we cherish never change

If everything falls into place as expected, I'll have two reasons to celebrate this weekend. One is a definite. It's my daughter's birthday today. The second cause for celebration is a bit iffy, and we'll get back to that one in a moment.

Jamie's birthday falls exactly three weeks after mine, and it's one of many close ties we've shared for more years than I'm sure she wants to count.

I can still remember the day Jamie was born. She came into this world just two weeks before I completed a two year tour of duty in the Army, and that meant a tremendous savings for a struggling young couple.

The years that have come and gone for Jo Ann and me since then have been enriched beyond measure by Jamie and later by our son Bryan. Their spouses and our grandchildren have strengthened our family ties.

Jamie is my walking partner, and those are cherished moments we share every week. It also works wonders for our physical and mental well-being.

Jo Ann has been a good mother, and Jamie has followed in her footsteps. I am often amazed at how loving and caring Jamie has been to Jessica, our 13-year-old granddaughter who has been known to occasionally try her mother's patience.

Thursday was a good example of how Jamie goes the extra mile. She drove Jessica to Baton Rouge for a school field trip, and they had a grand time. They have become good friends.

Birthdays are major events in our lives, and the eight of us will be getting together today so Jamie will know how special she is to us. Jo Ann's birthday is Nov. 1, so our meal together will honor two of the four women in our family.

Now, for that iffy situation.

According to my wife's construction schedule, I'm supposed to get my bathroom back by the first of the week. It's only a half-bath, but it's all mine.

My wife is remodeling her bathroom with help from Lisa, a talented friend. While the big bathroom has been out of commission, Jo Ann has been sharing mine for weeks now. I will say this, though. She followed all the rules I laid down when she was forced to invade my territory and has been a model occupant.

You would think a fellow who shared one bathroom with his parents and four siblings while growing up wouldn't be complaining about a few weeks of inconvenience. We also had only one bathroom in our house while our two children were young.

Looking back on those years, I've often wondered how we managed it. There are only two of us now, and you wouldn't believe how many bathroom conflicts we've had over the past few weeks.

I suppose it just depends on what you're used to that makes a difference.

With one major exception, the remodeling has gone well. We told everyone involved the only thing we wanted to save was our toilet bowl and tank. You can't buy them like that one anymore, thanks to do-gooders like former U.S. Sen. J. Bennett Johnston.

Our former senator and others in their exclusive Washington, D.C., club a number of years ago decided a great way to conserve water was to reduce the amount you could legally use in a toilet bowl tank. And despite the folly of their new law, it's still on the books.

I read a story a few years back that said although the law is extremely unpopular, efforts to repeal it weren't going anywhere. Johnston, who had left the Senate by that time, was quoted as saying he still thought it was a good idea.

Obviously, promoters of that law never talked to homeowners about their wild-eyed plan. I haven't found anyone who likes those new-fangled commodes.

So now you know why we wanted to save that water tank.

Unfortunately, one of the first things that had to be done to remodel my wife's bathroom was to remove old tile from the wall.

I heard some hammering but didn't give it a second thought. That is until a young man walked outside where I was working.

"I owe you a toilet bowl tank," he said. "I cut my finger and accidentally swung my hammer backwards and hit the tank. It broke and water spilled everywhere."

How could I get angry while the young man was standing there bleeding? It was an accident, I kept telling myself, but I was still upset.

"I'll get you another one," he said.

"Not like that one," I replied. "You can't buy that kind anymore."

"Oh, I'll find one," he insisted.

I waited but knew he would never be able to live up to his promise.

Jo Ann eventually had to buy a new toilet bowl and tank, but the young man's boss did give us that much credit on his bill.

As beautiful as the remodeled bathroom looks, I know the flushes will never be the same again.

Thank goodness my other reason to celebrate is a constant in our lives. Jamie's birthday will turn up again next year just as it has for a long time. And meddling congressmen can't do anything that will destroy the love we share.

Oct. 28, 2001

Chapter 2

You Don't Forget Them

They're just outside the door

What do you know about the fellow next door? Oh, you see him cutting his grass now and then, watch him drive off to work or come home in the afternoon and maybe stop and say hello once or twice a month. But what's the guy really like?

Some people say the Good Neighbor Policy is dead, and maybe it is in too many parts of this great country. Perhaps television and selfish interests keep us inside and preoccupied with our own little world.

But there are still a lot of nice people around, and I've got a neighborhood full of 'em. I only regret that I've lived around some of them for years and didn't know there was a gold mine of concern right under my nose.

A few weeks back, I noticed an awful lot of water standing around the carport. It hadn't rained, and even with my limited technical skills, it didn't take long to determine a water line had sprouted a leak.

Someone at work told me the first thing to do was cut off the water so you can get an idea of where the leak is located.

I called Melvin — he's the guy next door — and asked him if he'd cut off my water. When I got home, I found out Melvin not only cut off the water, but also had started digging to locate the leak.

Melvin has helped me out of a lot of jams. He and I have worked on my car so many times I feel like he's got part interest in the bundle of bolts.

When Melvin is stumped, which isn't often, he doesn't worry. He's got friends who are experts in a number of fields. One night after hours of tinkering around with a new fuel pump, we gave up. Melvin called a friend who had the old motor purring in minutes.

I'll tell you the kind of guy Melvin is. He still carries a pocketknife. If you'd seen how many times he whipped out those blades to solve a problem, you'd wonder how anyone goes through life without a pocketknife.

Melvin is also an extremely resourceful fellow. Why, when he re-roofed his house some time ago, he recruited all his relatives and friends. I'll bet no one had to lay more than 10 shingles. I was afraid the roof would fall in from the weight.

He painted his house about a month ago and did the job in one day. "How'd you get through so fast?" I asked. Melvin said he got some newfangled applicators and Russell — he lives across the street — came over to help out. "I told Russell there'd be a can of beer waiting for him at each corner of the house, and you'd be surprised how fast he painted," Melvin said.

Just this past week, I had trouble fixing the edger. Melvin's got a sixth sense about trouble and was over in minutes. He got that trimmer spinning in short order.

But back to the water leak.

Shoveling is something I can do without, but I started digging where Melvin left off. Before long, he was over with his shovel. We got the project under way about 4 p.m.

Richard — he lives on the corner — smelled activity and showed up with his spade. Talk about dig! Melvin and Richard are both about six feet and have the weight to match. You talk about earth moving!

We changed half the line going to the water meter. But it wasn't going to be that easy. We noticed the other half of the line was leaking. Then it was back to the trenches. Why do they put those lines so far underground?

Darkness came and those guys were working so fast all I could do was hold the light and stand out of the way. To cap things off, we needed a reducer for the faucet. The stores were closed by that time, but Bob — he's another neighbor from across the street — had just what we needed.

Finally, at 10 p.m. and $22 worth of pipe and fittings later, the job was finished. Those rascals saved me over $100 in labor costs and hours of manual labor.

It was a big job and probably the best example of what good neighbors are made of. But there have been numerous other times when I got a helping hand — like Allen with the upholstering and wall papering and Mr. Nichols with samples from his garden.

I'm here to say the Good Neighbor Policy is alive and well. Just open the door and step outside. If you're as lucky as I am, you'll find that's all it takes.

April 16, 1972

Will Rogers' wit is ageless

Humorist Will Rogers died in an airplane crash on Aug. 15, 1935, and singer John McCormack summed up the loss when he said, "A smile has disappeared from the lips of America."

The world was shocked and saddened when it heard of Rogers' death, but although the man was gone, he left a legacy that even today is evoking those smiles many thought they had lost forever.

Lake Charles American Press readers are finding out daily from reprints of Rogers' witticisms that the man's sense of humor and feel of the public pulse are timeless.

A new biography of the humorist — "Will Rogers: The Man and His Times"— gives Americans a rare insight into the man who still captures their hearts.

The American Heritage biography by Richard M. Ketchum was prepared in cooperation with the Will Rogers Memorial Commission and the staff of the Will Rogers Memorial at Claremore, Oklahoma.

Readers are treated to 415 pages of revealing narrative, anthologies of his comments and more than 300 illustrations showing the public and private Rogers.

Born part Cherokee in 1879, Rogers' first ambition was to become the world's best trick-roper. He realized his goal and became a genuine representative of the Wild West in remote parts of the world.

"Will's roping act is virtually impossible to describe, notes Ketchum, "and the way to appreciate the complexity and artistry it combined is to see the various tricks on one of his early silent films, 'The Ropin' Fool,' in which he did 53 of them ranging from the simple to the nearly impossible."

Rogers joined the Ziegfeld Follies in 1916 and was an instant hit. He was proudest of the night President Woodrow Wilson was in the audience in Baltimore. Nothing was sacred to Rogers as he commented on military preparedness, a subject for which Wilson was constantly criticized.

"There is some talk of getting a machine gun if we can borrow one. The one we have now they are using to train our Army with in Plattsburg. If we go to war, we will just about have to go to the trouble of getting another gun."

Movies followed the Follies and Rogers made 12 pictures for Samuel Goldwyn.

"He had embarked on two new professions, in both of which he succeeded simply by being himself," writes Ketchum.

Rogers then turned to after-dinner speaking and writing a syndicated newspaper column. His articles appeared in the New York Times from 1922 until his death.

His talks began by startling or insulting his audience. Automobile dealers were "old time Horse-trading Gyps with white collars on." Advertising men were "Robbing Hoods of America." He told the Association of Woolen Men to stay indoors in case of rain or there would be "about 500 men choked to death by their own suits."

Bankers heard that borrowing money on easy terms was a one-way ticket to the poorhouse. "If you think it ain't a sucker game, why is the banker the richest man in town?"

Rogers opened his column with the line, which began his Follies act: "Well, all I know is just what I read in the papers." He told his readers "Congress has been writing my material for years."

Aviation became another love of Rogers and he flew whenever possible. The lure of Alaska brought Rogers and Wiley Post together and their adventurous spirit ended in their air crash and death at Point Barrow, Alaska.

Although only in his 50s, Rogers had become the most popular columnist, speaker, broadcaster and movie actor in American history.

Thanks to the written word, those of us who missed that golden era can still enjoy that ageless Will Rogers humor.

Nothing is more appropriate for our time, for example, than Rogers' comment that "you can't make the Republican Party pure by more contributions; because contributions are what got it where it is today."

July 7, 1974

Apathy has consequences

Gene Pohorelsky has lived under tyranny during his lifetime, and he's worried.

A familiar face to many Lake Charles citizens, Pohorelsky is in charge of food service at St. Patrick Hospital and a co-owner of Joseph's Drive-In, a familiar hangout for decades.

Pohorelsky is retiring Jan. 5, and he feels it's time to repay Lake Charles for the many kindnesses its people have extended to him over the years.

What does he plan to do?

"Apathy concerns me, and I would like to do whatever I can to alert citizens to what happens when people become apathetic," he said.

Born in Russia in 1913, Pohorelsky was just a toddler during the Bolshevik Revolution. His father had been a town councilman, and he remembers how lucky his father was to survive the purges. "We lived in constant fear," Pohorelsky said.

A brew master by trade, the senior Pohorelsky moved away from the population centers to blend in with the country scenery.

Czechoslovakia became their home in 1925, a country that enjoyed freedom between the two world wars. It was there that the younger Pohorelsky began school.

The nation came into being in October of 1918 following the collapse of the Austro-Hungarian Empire. The new government was liberal and democratic, modeled after the government of the United States.

Freedom was to last only until March 15, 1939, when Hitler sent troops into Prague. The nation was dismembered throughout World War II, and a resistance movement constantly defied the German rulers despite cruel reprisals.

Following the war, the government became a coalition of Socialists and Communists. Eventually, in 1948, the Communists seized control of the country.

What does Pohorelsky remember about those days?

"The people of Czechoslovakia were never really concerned about the Communists. After the war, people just wouldn't get involved," he said.

Apathy was rampant. "And then one day we woke up and the Communists had seized power," Pohorelsky said.

Roaming the countryside picking mushrooms, Pohorelsky waited for the chance to escape to freedom. He and his wife had that opportunity the day after their wedding in 1948.

"We were near the border that day, which was just across the railroad tracks from where we were picking mushrooms. We waited for the guards to pass and made our dash to freedom," he said. The Pohorelskys escaped with only the clothes on their backs. "We left everything else behind," he added.

They settled in a German refugee camp and remained there until January of 1950.

Through the efforts of the Rev. Theo Hassink of Lake Charles, the Pohorelskys were relocated on a farm in Iowa, La.

Lacking experience in farm work, the job only lasted two days. From there, Pohorelsky went to work in the kitchen at the Pioneer Club. He stayed there until 1951 when he became a parts manager for a local auto dealer.

While there, Pohorelsky bought the Hob Nob restaurant on Broad Street, which he operated for 2 1/2 years while he was working at the car company.

He leased Joseph's Drive-In in 1956. The St. Patrick job came along in 1967.

What prompted him to speak out about his past and his concern for the future?

"The comments I hear in America these days remind me so much of the remarks I heard in Czechoslovakia before the Communists took over," he said.

What are they? Here are some examples:

"Politics are rotten, and there is nothing we can do about it."

"If we get rid of one crook, we just replace him with another."

"I've got a nice home, a good job, a boat and motor, so why should I concern myself with politics?"

"Let someone else worry about politics. I'm not interested."

"Those attitudes are dangerous," says Pohorelsky. "The belief that we can let someone else be responsible doesn't work.

"Our politicians are only as good as we elect," he adds.

I asked Pohorelsky if the 71 percent turnout in the Nov. 7 district attorney election changed his outlook.

"I'm optimistic, but I'm still concerned for America. It's the best turnout I've seen since I've been in this country, but will it last?" he asked.

I couldn't answer that question, but one thing is certain. Pohorelsky's been there before, and he has some insight worth sharing.

"Freedom is a very delicate property," he said as he departed.

The words stuck in my mind.

Dec. 10, 1978

Flooding had its good sides

There you are standing beneath Interstate 210 out of the rain during Friday's flooding, waiting for a ride to work. Cars and trucks keep inching by along Enterprise Boulevard on their way northward, but all you get are long stares.

After about 30 minutes, you look up and see your thoroughly soaked son walking your way. "Buddy said he couldn't get here, Dad. He said you might as well go on back home."

What to do? What to do?

Suddenly I remembered what Buddy had said on the phone earlier. One of our reporters had walked to work that morning. And he lives farther south than I do — on Louisiana Avenue about four blocks north of West McNeese Street.

"No, I think I'll wait here and hope for a ride," I told my son. "I'll walk if I have to." (If that reporter could walk more than three miles to work, I had to try).

"Dad, no one's going to pick you up dressed like that," he replied.

I hadn't thought much about how I looked, but his comments made me realize why I was getting the harsh stares.

I must have looked awfully cruddy standing there dressed in a 14-gallon cowboy hat, a raincoat, brown slacks rolled up to my knees, loud blue socks sticking out of my soaked shoes and a bright orange flight bag containing dry clothes and shoes draped over my shoulder.

Folks driving by must have thought I was a derelict seeking shelter while trying to hoof it out to California.

It was raining hard at the time, so I delayed my walk to town. Again, car and truck occupants just gave me hard, cold looks.

Then along came John Snody of Westlake in a pickup truck. He pulled over to the curb and asked where I was headed.

"Downtown to the American Press," I answered.

"Hop in, I'll take you right to the front door," he said.

Snody had taken his wife to work at Lake Charles Memorial Hospital. Afterward, he had been driving around helping folks in trouble. I assumed he was headed back to Westlake and that the Press was on his way. I found out later I had guessed wrong.

"If people wouldn't drive so fast, they could make it," he said. "I've been all over the city without any problem," he added.

Snody stopped behind a stalled car on Enterprise Boulevard near the State Employment Service Office. When a push didn't dislodge the stuck auto, Snody pulled around front and the car driver attached a chain Snody had in the back of his pickup.

The car came right out of he mud, and Snody and I were on our way again.

Rain was coming down hard when we drove into the back of the press, but Snody let me out near the back door. He refused to accept anything for the lift.

"Are you going home?" I asked.

"No, I think I'll keep driving around and see if anyone needs help," he said.

What a genuine Good Samaritan, I thought as I ran into the building.

Snody's kindness made me stop and think a moment about events earlier that morning.

Two neighbors had stopped by about 4:30 a.m. to tell my son about the rising water. They had walked down to the end of the block to clear out debris that had piled up and that was holding back the water.

A phone call got us all up at 5 a.m. A neighbor down the street had water in her home, but she found time to alert others. Suddenly we realized disaster was at our doorstep, thanks to a woman who thought about others even though she and her family had more than their share of problems.

Some water crept under the front door, but we were spared the damage suffered by thousands of others throughout the area. It could have been worse without that phone call.

Once I got to work Friday, I learned that three of our reporters had been given a ride on a city Department of Public Works truck. If the considerate driver of that truck only knew how much we needed those three guys.

A sports reporter, the only one who could make it, walked in all the way from the Piccadilly Cafeteria on Ryan Street. Was I glad I had decided not to turn tail and run! Can't let the sports department get ahead of the news staff at any cost.

We heard some bad news throughout the evening – residents telling of inconsiderate drivers flooding their homes and scattered stories of looting – but many of the reports told of man's thoughtfulness in the face of turmoil.

I know that the Good Samaritan I found Friday restored my faith in humanity. Other stories told of neighbor helping neighbor and stranger aiding stranger.

The cleanup will continue for some time and heartbreak is everywhere, but optimism seems to prevail.

I don't want to rush to judgment, but maybe there's hope for us all yet.

May 18, 1980

Lunchtime won't be same

The man is a Lake Charles institution. And when he leaves our city soon — he refuses to say exactly when — he'll take a piece of our hearts and our history with him.

He's George Petrou, the proprietor of Mary Ann's Cafe, the most famous hamburger establishment between here and Timbuktu.

If you don't know George, you've missed a big chunk of lunchtime life over the last 27-plus years.

Something tells me I ate my last George Petrou hamburger last Wednesday, and the thought disturbed me Friday evening when I realized the finality of it all. First, Borden's closed and now George. Is nothing sacred anymore?

I first saw George Petrou when he was cooking at the Colonial Inn, another Lake Charles hamburger landmark. It's a favorite of old-timers, and they will also tell you about its predecessor, the Palace Sandwich Shop, which was operated by the Yianaridis brothers. I heard my dad speak fondly of their hamburgers many times.

I'm not sure when I ate my first George Petrou hamburger after he took over Mary Ann's Cafe, but it's an experience no novice ever forgets.

There was this little thin guy working the register in the early 1970s. I never knew his name then, but he handled diners at the lunch counter. It was only after he left Mary Ann's that I learned his name was Kyriacos Papadimitriou.

Papadimitriou is a quiet man. I could never understand what he was telling George because he spoke so softly, but they had no problem communicating with each other. George, you see, was as loud as Papadimitriou was quiet.

A waitress took orders at the tables and booths. George was forever hollering at the waitresses who worked there over the years.

"When I want your order, I'll ask for it," he used to scream above the noisy crowd. Sometimes I think they gave him orders at the wrong time just to hear him howl.

If they got their orders mixed up, he'd ask them where they learned to count.

The first time you heard George dress down a waitress, you didn't dare look up for fear he'd give you a piece of his mind, too.

When George ran out of plates or lettuce or onions, or whatever, he had no problem getting refills. "LETTUCE!" he'd shout loud enough to rattle the rooftops.

And George didn't reserve his tirades for the help. If you were there by yourself and sat in one of the booths against the wall, watch out! George wouldn't hesitate to yell across the room and ask you to move to a stool or a small table. He didn't want you taking up space for more paying customers.

In those earlier years you took your life into your own hands when you asked for an old-fashioned hamburger or cheeseburger on a busy, busy, day. George would let you know in no uncertain terms that you were out of line. "No old-fashions today; we haven't got time," he'd blast out without a warning.

For some strange reason, George always knew how to make you feel guilty when you really hadn't done anything wrong.

You could never hide your trips to Mary Ann's. George didn't always have an exhaust fan on the west side of the building. That's when your clothes became saturated with that famous hamburger aroma.

"You've been to the Greek's for lunch, haven't you?" someone would invariably ask when you returned to the newsroom.

Things improved when the fan was added, but you never escaped the telltale smell.

If the place was packed and you were in a hurry, you were smart never to open the front door. George had no patience with impatience.

"If you're in a hurry, go down the street," he used to say in those early years. Recently, he would tell anxious diners, "You don't want to wait? Go to Hardee's."

George was too brash for some folks, but most of us knew that, way down deep, George really didn't have many mean bones in his body. He talked tough at first but mellowed over the years. He only wanted you to think he was an old grouch. And there was a kind and considerate side of George that he rarely displayed in public.

Even when George was visibly upset because of the frantic pace at noontime, he could always smile for a pretty face. "I always have time for the girls," he would say.

You knew you had arrived when George recognized you as a regular. That's when you no longer had to order. Once you earned your stripes, you could just plop yourself down and minutes later be eating your specialty.

The greatest recognition George gave a customer after he became a regular was free French fries on the side of your hamburger plate. It was stature that money couldn't buy. And now and then he'd slice your hamburger down the middle for easier handling.

George has been saying for months now that he's served his time over the busy grill. "The old legs aren't as strong as they used to be," he said. His wife, who wants to be near two of her children who live in Florida, has already moved. George will probably join her in July.

Jake Johnson has purchased Mary Ann's. You'll recognize him from his former association with the Piccadilly Cafeteria. George has been hanging around the last couple of weeks to teach Jake the ropes.

"He'll be OK," George told me out on the sidewalk one day last week. "The quality of the food will continue to be tops and he'll have help. It will just take him a while to get the speed."

Jake will do well, of course, and we wish him the best. But even Jake knows there will only be one George Petrou where hamburgers are concerned, and there probably isn't a man alive who can match his speed and memory in that department.

George gained national recognition for himself and Lake Charles when he and his hamburgers and onion rings were featured in a story in the late *National Observer* newspaper. It was a real tribute to the man and his town.

His town is your town and my town, too, of course, and that's why George Petrou will take a piece of our hearts and our history with him when he leaves. But those of us who knew the man well will still have a place in our hearts for the one and only hamburger king.

June 9, 1985

Dumars experience says it all

Fathers have a tremendous influence on our lives, and that's one of the reasons we celebrate their contributions on a designated day each year. But do we really understand and appreciate the role fathers play?

Probably not. We observe Father's Day with appropriate gifts and special events, but many of us fail to grasp the significance of the celebration. And all too often because of manly pride our fathers are gone before we tell them how much we love them and how they have enriched our lives by their own example.

Not everyone fits that pattern, of course. There are exceptions to every rule. It has been the good fortune of the people of Louisiana to share one of those exceptions this year with other Americans across this great nation.

He's Joe Dumars III, a member of the world champion Detroit Pistons of the National Basketball Association. Dumars expressed his love for his father in a unique way after the Pistons won the NBA championship last year.

The special relationship Dumars had with his father was the subject of a story in the April 22 issue of Parade magazine entitled, "The Ring Goes To My Father."

Joe Dumars Jr., Joe's father, died last week, but the legacy he left lives on in the son and with others whose lives he touched. But more important than that, the father's influence reaches countless thousands who know and admire the son for his achievements on and off the basketball court.

Those of us who have never met Joe Dumars III and who aren't regular NBA fans follow his exploits and savor his successes. Why else, for example, would we put ourselves through five tortuous basketball games which ended Thursday night when the Pistons repeated as NBA champions?

We like to see nice guys finish first occasionally, that's why, and Dumars fits that bill perfectly. Seeing him named most valuable player in last year's championship series against the Los Angeles Lakers was especially satisfying for his fans.

Dumars had no special advantages growing up. Quite the opposite, in fact. As the Parade article mentioned, his first basketball goal was a bicycle rim hammered to a door sawed in half which was nailed to a post in the backyard of the family's Natchitoches home.

Joe's father drove an 18-wheeler. His day began at 4 a.m. and ended at 9 p.m. He wanted the best for his children, but he had no idle time as they were growing up. He did find time, however, to instill a sense of human values and what it takes to succeed in life.

Although the father dropped out of school in the seventh grade, all seven of his children attended college. As folks around here are well aware, Joe attended McNeese State University and has given McNeese national recognition.

Joe told Parade magazine his father explained life this way: "As hard as I had it growing up, as hard as your mother had it growing up, we made it. You kids have got it great today, so don't sit here complaining about what you don't have and the reason this didn't work out. Just get it done and don't say anything about it."

Those words really hit home last year when Joe learned that his father, stricken with diabetes, had suffered another heart attack. He eventually lost both his legs because of the diabetes, which contributed to strokes and congestive heart failure.

Joe didn't tell anyone about his problems back home. He remembered what his dad had said about getting it done. But he said he sure wished he could "be sitting on the edge of the bathtub or in the backyard talking to Pop. Sometimes I needed that."

Joe learned Sunday that his father had died 90 minutes before the Pistons' third playoff game with the Portland Trail Blazers. It was an agonizing decision, but he eventually decided to stay in Portland for two more games through Thursday night.

"He was confused," Joe's mother told the Gannett News Service on Monday. "He didn't know what he wanted to do, if he wanted to fly in yesterday, or today, or what.

"I said, if he wanted to, we could have the funeral Saturday, and that would give him a chance to play Tuesday and Thursday. He told me yesterday he'd rest overnight, and make a decision today, and that's what he decided to do," Mrs. Dumars said.

"I knew my papa would want me to stay," Dumars said. "I put myself in his situation. He's gone through adversity for 21 years and he toughed it out."

Joe told Parade in April that the best things his parents gave him were "teaching me about hard work and learning to accept things as they are."

A father's words rang true even after his death. Although a nation knew Joe Dumars Jr. had died, his son was silent. His father had told him many times how to react to trial and tribulation. "Just get it done and don't say anything about it."

An Associated Press writer paid special tribute to Joe following Thursday night's fifth and deciding NBA game.

"Isiah Thomas was the most valuable player. Joe Dumars may have been the most valuable person," he wrote.

"Detroit's two MVPs, one through his brilliant play, the other through his personality and perseverance after his father's death, led the Pistons to their second consecutive NBA title Thursday night."

Joe gave his NBA championship ring to his dad last year. "I'm just as proud of it, but it will bring him a lot more enjoyment than me. I'm happy to have earned the right, but as far as having it on my finger, I don't need that."

Joe offered his parents a new home after making it big in the NBA, but they declined. His dad said, "I tell all our children that I ain't looking for nothing from them except that I want them to do by their offspring as I did for them. The thing that's most gratifying to me is he maintains a low profile..."

And how does Joe feel about his phenomenal success? He's worked hard and he's proud, he told Parade, but mostly he's glad his parents are able to enjoy his success.

"They've just been common working people all their lives, and now not that they are looking for publicity but just to be recognized as being somebody, that part makes me real happy," Dumars said.

Ask anyone who knows him and they will tell you Joe Dumars III is a class act. He has earned the respect of everyone he meets on and off the basketball floor.

Detroit center Bill Laimbeer said of his teammate, "He knows what to do in every situation, both from a basketball standpoint and a life standpoint."

Michael Jordan of the Chicago Bulls said getting to know and become a close friend of Dumars was the highlight of his experiences at the All Star weekend.

A Houston Chronicle writer referred to the two men as "Quiet Joe and Air Jordan," two superstars who have maintained a sense of humility.

Dumars lives by his dad's example, and the values he learned while growing up are being passed along to others. He speaks to youngsters often, many of them in his home state.

"A lot of kids in this area are not exposed to much," he told Parade. "A lot of kids haven't been any farther than Houston on the west and New Orleans on the east. And those are the lucky ones. I tell them they can do the same things as anybody else, because I was one of them. I tell them not to think of themselves as any less or any different."

The relationship enjoyed by Joe Dumars III and his dad is what this special day is all about.

Have an enjoyable Father's Day.

June 17, 1990

New mayor sees bright future

The two events that launched a new city administration Thursday were impressive and inspiring. If the citywide prayer service and swearing-in celebration are a sample of what Mayor Willie Mount can offer Lake Charles, we're in good hands for the next four years.

"Moving Forward Together" is Mount's campaign to enhance the city's self-image, and both ceremonies on her first day in office were all-inclusive.

The new mayor made it clear from the start that everyone was welcome at those events, and it was a privilege to be there. Citizens who couldn't make it weren't forgotten. Mount promised she would be mayor for all of the people of Lake Charles.

The prayer service brought people from all parts of the city to Warren United Methodist Church in northern Lake Charles. For many, it was probably the first time they have been in that area for a long, long time, if ever.

Here's hoping that visit sets the tone for closer contact in the future between all sections of the city.

The celebration moved to the Civic Center Thursday evening, and it, too, was a community-wide event.

Young and old, black and white and rich and poor were represented. They had to come away enriched by the experience.

Music by the Eastwood Pentecostal Church and Mount Pilgrim Baptist Church choirs was as moving as any I've heard in years. Tom Bergsteadt, the master of ceremonies, put it this way:

"If you can listen to that kind of singing and not shed a few tears, then I'm not sure I want to know you," he said.

Mount's address was masterful in content and tone.

"I am a dreamer," she said. "As I dream of Lake Charles moving forward together, I know that we can ... because the heart and soul of this city longs for justice, longs for harmony.

"But now I am your mayor and to the people of our city I simply say this: This administration will unite people, build togetherness, and promote a sense of community. And this new attitude in government begins today."

Mount said being mayor wouldn't give her any special privileges.

"I have a job just like you do. The only difference is you are my boss. I believe that most of what we do in life is about attitude. If we begin with the right attitude, things will turn out good," she said.

"A bad attitude almost ensures bad results. As I stand here today I believe the attitude of our people is upbeat and optimistic."

Mount ended her speech by asking God to bless Lake Charles and its people. Then some of those tears Bergstedt talked about flowed freely as the choirs and platform guests joined hands and the crowd sang the "Battle Hymn of the Republic."

"Has Lake Charles ever sworn in a new mayor with anything like this?" someone asked during a reception that followed the formal ceremony.

"If they did, I wasn't invited," I answered.

Only time will tell whether Mount can achieve her goal of uniting Lake Charles. But if desire means anything, she'll make it.

As I listened to Mount, I thought about the lifetime I've spent in Lake Charles.

Ryan Street was our main street in the early years, as it is today, but it was called South Street then. We were a small city, and no one talked about north, or east or south Lake Charles. Maybe we were more community-minded in those days.

Local government handled most of our basic needs, and we had mayors and other public officials who demonstrated leadership qualities that served us well.

World War II helped expand our economic base with construction of the petro-chemical plants west of the Calcasieu River. And we had our on-and-off U.S. Air Force base that created jobs, stimulated small businesses and brought new residents. Many of them are still here.

We have come a long way in the nearly 60 years I've been here, but there has always been a lingering question: Have we made the best use of the many blessings this area and its talented people have to offer?

I wondered as Mount spoke if she could maybe more successfully than others help this city realize its true potential.

The people have definitely shown courage and determination in the past, but it was often in times of crisis. They dug the ship channel that helped make Lake Charles a leading port city. When public officials were corrupted by illegal gambling influences, citizens organized to fight and clean up the corruption.

People made it clear they wouldn't tolerate labor violence, which erupted in the mid-1970s. And when the U.S. Navy and Boeing talked about coming here, they worked hard to make it a reality.

However, without high-visibility challenges like those, citizens have tended to become more concerned about self-interests. And that has fueled factionalism among people and division among parts of the city.

Mount wants to change that, and she believes the place to start is with our attitude. If we believe it can happen, it will, she said.

The new mayor wasted no time meeting and talking with the men and women who keep this city on the move 24 hours a day. She wants them to feel they are part of the team.

More important than anything else Mount might accomplish will be her role as our ambassador to the outside world. She has already proved that will be one of her strong suits.

Other areas of the state are watching us with interest. That marks a change from the past when we often wondered whether Lake Charles was really considered to be part of Louisiana.

I'm confident about Mount's vision for the future. Time is running short for me, and I want to be around to see progressive things happen to the city that I have loved for so long.

If Mount succeeds, we all succeed. And when she does it will be an inspiration for the young people of Lake Charles who will have to finish the job the new mayor starts.

Won't you join the effort? Working together, we can make Lake Charles the great city it was meant to be.

July 4, 1993

Grizzard covering a new beat

"Who are you going to get to replace Lewis Grizzard?" the doctor asked as we left a church meeting Tuesday evening.

Grizzard, the Georgia-based columnist, lost a long bout with heart problems Sunday when he died at age 47. Recent surgery led to extensive brain damage.

We aren't certain at this point who might fill the void, but we know you really can't replace a writer like Grizzard. He was one of a kind.

It was only natural that Southerners were Grizzard's biggest fans because they could identify with his writings. However, his appeal was universal as evidenced by the fact his columns were carried by 450 newspapers across the country.

I first met Grizzard back in May of 1979. He was one of the speakers at an annual workshop sponsored by the National Society of Columnists in New Orleans.

I heard him again when he spoke to the Louisiana Press Association convention in New Orleans and when he was principal speaker at the annual banquet of the Chamber/Southwest Louisiana.

The man never ran out of great stories to tell, and he captivated audiences wherever he spoke.

Although I was older than Grizzard when I first met him in New Orleans, I was a beginner in the column-writing business. Those were my carousing days, and that's another reason why he became my idol.

When Grizzard spoke about honky-tonks, longnecks and rednecks, I could really identify with the subject matter.

His topic at that workshop was right down my alley. It was titled, "How You, Too, Could Launch a Search for the Perfect Beer Joint in Your Circulation Area and Justify the Expense Account."

I have been a long-time and frequent patron of the infamous John's Barn on 18th near Ryan Street. I wondered whether it could be a contender for such a title.

By the time Grizzard finished his talk, I was convinced John's came as close as anything I've ever seen to being the Perfect Beer Joint in this neck of the woods.

Start with the jukebox, Grizzard said. The music has to be real country — no Elvis Presley or Linda Ronstadt. He suggested you look for songs like, "My Wife Ran Away With My Best Friend — Gee I Miss Him."

Or, "I Gave Her the Ring and She Gave Me the Finger."

The bartender's name comes next. Grizzard said a handle like "Scoobie T" fits the bill perfectly.

Grizzard said if the women in the place are married, going steady or have more than four teeth, the place is a loser. He said they also have to have beer joint names — like Betty Sue, Betty Jean or Emma Lou.

You might also find a "Veeanna Sausage" sign on the wall, he said. There may be an old beer sign that has those multi-colored lights that blink up and down like a roller coaster and put you in a trance after six beers.

There is no room in the Perfect Beer Joint for those "smart college kids wearing school T-shirts."

Customers drink beer out of longneck bottles. Grizzard said that's the kind you need for protection in the event you are attacked from behind. You can grab it around the neck, whack it on the bar rail and have a jagged weapon for self-defense.

Grizzard said once he had the ground rules firmly fixed in his mind, he launched his search for the Perfect Beer Joint in the hills of Georgia. He said the response was phenomenal.

The third-place winner won a free beer, second got a six-pack and the winner got to drink beer with Grizzard.

"No Name Tavern," an out-of-the-way establishment in an unheard of Georgia town, met all of Grizzard's qualifications.

There were two pool tables in the corner over which a sign hung, which read, "No gambling. Gamblers will be prosecuted."

Like many beer joints, it had pets — a coon and a monkey. The coon had died of loneliness and the monkey had only one claim to fame — it picked the pockets of patrons who had had one too many.

Grizzard said one place had a dog, which was noted for catching beer bottle caps thrown into the air. The hound had the misfortune, however, of swallowing one of the caps and died while a sawmill worker was performing an emergency tracheotomy.

The columnist said his visit to the Perfect Beer Joint was the occasion for a town wide celebration.

"I tried to buy my own beer," he said, "but my money wasn't any good anywhere in town. And even though I spent only $19.75, I turned in an expense account for $211."

Find a newspaper writer who can't identify with that expense account story, and I'll show you someone who doesn't belong in the club.

After his entertaining speech that day, Grizzard spent a few minutes out on a French Quarter balcony. Then he was gone before anyone even noticed.

I've often wondered where he went that day, and would have loved to tag along.

I figured he was probably roaming around New Orleans looking for one of those joints he loved to write about. You always sensed that Grizzard would feel at home in any place where he could belly up to the bar, enjoy a longneck and soak up some local flavor.

It was obvious from his columns that he spoke from experience. That's why so many common folk identified with Grizzard. He came across as one of them, and that's why he's going to be hard to replace.

Now Grizzard is traipsing around a news beat he hasn't covered before. Wherever that is, do you suppose he'll be able to find his Perfect Beer Joint?

March 24, 1994

Smitty at home in his yard

From now on, whenever I look out the back door and see leaves piling up on the ground, I'm going to remember Smitty. Smitty was my next-door neighbor who lost his fight against cancer just over a week ago. Luther G. Smith was his name, but Smitty is what everyone called him.

I had known Smitty since moving into the neighborhood 12 years ago. We had less than a dozen conversations longer than five minutes during that time. However, Smitty was the kind of fellow who made a lasting impression. He was a lot like my dad, and maybe that's why we hit it off.

Most of our discussions were over the back yard fence. Neither one of us could hear very well, so I'm not sure how much of what we said got through. However, we both faked it well.

Smitty had retired and yard work was his passion. I never understood why, but he loved to work outside during the heat of the day when the experts tell you to stay inside.

The shrubbery in front of Smitty's house is perfectly manicured. I've never seen any that looked any better. I picked up some pointers watching him work, but I could never duplicate his skills with a hedge trimmer.

One of the neat things I learned from Smitty was to keep a no-grass strip along the fence line. By using his sidewalk edger, he was able to maintain an area 8 to 10 inches wide all around his yard. It helps with drainage after heavy rains.

Although he never complained about them, I'm sure Smitty wasn't happy about the two pine trees I had next to his fence. Falling pinecones and needles kept cluttering his turf.

Another tree I had along his fence line looked pretty sick for a few years.

"Looks like that tree's dead," he'd say every spring.

I refused to pronounce the benediction, however, and the tree lived to see another couple of years. I'm sure Smitty was relieved when we finally decided it had to go.

When I bought a new lawn mower last year, I knew it was only a matter of time before Smitty would come over to check it out.

"What kind of mower did you get?" he asked after ambling over for a look-see.

I knew what Smitty was going to say the minute I told him it was a Honda.

"One of those Jap mowers, huh?" he fired back.

Smitty had served in Africa and Europe during World War II, and that's why I wasn't surprised.

"But I think it was made in North Carolina," I said.

"It doesn't matter," he countered, "it's still a Jap mower."

I know it's politically incorrect to use that word these days, but that's what he said.

As I mentioned earlier, Smitty was like my dad and I knew what to expect. That's exactly what my dad would have said, so I handled Smitty like I had treated my dad. I just let his words roll off my back.

Later, Smitty came out with a newspaper insert to show me how I could have saved some money if I had bought a mower someplace else.

That's when he asked me to turn my new mower on its side so he could see the mulching blades.

"I'll bet I could put blades like that on my riding mower," he said.

Smitty occasionally hired outsiders to cut his grass and trim his hedges, sidewalks and driveway. I knew he wouldn't like the way they did the job, but kept my mouth shut. As expected, most of them never came back a second time.

When Smitty wasn't feeling well, his son, Philip, did the yard work. He's good at it, too, but I'll bet he never heard his dad say so. Dads like ours weren't much on praise for their offspring.

One of the few conversations I heard between Philip and Smitty was pretty spirited. Smitty was complaining about Philip driving his mower too fast.

Although he had a tough exterior, Smitty also had a gentle side. Like my wife, he had a dog at one time. They used to talk about their dogs while Jo Ann was sitting on the patio to read or work her crossword puzzle.

Smitty had to put his dog to sleep, and Jo Ann said he always wondered whether he had done the right thing.

Then there was the time a bird fell out of the tree onto the ground in our yard. Jo Ann held Levi back and asked Smitty to come over and pick up the ailing bird. She said he treated it gently and tried unsuccessfully to nurse it back to health.

Like Smith's other neighbors, we could always count on him to put out our trashcan and bring it in when we were out of town. You always knew he'd keep watch over things while you were gone.

Smitty showed unusual courage during his last days. He seemed to accept the hand fate had dealt him — as bravely as anyone can — and kept his suffering and pain to himself and his family.

One of the last conversations we had was after I had been raking big, brown leaves, which had fallen from the tree in the middle of my back yard. I was competing with a stiff breeze.

"I saw you fighting those leaves," he said. "Why don't you get your mower out and mulch the leaves. All you have to do is raise the blade and crank it up."

I had forgotten about using the mower for mulching, and it worked like a charm.

When I looked out the kitchen window Saturday morning, those leaves had piled up again. I thought about Smitty and the need to get out there today if the weather lets up.

Most of us go through life with little inkling of the impact we have on other people, but we do touch them in ways like Smitty touched me. We'd probably all be better persons if we kept that in mind.

Somehow it seems fitting that I should remember Smitty in connection with my yard. That's where he was the old pro and I was just an amateur.

Dec. 11, 1994

Brinkley doesn't pull punches

BATON ROUGE — It's always difficult to get straight answers from a Washington politician. That's why it was refreshing here Tuesday to hear one of this country's most-respected newsmen tell it like it is.

David Brinkley, host of ABC-TV's "This Week With David Brinkley," delivered the 15th annual Greer Lecture in the LSU Union Theater.

Brinkley set the tone for his comments on the nation's capital when he said he would like to rename the city "Hypocrisy, D.C. 20515." He said decisions in Washington are based on their political impact rather than on what's good for the country. He added that you could often learn more by what a politician doesn't say.

Congress has total dedication only to itself, Brinkley said. That's why the nation's lawmakers don't have the guts to do anything about problems like the mounting national debt, the deplorable welfare system and illegal immigration.

Some examples of their folly:

The Senate wouldn't confirm Robert Bork for the U.S. Supreme Court because he was too intelligent.

Congress voted against making English the official language of this country.

Members of Congress defeated the balanced budget amendment

because they don't want to be forced to cut spending. "They want to continue re-electing themselves with our money," Brinkley said.

It takes 13 railroad freight cars to haul away waste paper from the U.S. Capitol every day.

The award-winning newsman and longtime observer of the Washington political scene touched on a wide variety of topics during his address and a question-and-answer session.

Brinkley said if it were up to him Louisiana Sen. John Breaux would be the next Majority Leader of the U.S. Senate. George Mitchell is stepping down, and Breaux is considered one of the front-runners for the job.

Breaux is a good man, he said, and is well liked by his colleagues. However, Brinkley said the final decision would rest on whose election to that post will be most beneficial to the most political careers.

Here are some of his other observations:

Term limits — Brinkley thinks they are the only way to improve the political climate in Washington. Otherwise, some congressmen will stay in office until they are carried out in a box.

Term limits aren't new. The president is limited to two terms, and 15 states have voted for term limits. Forty governors are also limited to one or two terms.

The economy — an improving economy will help Clinton and will get him re-elected if prosperity continues. It's a fact of political life that presidents get credit for the good and blame for the bad.

Brinkley said he had three economic experts on his program last Sunday, and none of them said anything he could understand. Like most small investors, he said he's decided to leave his money in the market and take his chances.

Health care reform — it won't become law this year, and Clinton will get only 10 or 20 percent of what he's asking for. Members of Congress seem to favor the Canadian system, which makes use of "health care credit cards." However, the Canadian system is in financial trouble.

Whitewater — it appears to be a story of small-time chiseling, which goes on in most small towns.

Hillary Clinton — the president's wife parlayed a $1,000

commodities market investment into almost $100,000, and that's quite literally impossible.

Bosnia — Clinton is being pressured to get involved in the conflict in the former Yugoslavia. He's made the right choice to stay out of that country's turmoil.

Brinkley said Germany sent 20 divisions into Yugoslavia in World War II and failed, and the United States doesn't even have 20 divisions.

The hatreds in that country existed even before the United States became a nation. He said the nationalities in Yugoslavia hate each other and seem to enjoy it.

Although it's painful to see the wounded and dying on television, Brinkley said Bosnia could become another Vietnam. That war couldn't be won and wasn't, he added. He called Vietnam a national embarrassment.

Somalia — The United States went in and fed and housed the people of Somalia and conditions are worse now than before we became involved.

Television — It has helped us become the best-informed people in the world. We know about everything from the backside of the moon to the bottom of the ocean.

New trends, like more nudity on TV, become acceptable in the daily lives of many Americans before they become fashionable on the small screen.

Local news isn't always hard news because sometimes there isn't any. So if you have a half-hour to fill, you put on whatever you can find. Brinkley said he wasn't being critical of local news, but that's a fact of life.

North Korea — Kim Il-sung, the 81-year-old leader of that country, is insane and that's why he's making nuclear threats. Conditions won't improve until he dies and his son is thrown out of office.

Vladimir Zhirinovsky — The Russian nationalist leader is a hard-liner, anti-Semitic, anti-American and a monster. "He's dangerous," Brinkley said.

Singapore vandalism — Michael Fay of Dayton, Ohio, will be flogged with a cane as punishment for acts of vandalism in Singapore. Brinkley said Fay is 18, and he knows the law. He added that the

American people have little sympathy for Fay.

My wife is one of Brinkley's biggest fans, so I wasn't surprised when she asked a question. She wanted to know why newswoman Cokie Roberts doesn't play a bigger role on his "This Week" program on Sundays. He said that's a question he is asked often by viewers.

Brinkley said he, George Will and Sam Donaldson had been doing the first part of the program for 12 years. "Whom do you cut to make room for Cokie?" he asked. He added that Roberts, the daughter of Lindy Boggs and the late Hale Boggs, both of Louisiana, comes in on the best part of the program anyway.

"I hired Cokie, and she's a real asset," Brinkley said. "She knows the U.S. Congress better than any of its members."

Brinkley ended his address with a story he said President Lyndon Johnson told him a number of times.

Johnson said he and some of his cohorts were going through a graveyard adding names to the election rolls the first time he sought elective office. One fellow got to a tombstone covered with moss and it was hard to see the name.

"I can't read this one," he said.

Johnson replied, "Nonsense. He has as much right to vote as anyone else."

That says a lot about the kind of political reasoning we get all too often out of "Hypocrisy, D.C."

April 7, 1994

Rex saw lighter side of news

Any time people get an overblown sense of their importance in the overall scheme of things, there is usually someone around to bring them back down to earth.

Rex Miller Jr., a former colleague and classmate of mine, was the resident wit in our newsroom for a number of years. He helped us keep things on an even keel. Miller lost a lifelong battle against multiple sclerosis (MS) recently, and I remembered the man for his courage and clever way with words.

Miller's courage was perhaps best demonstrated when despite his muscle problems he went out for high school football. Robert Benoit and I were on that same team, and we admired Miller's determination.

All three of us ended up on the "B" squad, and Benoit was the only one who ever got into a game. Unfortunately, he broke his leg on that occasion, so our gridiron days were anything but glorious.

We attended McNeese State University after high school graduation, where Miller became editor of the college newspaper. Benoit and I went into teaching.

Eventually, Miller and I ended up in the American Press newsroom.

Whenever Miller saw the humor in a news event, he put it down on paper. It wasn't for public consumption, but it made great in-house reading.

I collected much of what Miller wrote and filed it away. After attending his funeral services, I pulled out a folder with his name on it and laughed all over again.

Here's part of a story he wrote after I appeared on local television and radio news shows:

"Jim Beam, American Press city editor, is reportedly considering a career in show business after what he termed 'smash successes' on local television and radio programs.

"Beam neglected to say that his TV appearance lost out in the ratings to a Leo Gorcey film festival, and that his radio guest spot ran third to one station's live coverage of a Home Demonstration Club meeting and another station's broadcast of the 109th anniversary celebration of the Zulu uprising in the Congo.

"'What the hell, chickie baby,' said Beam, who has taken up the language of show business. 'You can't win 'em all. But that star image is there. That's what counts, baby.'

"Beam has reportedly been going to a man's hair stylist and buying expensive tailored suits."

Once when a member of the women's news staff was complaining about having to write a long Sulphur wedding story, Miller dropped this gem on her desk:

"Add this to wedding story.

"A high point of the ceremony will be when a pure young maiden is thrown from atop the Vinton rice dryer in a fertility rite."

Miller had a field day poking good-natured fun at Gene Dolan's efforts to build local birdhouses for Purple Martins. He typed up a fictitious flyer proclaiming Purple Martin Day, which touted the following:

"See a bearded Gene Dolan dive from a speeding plane at 5,000 feet without a parachute and be carried gently to earth by a flock of Purple Martins.

"Hear Hank Williams sing (sober).

"See Rudolph, the red-beaked Purple Martin.

"(Celebration void if Martins don't show up)."

When Mardi Gras season rolled around, Miller wrote about the formation of a new krewe for the Lake Charles area.

"The group will be known as the Kalcasieu Karnival Krewe (KKK). Unlike other Mardi Gras events, it will not be expensive for the average member. The gala masked ball may be attended by anyone owning a sheet."

Miller wrote a speech for me that was the culmination of a hoax. A handful of plotters pulled off the caper a number of years ago on members of the Louisiana Tarpon Fishing Club.

Russell Tritico Sr. and Red Kohnke were members of that club and they cooked up the scheme. They asked Bill McMahon, another former colleague of mine, and me to help with the devious plan.

McMahon and I showed up in Baton Rouge at the club's state convention posing as marine biologists from the Woods Hole Oceanographic Institute in Falmouth, Maine.

Our wives went along on the daylong masquerade, and club members swallowed it hook, line and sinker.

The speech Miller put together was entitled, "The Migration, Feeding and Breeding Habits of Tarpon."

I talked about a "tarpon trip tipper,' which was being laid from Grand Chenier to a point 10 miles out into the Gulf of Mexico. It was designed to count and estimate the size of each tarpon, which swam past it.

Then there was mention of our laboratory imitating the breeding call of tarpon which "sent whole schools of tarpon into, if you will pardon the expression, sexual rages."

"We intend to employ this method on the Louisiana Gulf Coast this summer, and the result will be thousands of baby tarpon next year."

I told the group that tarpon actually lived off sand crabs, which they caught by crawling up on the beach at night. I added that tarpon in search of sand crabs had actually been run over by cars on the Grand Chenier to Cameron highway.

Club members had to be fidgeting in their seats by that time, but no one said anything.

The hoax ended abruptly when I mentioned that tarpon had been caught in 1907 as far north as Alexandria in the Red River. An elderly gentleman who had been a longtime weigh master at fishing rodeos had heard all he could take.

"That's a lie," he said as he jumped out of his chair.

I never got to that part of the speech about the possibility that the Jonah's whale in the Bible might have been an oversized tarpon.

However, Miller's superb writing effort had carried me a long way.

Miller and his brother, Walter, owned a charter fishing boat, so the tarpon speech was a natural.

No one seemed offended by the deception, and the hoax is part of my past I'll never forget.

Anytime I get too wrapped up in the news business and stressed out by the nature of the work, I try to remember people like Rex Miller. With a little humor at the right time, they are a great leveling influence.

Sept. 18, 1994

Brooms were his calling card

The first time I met John G. Schwegmann he was walking into the American Press newsroom in 1971 with a handful of brooms. Schwegmann was running for governor, and he was touring the state promising to sweep the deadheads out of Baton Rouge.

Those brooms were an appropriate campaign symbol for Schwegmann. He had built a supermarket empire in the New Orleans area and earned a reputation as a crusader for consumers.

Schwegmann died last week at 83, and his death deserves more than a passing mention.

Having worked at the corner grocery store as a young man, I have always closely identified with the business. Maybe that's why I've been doing my family's grocery shopping longer than I can remember.

Schwegmann and two of his brothers opened their first supermarket in 1946. By the time of his death it had grown to 18 stores with 5,000 employees.

However, as great as that accomplishment was, it isn't the only reason Schwegmann will be remembered. His name became a household word because of his challenge of unfair trade laws.

In 1948, Schwegmann took on the Legislature and liquor interests, and he beat them both.

The Legislature had passed a law requiring a minimum markup on alcoholic beverages. Schwegmann always believed grocers should be able to set their own prices, so he filed suit.

The case went all the way to the state Supreme Court, which declared the law unconstitutional.

Next came a challenge of the state's fair trade law. It let manufacturers set retail prices for an entire trade area.

The case went all the way to the U.S. Supreme Court, which ruled that merchants couldn't be forced to charge certain prices.

Schwegmann's determination to sell cheaper milk from out of state brought one of his biggest court victories. He took on milk price-fixing by the state commissioner of agriculture and the Milk Commission.

It took eight years, but Schwegmann won a federal ruling that said he couldn't be barred from buying cheaper milk.

"He favored unrestricted, free competition," Schwegmann's attorney said. "It's principle, nothing personal with it. He had nothing to gain at all."

Schwegmann got into politics in 1961 when he was elected to the state House. He became a state senator seven years later and was elected to the state Public Service Commission (PSC) in 1975.

A son, John F. Schwegmann, is a current member of the PSC and his daughter-in-law, Melinda Schwegmann, is lieutenant governor.

When the older Schwegmann ran grocery advertisements in newspapers, he included mini-editorials espousing his opinions. He also had the names of candidates he supported printed on his supermarket shopping bags.

While in the Legislature, Schwegmann voted against pay raises for public officials, tax increases and the use of state bonds to construct the Superdome in New Orleans. He predicted the $35 million Superdome would eventually cost between $150 million and $200 million. It cost $179 million.

The Picayune said Gov. John McKeithen was convinced he could win Schwegmann over on the Superdome issue.

Schwegmann had his usual quick response: "Governor, you can't do nothin' for me."

He was right, of course, because Schwegmann was a wealthy man.

When Schwegmann walked into our newsroom with those brooms that day, I knew he'd find a sympathetic ear. Everything I had read about Schwegmann indicated he was Mr. Tom's kind of guy.

That's the late Tom Shearman, our publisher emeritus who had purchased the American Press in 1943. Like Schwegmann, Mr. Tom was a crusader who wasn't afraid to take on the political power structure.

Mr. Tom loved the broom gimmick, and he and I kept our Schwegmann brooms a long time after that initial visit.

Schwegmann said, if elected, he was going to do his best to expose graft in state government. He said he wanted to find out why "a man will pay one million dollars for a $25,000 a year job."

"If I'm elected, the politicians are either going to commit suicide or leave Louisiana," he said.

Here's what he said about other candidates, public figures and the Legislature:

Edwin W. Edwards — "Pretty Boy Chanel No. 5 Edwards. He hasn't yet decided if he wants to run for governor or (U.S.) representative. He won't be either if he doesn't straighten up. He is the biggest deadhead in the State of Louisiana."

Gillis Long — "Gillis Long has been in the public trough all his life. How can you be against deadheads if you are one yourself?"

Former Gov. Jimmie Davis" — You got to realize that all Davis says is, 'Don't ask me no questions and I won't tell you no lies.'"

Davis came under fire for state contracts awarded to his friends, like the one to build the Sunshine Bridge at Donaldsonville, which became known as "The Bridge To Nowhere."

Gov. John McKeithen — "McKeithen is building a Sunshine Bridge. Only thing is he's putting a dome over it."

Bill Dodd — Schwegmann said Dodd (superintendent) had turned the state Department of Education into "a rest home for incurable political deadheads."

The Legislature — "The governor has control of 80 percent of the Legislature, and they are slick, slimy, ambulance-chasing liars."

Schwegmann financed most of his own campaign. He said, "As far as John Schwegmann is concerned, he never asked anybody for anything. He doesn't have any red beans and rice dinners, any steak dinners, no $100 dinners, no $25 dinners, no $50 dinners. John Schwegmann can spend his own money and be his own boss."

Mr. Tom and Schwegmann hit it off so well, I knew Schwegmann would be a factor when it came time to endorse a candidate. As it turned out, the American Press said Edwards, Bennett Johnston and Schwegmann were all well qualified to serve as governor.

It would have been interesting to see how Schwegmann would have handled the state's top political job, but he finished fifth in a field of 17 behind Edwards, Bennett Johnston, Gillis Long and Davis. He was also fifth in Calcasieu Parish.

Edwards and Johnston made the runoff. Edwards won the runoff by 4,600 votes out of nearly 1.2 million cast and went on to defeat Republican Dave Treen in the general election.

Schwegmann didn't achieve the ultimate victory on the Louisiana political scene, but he won numerous consumer battles that served us all well.

I wish I still had that broom Schwegmann gave me back in 1971. The state Capitol he wanted to clean out 24 years ago could still use a good sweeping.

March 12, 1995

Don't look for Eddie behind bar

"Eddie died tonight," sports editor Scooter Hobbs said after I picked up the telephone at home Sunday evening. Scooter didn't have to say much more. I knew he was talking about a good friend and a gentle man who was the best-known bartender in these parts.

I met Eddie in the 1970s when Papania's restaurant was located at 2601 Broad St. It has always been a popular nightspot and a great place to unwind after work, particularly on election night.

After our first meeting, I never had to ask Eddie for another drink. As I said in a 1982 column, "Just open the front door to the lounge and Eddie would have your brand of beer on the bar before you bellied up."

That column was written after Papania's Broad Street location was destroyed by fire on Sept. 21, 1982. The restaurant eventually reopened at its current Fifth Avenue location.

Scooter told me about Eddie, and it was Bobby Dower, who was sports editor at the time, who called me the morning Papania's burned. Sports writers and others in our profession have little in common most of the time, except when it comes to the social side of life.

The late Ward "Buddy" Threatt, another friend and longtime colleague, had known Eddie much longer than I had. I asked Buddy's wife this week how the two men met. Buddy was from Charlotte, N.C.

"Buddy said — outside of me — he had known Eddie longer than anyone else in Lake Charles," she said. Vi said the two men met at the Aragon Supper Club, where Eddie was tending bar.

The Aragon was located at 2519 Broad St. in the block just west of Papania's. Editor Brett Downer, who collects old matchbook covers, found one for the Aragon on Wednesday, which described it as a "Doggone Good Place to Drink & Eat."

The same thing can be said about Papania's, and Eddie definitely made it someplace special. Although it might not be considered "a place where the elite meet" on a regular basis, Papania's has drawn people from all walks of life over the years.

I've seen judges, lawyers, doctors, politicians of every persuasion, union and business leaders — you name it and they've probably been there. Crowds are especially large during Mardi Gras and football seasons.

American Press reporters and editors have a tradition of gathering there on election nights to relax, talk politics and wait for a copy of Sunday's newspaper. It's a place where even your toughest critics will, for the most part, respect your right to put your work behind you for a few hours of relaxation.

Things did get rather tense a few times. The relative of a losing candidate — whom the newspaper didn't endorse — wanted me to meet him outside one election night. I knew better, but Eddie didn't take any chances. He was right there to defuse the situation.

On another occasion, Eddie walked me out to the car after an area contractor took issue with some investigative work the newspaper was doing.

A union leader's wife was on the warpath one night, but I escaped her wrath. Eddie said I was lucky she had cooled down because she had broken her arm on a previous occasion while whacking another foe over the head.

I ran into a number of notables who were subjects of columns I had written, but most of them respected my right to relax in a neutral zone.

Politics was always a favorite subject, however, and customers like the late Johnnie Caldarera made it difficult to get a word in edgewise.

Eddie would have never written a book — it's probably against the bartender code of ethics — but I'd sure love to read about some of the stories he's heard over the years.

Customers knew very little about the private life of Eddie. In fact, most of them didn't even know his last name. However, from what he did say and what you picked up here and there, you knew he was a good father who was extremely proud of his family.

Eddie had some heart problems in recent years, and that caused his death at age 67.

Edward Chretien Sr. was his given name, but the thousands of people who knew him as just Eddie will always remember him.

Each time we lose a friend or loved one, I suppose a little piece of us goes with them. However, we also gain something as well — the memories they leave behind.

I'd like to think that Eddie is having a reunion about now with Buddy, the late Wayne Owens, Caldarera and some of the other people who were a big part of my life and his. I'm not sure there's a bar to belly-up to where those fellows are — but if Wayne's there, you can bet Eddie is hearing some wild stories again.

If we are truly enriched by the lives we touch, Eddie left this earth an extremely wealthy man.

Sept. 10, 1998

Ernie Pyle was our man at front

The movie "Saving Private Ryan" has generated renewed interest in America's involvement in World War II. The film is considered by many to be a realistic depiction of the brutality of war.

Some actual battlefield footage is also beginning to surface, but it wasn't available for those of us who were approaching our teen-age years during the war. Censorship denied us the gruesome details, but that didn't mean we were totally in the dark about the war in Europe and in the Pacific from 1941 to 1945.

Newspaper correspondents like Ernie Pyle and Hal Boyle wrote about the war, and Bill Mauldin brought the conflict back to the home front with cartoons featuring unshaven and bleary-eyed characters called Willie and Joe.

I ran across an April 20, 1945, story about Pyle recently while researching through past issues of the American Press, and it piqued my interest in his contribution to the war effort. "Hal Boyle writes his tribute to Ernie Pyle," said the headline, and I wanted to know more.

Pyle had been killed two days earlier by Japanese machine gun fire. "The little guy, beloved by every GI Joe, fell in action yesterday mid-morning on Ie — a little island nobody ever heard of before Pearl Harbor," wrote Grant Macdonald of The Associated Press.

It happened April 18, 1945, while Pyle was riding in a jeep with Lt. Col. Joseph B. Coolidge of Helens, Ark.

"We were riding along," said Coolidge, "when we were fired on by a Jap machinegun. We dove into a ditch. A little later, Pyle and I rose up to look around. Another burst hit. I looked at Ernie and he was dead. A bullet had entered his left temple just under his helmet."

Pyle, 45, reportedly had a premonition something might happen to him and told a friend, "I try not to take any foolish chances but there's just no way to play it completely safe and still do your job."

He covered the war against Germany in Europe and came home a national hero before transferring to the Pacific Theater. Here is how Marquis Childs of United Feature Syndicate described the work of Pyle in another tribute:

"There is no substitute for experience — for the kind of hell that hundreds of thousands of Americans are going through. Not all our modern techniques of radio and motion picture can halfway bridge the gap. But the shy little man whom people all over America spoke of as Ernie came as close to it as anyone has."

Boyle was with Pyle in Tunisia. "We slept next to each other on lumpy flea-ridden piles of straw under a farm wagon with bent pieces of tin between the wheels to keep out the winter wind," Boyle said. "Rain leaked on us and he shivered and said how much he hated war. But already he had fallen in love with the Infantry."

Pyle was nearly killed in a bombing raid at Anzio, Boyle said. "He never overcame the dark feeling of terror it left in him, but he drove himself again and again to expose himself to frontline danger because he knew he could never write honestly of the terrible loneliness of battle unless he shared it. He had become the symbol of all fighting men, the doughboy articulate."

After his death, the American Press published a number of Pyle's columns, which were written before he was killed.

Americans saw the human side of war through Pyle. He wrote about individual soldiers like Corporal Martin "Bird Dog" Clayton Jr. of Dallas, Texas, and Private First Class William Gross of Lansing, Mich.

"Gross is simply called Gross," Pyle wrote. "He is very quiet, but thoughtful of little things, and they both sort of looked after me for several days. These two have become very close friends, and after the war they intend to go to UCLA together and finish their education."

He added, "The boys tell jokes, they cuss a lot and constantly drag out stories of their past blitzes and sometimes they speak gravely about war and what will happen to them when they finally get home."

Pyle talked about the discomforts of war: "Right after dark the mosquitoes started buzzing around our heads. These Okinawa mosquitoes sound like a flamethrower. They can't be driven off or brushed away."

He described two Japanese soldiers, one 30 and the other 16 or 17, who surrendered without a fight.

"They were both trembling all over," he said. "The kid's face turned a sickly white. Their hands shook. The muscles in the corporal's jaw were twitching. The kid was so paralyzed he couldn't even understand sign language."

Pyle added, "My contribution to the capture consisted of standing to one side looking as mean as I could."

He talked about the time Marines found some Japanese kimonos in a smashed house. "If there ever is a war play about Marines, I hope they include one tough-looking private in a pink-and-white kimono, stewing chicken and trying to ride a one-pedaled bicycle through a shattered Japanese village."

Here are others Pyle wrote about:

After washing off several days of grime inside a house on Okinawa, Lt. "Bones" Carstens said, "I cleaned my fingernails this morning, and it sure does feel good."

Pfc. Buzz Vitere of the Bronx, N.Y., was known as the Bing Crosby of the Marines. "If you shut your eyes and don't listen very hard, you can hardly tell the difference," Pyle said.

Pfc. Johnny Marturello, an Italian from Des Moines, Iowa, played the accordion. Pyle said, "He sings, too, but he says as a singer his name is 'Frank Not-so-hotra.'"

One paragraph in Pyle's last column captures the essence of what Steven Spielberg was trying to say in "Saving Private Ryan."

"The wear and the weariness of war is cumulative," Pyle wrote. "To many a man in the line today fear is not so much of death itself, but fear of the terror and anguish and utter horror that precedes death in battle."

If you saw the movie, you know exactly what Ernie Pyle was talking about — and why he has earned a place in American history.

Sept. 17, 1998

GI Joe earns 20th century title

We were a bunch of scared kids who had a job to do. We were in it to get it over with, so we could go home and do what we wanted to do with our lives

If noted World War II historian Stephen E. Ambrose has his way, those would become the sentiments of the most important person of the 20th century — GI Joe. It was a typical answer from American servicemen who, when the war ended in 1945, didn't consider themselves heroes.

Ambrose said a number of people qualify to be named the most important person of the century. He mentions Presidents Franklin D. Roosevelt and Dwight D. Eisenhower, Winston Churchill, Henry Ford, John D. Rockefeller, Bill Gates and many others. However, Ambrose is convinced GI Joe is the obvious winner.

"He was called Doughboy in World War I, when he stopped the Kaiser from taking control of Europe, and GI Joe in World War II, when he stopped Hitler and Mussolini, Tojo and Hirohito," Ambrose said.

"From 1950 to 1953, he kept the Communists out of South Korea. Throughout the half-century from 1945 on, he stopped Stalin and his successors and won the Cold War. In Vietnam, he was called Grunt. He was unable to keep the North Vietnamese from taking control of

South Vietnam, but that was not his fault.

"In Kuwait, he hurled back Saddam Hussein's army. In Kosovo, along with NATO allies, he did the same to the Serbian army."

Ambrose said there are millions of people around the world who owe their freedom to GI Joe. What made American servicemen and women different from their counterparts in Germany, Japan and the Soviet Union?

"Listen, I was 18 years old and had my whole life ahead of me," one of them told Ambrose during an interview. "I had been taught the difference between right and wrong. And I didn't want to live in a world in which wrong prevailed. So I fought."

Ambrose calls that "the hallmark of GI Joe."

For those too young to remember much about World War II, the term "GI" traces its origin to two sources. Some say it comes from galvanized-iron (GI) Army garbage cans. However, the prevalent and most popular view is that GI comes from Government Issue, the term that was stamped on everything from underwear to tank parts.

Ernie Pyle, the correspondent who died covering World War II, called GIs "the mud-rain-frost-and-wind boys. They have no comforts, and they even learn to live without necessities. And in the end they are the guys that wars can't be won without."

Ambrose, who was in the second grade when the United States entered the war in 1941, has probably interviewed more American servicemen than anyone. He has told their stories in over a dozen books. "Citizen Soldiers," written in 1997, and "D-Day June 6, 1944," written in 1994, were best sellers. His latest is, "The Victors: Eisenhower and His Boys, the Men of World War II," written in 1998.

Beginning next month, Ambrose will start research for a book on the soldiers, sailors and airmen who served in the Pacific Theater during World War II.

"I want this book to be much like the history I wrote of the soldiers in the European Theater called 'Citizen Solders,'" he said.

Persons who served in the Pacific in World War II and those who know someone who did are asked to help with the research by contacting Ambrose at his Internet web site. It's www.stephenambrose.com.

Ambrose has a significant Louisiana connection. He taught at the

University of New Orleans, and is the founder of the National D-Day Museum, which opens June 6, 2000, in New Orleans. It is the only museum in this country dedicated to all of World War II.

Thanks to help from people like Tom Brokaw, George Bush, Steven Spielberg, Tom Hanks, citizens from across the country, the federal government and the state of Louisiana, the museum has raised over $20 million. Contributions are still needed, and details can be found on the Ambrose web site.

New Orleans was selected for the museum because it's the home of Andrew Higgins, who built the Higgins landing craft that were used to hit the beaches during the war. Eisenhower described Higgins as "the man who won the war for us."

Because of his close ties to the D-Day Museum and his books on World War II, Ambrose speaks with authority when he advocates that GI Joe be named the person of the 20th century.

"Today, thanks to GI Joe and the Americans and their many allies around the world, except in China, Vietnam and Cuba, the Communists have joined the Nazis and Fascists in the ash can of history, where they belong," Ambrose said. "Today it is democracy that is on the march. Today we can once again, as we did at the beginning of the 20th century, believe in progress....

"Which is but one of the reasons why I nominate GI Joe as the person of the 20th Century."

No doubt about it. GI Joe qualifies in every sense of the word. We can only hope the people who make that final decision will remember who it was that helped make this world safer and more democratic than ever before.

Nov. 28, 1999

Mr. Glenn patriarch at John's

The man who came to be known as "Mr. John's Barn" has died, but the memories he leaves behind will be with some of us for a long time.

Glenn Demarie Sr. was an intelligent fellow with a warm and friendly smile. Family members and others who knew him well called him a teacher, counselor, jokester, pack rat and storyteller all rolled into one. He was easily recognizable in his trademark polyester jumpsuit.

I knew Glenn most of my life. His family moved into a home my family had once lived in on Deaton Street as World War II erupted. I remember enjoying my first snowfall at that address.

Papa John and Mae "Mama" Demarie were Glenn's parents. They operated the bar across the street that was hard to miss because of its bright red color.

My first John's Barn experience came shortly after I enrolled at McNeese State University in 1951. My classmates and I were freed from high school restrictions, and we lived life to the fullest.

One afternoon while preparing to study for an exam, someone — Vernon Abraham, I believe — said we should drop by John's Barn and have a couple of beers before taking the test later in the day.

"Having a beer or two helps you retain information," he said.

The theory sounded solid, so off we went. Well, I couldn't remember anything once we sat down in class. My midterm grades showed it, too. So much for wild and unproved theories.

We didn't give up John's Barn over the next four years, but we never tried Vernon's theory again.

I saw my first bourre card game in a backroom at John's Barn. One of the dealers always slapped the trump card up against his sweaty forehead, and that made a lasting impression.

After getting married and graduating from McNeese, I spent two years in the Army and over four years teaching at Marion High School. There wasn't much time for John's Barn during those struggling economic times.

My newspaper career began in 1961, and my colleagues and I usually dropped by John's Barn after working the late shift on Friday and Saturday nights.

It was at John's Barn that the late Wayne Owens, a co-worker and running buddy, did his first wild dance to "Rockin' Robin." The familiar tune on the jukebox always got Owens out of his chair whenever and wherever it played.

During one of those weekend nights, a fire broke out around the corner on Ryan Street. The fire department ran a hose from a fire hydrant just east of John's Barn and it encircled the bar. Firemen insisted we couldn't drive over the hose and we had to stay put.

As the evening wore on, I decided I had better call Jo Ann and let her know I was locked in. You won't be surprised to know that she found the story awfully hard to swallow.

Someone eventually got desperate and found a path next to a nearby house that was wide enough to get a car through. The rest of us followed his lead.

Jo Ann asked me the next day why it took so long for us to find an escape route. I had to admit that, in the beginning, we weren't looking that hard.

The late Buddy Threatt, a dear friend and longtime colleague, believed an introduction to John's Barn was a requirement for all new reporters. I can still hear him issuing that first invitation.

"You'll have to join us after work for a beer at John's Barn," he would say.

There weren't many who turned him down. I recall the first time staff writer Sunny Brown saw the inside of the place.

"Is it me, or is this building leaning?" she said.

"If you had been here as long and seen as much as this old building has, you'd be leaning, too," I said.

Customers enjoyed Glenn's colorful stories. Sometimes he would write jokes on one of those small cocktail napkins.

No evening was complete unless you bought a small sausage link prepared by Glenn in a relic of a toaster oven. He would slice the sausage when it was done, coat it with mustard and stack some crackers alongside. What a treat it was!

Political junkies like me could pick up all kinds of gossip about public figures during visits to John's Barn.

While there may have been some serious scuffles outside the place, Glenn was always quick to quell disturbances inside. He was a little fellow, but big enough to put down a fight before it got out of hand.

My trips to John's Barn have been few and far between in recent years, but Glenn always made me feel at home when I did stop by. And I have always been amazed that he was able to attract new generations of customers.

Rodeo contestants and their followers are particularly fond of the place. When there was a rodeo in town, you knew it would be packed.

John's Barn will stay open, according to a family member. I'm not sure if John's Barn qualifies to be considered a local institution, but it's definitely earned the right to be called "the best little honky-tonk in town." And if you ever tried to get all of the people who have been there together at one time, there wouldn't be a place in town big enough to hold them all.

March 7, 2002

Stelly leaving legacy

Another in a long line of outstanding Southwest Louisiana legislators will bow out of politics at the end of his term next year. Rep. Vic Stelly, a Republican from Moss Bluff, said Friday he is serving his fourth — and last — term in the House.

Stelly could have run for another term. Term limits don't take effect in Louisiana until the statewide elections of 2007. Legislators were allowed to serve three full terms when limits were first imposed.

"I'd prefer to go out by my own choice, with head held high," Stelly told the local Republican Roundtable Friday.

Unlike some in public office, Stelly won't draw one penny of retirement benefits or have state health insurance coverage. He had that option before retirements for part-time public officials were ended by constitutional amendment, but turned it down.

Prior to his election to the House, Stelly served four years on the Calcasieu Parish School Board.

I have followed the Louisiana Legislature closely for over 40 years, and rank Stelly among the best we have sent to Baton Rouge. He said he sought the job in an effort to make a difference, and he has done that many times over.

Stelly has never shied from controversy. He once advocated giving voters an opportunity to vote on whether they would do away with the homestead exemption for school taxes.

Some wrongfully accused him of trying to do away with the homestead exemption altogether. However, it would have only been eliminated for school taxes after a vote of the people. The plan never had an opportunity to come to a public vote.

Two years ago, Stelly again tackled the difficult job of trying to change the Louisiana tax structure. He sponsored a plan to substitute higher income taxes for elimination of sales taxes on food and utilities. The state shouldn't balance its budget on the backs of the poor, he said.

Unfortunately, his plan was hijacked and became a vehicle for a $200 million tax increase for teachers. Voters approved elimination of sales taxes on food and utilities, but rejected higher income taxes. Both had to pass for either to take effect.

Most people would have thrown in the towel, but Stelly resurrected a much improved tax-swap plan that will be No. 2 on the Nov. 5 ballot. I was covering the Legislature when Stelly's new plan first surfaced earlier this year. Gov. Mike Foster and some leading legislators said it was "dead on arrival."

Stelly refused to buckle under the criticism and worked and reworked the plan to make it more acceptable. He began to win legislative converts one by one.

Legislators rejected Foster's proposal to renew those sales taxes on food and utilities for 10 years. And the governor and his advisers had to struggle to get them renewed at a slightly reduced rate for two more years.

The new Stelly plan sat in the wings waiting the proper time to try and get the two-thirds vote needed on taxes. It didn't come to a floor vote in the House until the waning days of the fiscal session.

Stelly's impassioned plea to his fellow legislators drew applause that is rare in the House chamber for fellow lawmakers. Like the former coach that he is, Stelly asked House members if they were playing for the name on the state Capitol (the state of Louisiana) or the name on their desk (their own).

The proposal drew 75 votes, five more than the required two-thirds. Stelly had cleared his first major hurdle by a wide margin.

Another stroke of genius was getting Sen. Jay Dardenne, R-Baton Rouge, to handle his bill in the Senate. Dardenne is well respected by his colleagues, and he fielded their questions like a pro. The plan got 29 votes, three more than the required two-thirds.

The next vote will come at the polls in November. Stelly said he has been considering giving up his House seat for some time now, and it has nothing to do with the outcome of the vote on his tax swap plan this November.

If voters give it a fair hearing, it has a good chance of passing. However, the critics are out there, and they are constantly looking for ways to try and shoot it down.

Much will be said and written about the plan in the coming months. Each of us will eventually be able to determine exactly how we are affected by the Stelly plan. So give it a fair hearing and make up your own mind.

Stelly has nothing to gain personally from his tax plan. In fact, he will pay more taxes because he is in a higher tax bracket. However, he is confident no one will bear an unfair burden under his tax swap.

Why is he taking on a controversy he doesn't need and one that demands much of his personal time promoting the tax swap?

"I went to Baton Rouge to make a difference and hope to leave our state better than I found it 16 years ago," he said.

Stelly has lived up to that goal, and his expertise, experience and dedication will be missed. In another unselfish act, Stelly plans to donate his campaign funds to an endowed professorship in health and physical education at McNeese State University.

People who work in state government have asked me over and over again since the 1960s how Southwest Louisiana manages to produce so many outstanding legislators. I have given them the same answer every time.

It is a tribute to the voters who send them to Baton Rouge. And I am confident the trend will continue.

July 14, 2002

Editor's Note: Voters approved the Stelly Plan on Nov. 5, 2002, by a margin of 51-to-49 percent. It was called one of the most significant tax reform measures in recent state history.

Chapter 3

A Personal Journey

Going after the big ones

Bill and I went "fishing" last weekend for what must certainly be one of the craziest outings on record. And we went after the big ones.

For most, a fishing trip is nothing out of the ordinary, but for me it's quite an achievement. Bill has been known to catch a few, but even last week's caper was out of his class.

It all began when Red Kohnke, our photo editor who had rather fish than flash, invited us as guests of the annual meeting of the Louisiana Tarpon Club in Baton Rouge. Red was president and planned the yearly get-together noted for its hilarity and tomfoolery.

Once we put our scheming heads together it was decided that Bill and I would pose as two experts on oceanography, with doctor of philosophy degrees in the field, mind you.

Red told members of the club he found us working on a project at the Rockefeller Refuge in Grand Chenier and had asked me to be guest speaker at the club banquet. Of all things, he said we were working on brown shrimp propagation as related to inland waters.

We arrived in the capital city about 1 p.m. Saturday afternoon and had to put on our "front" until the banquet at 8 p.m. that evening. Not knowing a tarpon from a tarpaulin, I stayed away from the avid anglers.

Bill was better at the game since he knew a little about fishing. But as luck would have it, we became engaged in a conversation with Marion Higgins, weigh master for most of the major state fishing rodeos.

When he started asking questions, I felt the game was over. Bill saved the day, however, when he said something to Marion about a tarpon's eyes giving a hint as to how long the catch had been out of water.

The meeting got under way that afternoon and I must admit I have never seen adults have such fun at what was supposed to be an annual meeting.

For instance, Higgins was awarded the door prize – a beautiful babe who was his personal slave for the afternoon. Then there was the wild lawsuit lodged by Walter Miller, noted tarpon captain from Lake Charles, against Dr. R.J. (Sonny) Young of Abbeville. The doctor had made comments about Miller's beard grown for the Lake Charles Centennial celebration.

Dr. Young felt so bad about the carryings-on that he cornered me and apologized. "I know this gathering must seem strange to a scholar like yourself, but I want to assure you we'll be quiet tonight when you deliver your speech." I began to feel like some sort of villain for the hoax we were perpetrating.

We made it through the afternoon, though, and then came my big moment. A hush fell over the audience as I began to read my treatise on the habits of tarpon. Rex Miller, a writer of keen wit and one of our copyreaders, wrote the speech for which I held zero qualifications.

The fraud lasted through Page 1, but when I mentioned development of a "tarpon trip tipper" for counting and sizing the silver king, Higgins jumped from his chair in amazement.

Then there was the part about the Job Corps being assigned to man the beaches to count tarpon as they passed. We made it through that part fairly well, but the wild story about discovering a way to imitate the sexual mating call of tarpon was more than the listeners could stand, particularly when Bill reproduced the call.

Deception ended when I told this group, which knew better, that the tarpon's actual diet is sand crabs that they caught by crawling up on the beach, and I mentioned the famous Tarpon Riots of 1897.

But we had succeeded in our original goal. We had taken most club members by surprise and deceived a group, which makes it a point to do just that to one another each year at the annual meeting.

Best wishes, silver king seekers, from "Drs." McMahon and Beam. How will you top us next year?

May 21, 1967

Where did wallet go?

When you're perfect, it's difficult to accept imperfection in others.

My wife's wallet was lost last week, and the disaster has turned my life upside down. I almost lost my appetite Thursday evening when she told me the bad news.

She advised my daughter and son to drop the subject, knowing it would only prolong my agony. "Your father never lost anything," she noted in a disdainful tone. "You remember when he wouldn't speak to me for two weeks that time I lost my keys."

I tried to dismiss the misfortune from my mind, but the misery lingered.

"Don't worry," I said, "we are only liable for up to $50 in purchases on our credit cards once we tell someone they are missing." The $50 times six cards equals $300, and that's piercing pain any way you size it up.

In addition, she will probably have to get a new driver's license, Social Security card and whatever other important documents she was carrying around. Thank goodness she only had $9 in cash.

The duplicates I have of those credit cards will apparently be useless once the companies involved are notified my wife's cards are missing.

Those keys she mentioned eventually turned up in the kitchen cabinet. She found them during her annual cleanup. They had been in a drawer and rolled out over the back when it was opened. I got over that traumatic experience, but the wallet episode won't be easy to forget.

Looking for sympathy, I discussed my plight with the boss's secretary. Her reply when she heard the story and my reaction to the loss only reinforced what I should have known all along. Women stick together most of the time.

"You must be a hard man to live with," she said.

From now on, I'll go somewhere else for a little compassion.

Before you take sides, I should explain that even though I might want to be more considerate during difficult times, something inside me clicks in the other direction. I suppose the same thing happens to most of us perfect mortals.

I'm really not as cruel as it might seem. If an armed robber had taken my wife's wallet by force, I could understand. Of course, I would hope she'd follow the lead of one of our legislator's wives who under similar circumstances whacked the would-be robber with her purse.

Meanwhile, I'm going to keep telling myself things could be worse. I probably won't buy my own rationale, but anything's worth the effort.

She could have lost the car or her paycheck or our life savings (meager as they are). There's even a good chance that once she reads this column she'll lose her husband, and it won't be by accident.

March 20, 1977

When spirit moves you, go

I almost danced with Susan Saint James. Unfortunately, almost isn't good enough.

The chance of a lifetime came my way last weekend in Austin, Texas, when the longtime star of the television series "McMillan and Wife" was in the Lone Star State promoting her latest movie, "Outlaw Blues."

Susan (pardon the familiarity) is no Jacqueline Bisset, sex star of "The Deep," but she's got class. It's like the movie promotion says, "She's a woman with street-smart savvy."

Those of us in Austin for the premiere of "Outlaw Blues" were sitting around the lobby when Susan and her co-star, Peter Fonda, arrived at the hotel. We all played it cool. After all, it isn't sophisticated to get goggle-eyed over a couple of movie stars.

We saw them again at the theater, but still no one got too excited.

A party followed the movie premiere. It was held at Soap Creek Saloon, one of the locations used in the film. Austin is considered the country music capital of the Southwest, and the Soap Creek is a real drawing card.

There was no air conditioning, nothing fancy, but, as the name implies, an actual saloon out of the Old West. Atmosphere at its finest.

Later in the evening, Peter and Susan came in with a party of four or five and sat down at a table next to ours. Both stars ordered beer. I thought to myself, "Anyone who likes beer has got to be down-to-earth good people."

Eventually we all moved over to the stars' table. I could see Susan swaying back and forth to the music. I'm a shy, reserved person, but I made up my mind I was going to ask her to dance before the evening was over.

Would she really dance with Jim Beam? I wondered. I decided to see if she would dance with someone else first. She did.

I sat around waiting for the right tune, and I was going to make my move. Someone on our tour bus was leaving. "Go ahead," I told the others in our party. "I'm going to stick around for that one dance."

The right song didn't come along in time. The stars got up and left, and my big moment had eluded me.

That was only the beginning. I walked outside and found out our bus had actually deserted me. There I was on a Texas hillside wondering how I was going to get back to town when I didn't even know where downtown was located.

I asked a young couple if they had any idea how I could get back to the Driskill Hotel. They said they were going in that direction and offered to give me a lift. Saved by that famous Texas hospitality.

You can imagine my shame when the people in my party asked me the next day if I had ever gotten that dance with Susan Saint James.

The worst was yet to come. I mentioned to Susan at a news conference that afternoon that I had come within an inch the night before of asking her to dance.

"I wish you had," she said. "I got awfully tired just sitting there all night."

The opportunity never came again. I came home a beaten man. No autographs, no personal mementoes from the stars, no tape recordings of interviews like my son had suggested and no dance with Susan Saint James.

An "Outlaw Blues" T-shirt for my daughter from a press kit was the only evidence I had even been there.

A failure, that's what I am. I'm going to punish myself for blowing such a rare opportunity. The next time a premiere comes along we'll send someone with guts.

Almost just isn't good enough.

July 10, 1977

'Experts' hold up progress

"You gotta be crazy" has been the universal reply when I've mentioned to anyone that I was going to re-roof my own house.

The project has been a major topic of discussion around the office for the last couple of months. In some cases, I have sought advice. Most of it, however, has come my way unsolicited.

"You had better wait until summer's over," said some "experts."

"Skinning off the old roof is back-breaking," said others.

"You're going to get caught by those summer showers," warned still others.

Throwing caution to the winds, I launched the project Thursday while a large black cloud hovered overhead.

Mother Nature was kind, though, and I managed to skin one of four roof sections and put down felt without a single drop of rain falling from the sky.

Hopefully, I can do a section a day and wrap up the difficult part of the job today.

I must admit the experts were right in most respects. The heat was stifling. I could only go about 15 minutes before taking a break. Muscles I probably haven't used since my high school days began to ache.

When I signed a check late that afternoon, I realized the nerves that control finger movements weren't working right. The signature looked like hen scratch.

There wasn't enough water and soft drinks to quench my thirst. Every ounce of energy had been drained from my body.

My wife has been opposed to me doing the work from the beginning, even though she knew it was do it myself or cancel our vacation plans.

Telling her about my worn and broken body Thursday evening brought a look of anguish to her face, but I told her I was determined to forge ahead.

My son was a lifesaver on the first day, and we both convinced her we could see the project through.

Buddy came over to look at our work and said he was amazed at how much we had done in a few hours.

"How does it look," I asked.

"Great," he answered.

That was all the catalyst we needed. Buddy, you see, was my real inspiration from the beginning. He had re-roofed his house and his roof has to rate as one of the most difficult around.

"If Buddy can do it, so can I," I had told myself for months. Buddy would be the first to admit neither one of us was cut out for physical work of any kind.

The word of my first day's accomplishments spread through the office Friday like wildfire. Colleagues who had been skeptical at first were now cheering me on.

You could tell they were all dying to get up there with me were it not for bad backs, tricky knees and previous commitments.

I left work Friday actually anxious to get back up on the roof. The prospect of getting that fellow who has been dating my daughter to lend a hand was added incentive. It provided me the opportunity to test his fortitude.

In all honesty, I must admit my decision to quit talking about the roofing job and to get started was brought about by more than the desire to accomplish a difficult task.

The roof has been leaking badly through one of the walls, and I got tired of seeing my floor tile floating around in the bathroom.

July 24, 1977

Take it one day at time

I've stopped smoking after puffing away for over 30 years. It may not be a big event for many people, but, for me, today marks the beginning of Month No. 3.

You'll notice I said, "stopped." I prefer stopped because I've seen too many people who quit start smoking again in months and even years. I could well fall into that category in time to come.

I haven't said too much about kicking the habit for that reason. Why look foolish when you don't have to?

No, I'm not going to start preaching about the evils of tobacco. There's nothing worse than a one-time smoker trying to reform everyone around him.

Former smokers who continually try to enlist everyone in their glorious cause probably do more harm than good when it comes to encouraging others to stop smoking. They might well consider living by example as being more productive. Quiet quitters have motivated me.

I labored long and hard over whether to even write about the subject. I've asked myself many times whether I should put my neck out on a limb.

I finally decided that my experience might help someone else make a decision about smoking — either to quite or continue. Those who have never smoked, of course, should never try it.

Smoking was the "in" thing when I was a youngster. Few teen-agers escaped the habit. We used to think we were big stuff smoking out behind the football stadium and after school.

My oldest brother hid his smoking from Mom, but I'm sure she knew. That's when I decided to be brave and smoke out in the open at the tender age of 16. Mom hit the ceiling, but it didn't make me stop. And I hadn't stopped for more than a couple of days at a time since then.

Yes, I had read everything the surgeon general said about smoking. I also knew that lung cancer was practically incurable. But I always figured I would be one of the lucky ones.

As the evidence against smoking accumulated over the years, I still refused to heed the warnings. Even during bouts with bronchial asthma, I never let up.

My father had smoked all his life, but the day of reckoning came a couple of years ago when emphysema made breathing almost impossible. He quit, and hasn't smoked since then. Even though I realized he could do it, I still lacked the determination.

An uncle died of lung cancer after smoking much of his life, but even then I didn't have the courage to try to kick the habit.

Like so many others, I refused to read anything about the hazards of smoking. I resented the anti-smoking commercials on television. I tried to close my mind to everything having to do with smoking.

When my doctor found out I smoked about a year ago, he was emphatic about quitting. He told me what I had already known — smoking was a leading cause of heart disease and death, in addition to the cancer hazard.

I enjoyed smoking, and doggone it, I wasn't going to stop. Besides, I had tried to cut back on smoking many times and it never worked.

Naturally, I was kidding myself. My common sense was in a constant tug of war with that side of me that enjoyed the pleasures of smoking.

One weekend late in October I just felt down physically. Sinus and postnasal problems seemed to be with me constantly. Was it simply advancing age or was it the smoking? I knew I'd never know if I didn't stop smoking for a while. But I had never been able to do it before. Could I do it now?

I made a decision Monday night, Oct. 27. My daughter's birthday was Tuesday, so why not stop smoking on such an occasion? But I had told myself that many times before and always ended up having a cigarette with that first cup of coffee, and the best of intentions always went down the drain. I would probably do it again on the morning of the 28th.

Well, I made it all that day and every day since. I follow the lead of alcoholics who take it "one day at a time." Some days are easier than others.

Suddenly it seemed that everyone was smoking but me. That first beer without a cigarette was especially trying. I don't know how many times I reached in my shirt pocket only to come up empty-handed. I don't mind telling you that it's one of the toughest things I've ever had to do in my lifetime.

Do I feel better? Not as much as one might have hoped. The psychological problems associated with quitting had an impact on my physical well-being. There's that constant problem of overeating and putting on pounds which are just as harmful to your health.

Gradually, though, things improved. That little cough disappeared. And I feel much better when I awaken each morning.

The best reward, however, is the satisfaction of knowing you can control your own destiny. You like yourself a little better, and that makes it all worthwhile.

Dec. 28, 1980

Editor's Note: Jim Beam is still smoke-free.

We are what we come from

An aunt of mine died last month, and it suddenly struck me that an era was ending in my life.

How can the loss of an aunt end an era?

My mother came from a family of 12, unusually large by today's standards. When Aunt Curry died April 14, only Uncle Walter remained from the original 12.

I had to be out of town and couldn't make the funeral. When I returned, I sat down to write the family a note to explain my absence.

While reflecting on what to say, I felt an emptiness I haven't felt since my mother's death. The words finally came, and after expressing my sentiments, I understood the reason for the strange feeling.

In that letter I said something about my mother's family having had a tremendous impact on my life. "If I've been successful to any degree, then I have to give much of the credit to that family," I wrote.

I've been asking myself since then why I felt as I did about that family. And the same phrase keeps rolling over and over in my mind: "We are what we come from."

That isn't a good way to end a sentence, but that's what I've been thinking, so why not go ahead and say it?

I've been accused of being like my dad so many times; I should know we inherit quite a bit from family members. I just never dwelled on it much before writing that letter to Aunt Curry's family.

My grandparents were pioneers in Cameron Parish and that has always been the place many of us called home.

As a youngster, I spent every summer with my Aunt Nona in Leesburg. It's now the town of Cameron. I can remember my dad getting me a ride to Cameron every summer on a bread truck. I cried when I boarded that truck a few days after school was out because I hated to leave home. And I'd cry when I had to leave Cameron to come back home at the end of the summer.

Boy, what a fun time I had once I got to Leesburg! Aunt Nona was on the ration board during the big war, and she had credit at Pete Henry's grocery. I'd just amble down there and "put it on Aunt Nona's charge account."

Mr. Henry always gave me a five-dollar bill at the beginning of each summer, and that was big money in those days. I can still remember the joy of seeing Mr. Henry for the first time during those visits. That was enough spending money for the entire summer.

The women in the ration board office always bragged about how much they enjoyed seeing Jimmy every summer. "He's such a nice little fellow," they'd say. They were pretty as I recall, and I loved the extra attention. I guess I've liked girls ever since.

On weekends, we'd drive down to the old home place at Oak Grove near Creole. I'll never forget the Friday and Saturday nights when Uncle C.B., my bachelor uncle, would get all slicked up and head out for Creole and Hebert's dance hall. He'd be gone until the wee hours of the morning.

I always wanted to go with Uncle C.B., but I was too young. I told myself, though, that one day I'd be able to enjoy those good times on Friday and Saturday nights just like Uncle C.B.

I'm certain my wife will never forgive Uncle C.B. for that influence in my life. In his later years, Uncle C.B. always complained about me wearing dress slacks all the time. "Don't you have any khakis?" he'd ask.

Uncle L.B., I suppose, was considered the best-educated member of the family. I always stood taller when people said I looked like L.B.

If there is any kindness in my bones, the credit goes partly to Uncle

Buster. He was Mr. Nice Guy and always made life a little brighter. The only thing I didn't like about Uncle Buster was having to scratch his feet. But that was something every niece and nephew had to take his turn doing.

I supposed I'm tight-fisted with a dollar because of Uncle Shine. That wasn't his real name, of course, but that's how everyone knew him. He probably had the first dollar he ever earned.

We had a Texas branch in the family. They moved on to Port Arthur, and I didn't know them as well as the rest. Even so, Uncles Walter, Will and Monroe raised fine families. And Aunt Dora's family still had strong ties to Cameron.

Aunt Lucille died early, and I never knew her at all. Aunt Nona, however, was tops in my book. If there is such a thing as a second mother, she was it.

Aunt Curry, bless her soul, was pleasant every time I saw her and she always had a kind word for everybody. She would always greet you with, "How you doin', Pud?"

Yes, there is one more from that original 12. My cousins call her Aunt Carrie. For me, though, she is Mother No. 1 and, along with my dad, the greatest influence in my life.

And I mustn't forget the in-laws. They, too, exerted tremendous influences while we were growing up.

So add it up anyway you want, but it still comes out the same for me: "We are what we come from." And when the living examples of our heritage slip away from our day-to-day living, we can't help but feel a certain emptiness and the closing of an era in our lives.

We can fill that emptiness, however, by reflecting on the mighty fine people who have had a part in helping to mold our character and who have helped bring meaning to our very existence.

I suppose Mother's Day is as good a time as any for all of us to remember those wonderful people who influenced our lives.

Happy Mother's Day.

May 9, 1982

Guess who came to lunch

Buddy was right, of course. Lunch with the President of the United States is definitely a once-in-a-lifetime opportunity. And thanks to the generosity of my fellow editor and our boss, I got my shot at the political big time last Tuesday.

Buddy had attended a similar briefing with President Reagan two years ago, and insisted I should grab this latest opportunity.

The Mailgram from the White House was simple and direct: "On behalf of President Reagan, I wish to cordially invite you to an on-the-record briefing and luncheon for editors and broadcasters on Tuesday, March 11. Discussion will focus on foreign policy, defense matters and Central America.

"Please plan to arrive at the 17th Street entrance to the Old Executive Office building at 9:15 am. Following a morning session with Cabinet members, President Reagan will host a luncheon, concluding at approximately 1:30 p.m."

A quick telephone call the next morning, and I was on the list.

Gary, God bless him, got excited when I told him about the invitation. I knew I could count on my son-in-law to show some enthusiasm.

My wife, a pro when it comes to taking the wind out of your sails, said something like, "Yes, but there'll be about a hundred other editors there, too."

Actually, there were only about 80 other editors and broadcasters, but Gary fielded that one like a champ. He asked, "Lilly (that's what he calls my wife), when is the last time you were even in the same room with the President of the United States?"

I had to give him five on that one.

You don't take chances on a trip like that, so I left a day early. And you can bet old Jim Beam was at that 17th Street entrance in plenty of time Tuesday morning.

When I saw Sylvia Chase, the former TV reporter for ABC's "20/20," I knew it had to be the right place.

It was only about 8:45 a.m., but what are a few minutes standing around when you're getting ready to hear from some of the biggest names in national politics and have lunch with the Great White Father in Washington?

Our security checks started at 9:30 a.m. We produced our picture IDs; security personnel searched all camera bags and briefcases; we had to click our cameras then walk through a metal detector. Background checks had apparently been completed earlier with the birth dates and Social Security numbers we supplied.

Patrick J. Buchanan, the controversial and outspoken assistant to the president, opened our briefing. He set the tone for the rest of the day – aid to the Contras in Nicaragua was on all their minds.

The president and his advisers are firmly convinced Nicaragua adds up to another Cuba at our doorsteps, and they believe $100 million in aid to those forces fighting the Sandinistas is the only answer.

Other speakers include Elliott Abrams, assistant secretary of state for Inter-American affairs, Caspar Weinberger, secretary of defense, and Donald T. Regan, the president's chief of staff.

By the time Regan completed his part of the program the appointed hour had arrived. We walked across the street to the White House.

Anyone who says walking through the front door of the White House for lunch with one of the world's most powerful politicians is not an impressive experience isn't being completely honest about his feelings.

We selected our own seats at the 10 tables in the State Dining Room, wondering where the president would sit. A few minutes after 12 noon someone announced, "The President of the United States."

We stood up and applauded his entrance, but as luck would have it, my table wasn't close to his. However, it was only 15 to 20 feet away. But I was close enough to see that President Reagan looked even better and younger than he does on television, if that's possible.

A card at each plate spelled out the menu, and it's a souvenir you cherish a lifetime.

We dined on green pea soup with croutons, Supreme of Chicken in fennel sauce, Spaetzle Noodles, Zucchini Romano, caramel custard with fresh fruit and coconut macaroons.

For wine, we sipped on Charmenet Lauvignon Blanc 1982.

How do you make sure you use the right fork and correct table manners when you dine with the president? You just follow the lead of the White House staffer at your table.

One of the hosts at our table was a personable young man named Mitchell E. Daniels Jr. He's an assistant to the president for political and intergovernmental affairs.

I sat down next to Daniels, and shadowed his every move. It must have worked because the eight editors and broadcasters at our table came through with flying colors.

I looked at the president's table four or five times during the luncheon, trying not to stare but hoping for a chance to at least get in a nod. Unfortunately, the opportunity never came.

After lunch, President Reagan followed the lead of his advisers and hammered away at the necessity for aid to the Contras in Nicaragua.

When asked why the public seemed to be opposed to his $100 million aid package, Reagan blamed it on the public getting bad information or no information. He added, "Jefferson said if the American people know all the facts, they won't make a mistake. We haven't done our job."

Maybe it's the Western influence or his movie background, but President Reagan reduces most problems to their simplest terms. His philosophy about the Nicaraguan problem is like most others. For him, it boils down to "them against us." And if you're against us, you're for them.

Our once-in-a-lifetime experience ended about 1:20 p.m. after the president fielded some questions. We turned in our badges and walked out a front gate at the White House. While those rare moments may have ended, you can bet they won't ever be forgotten.

March 16, 1986

Memories should be cherished

...Middle age is reached the day you realize your memories have become more important to you than your dreams...
Robert J. Davis Santa Rosa, Calif.

◈

Davis told Newsweek magazine he didn't intend to reach that point in his life. I'm not sure how he plans to avoid middle age, but we wish him luck.

Those of us on the down side of middle age don't have any choice. Our time for dreams is short, so our memories are something we are happy to have around.

Maybe that's why a recent picture we published brought back memories of a time over 40 years ago. It was a photograph of Chris Verret of Lafayette receiving a plaque paying tribute to his late father, Jesse J. Verret.

Mr. Verret was my principal at LaGrange High School. It was pretty much a country school in those days on the northwest corner of Ryan and West School streets. The buildings are gone, and it's a soccer field now. However, I can sometimes hear that sound to which so many of us grew accustomed.

"Move on, Sonny," Mr. Verret would say.

He called everybody Sonny all the time. If you heard it, you knew you could be in real trouble. Like the time a couple of us went down to the principal's office to help Mr. Verret move some school supplies.

I had forgotten about the mustache someone had earlier penciled on my upper lip.

"What's this, Sonny?" Mr. Verret asked.

I was completely puzzled by the question, and he saw I was confused.

"This," he said as he pointed to his own upper lip.

That was the only clue I needed. I knew immediately what he was talking about, and I felt much like the fool I must have looked.

Another time Mrs. Dorothy McFatter, the librarian, sent a couple of us to Mr. Verret's office for cutting up in study hall.

"Go on home," he said in a frustrated tone. "I'm tired of fooling around with you boys."

We knew we had been expelled for the rest of that day, and the prospect of our parents finding out scared us to death. I was so shook up I ran two miles to get home at the same time as the bus. It was the only hope I had that my mother wouldn't find out what had happened.

I made it, and suddenly realized how panicked I had been. School was going to be out 15 minutes after we were booted out the door. All I had to do was wait that long and get on the school bus. No one would have been the wiser, but because of Mr. Verret's anger I wasn't thinking straight.

The worst incident of my high school days occurred when five or six of us decided to skip school and head downtown to the pool hall.

I don't recall who went along on that wild excursion, but they would remember. I bummed around in those days with Robert Benoit, Gerry Firmature, Mack Nevils, Bill Gossett, Val Sweeney, Jerry Corbello, Hulen Landry, Mural Cormie, Carl Williams, Don Daigle, Dickie Landry, John Ney, Charles "Sam" Reeves and Ira Landry.

Any of them who may have been in the group that day will recall the weird chain of events.

We planned to ride a city bus to town, but walked the back roads until we got out of the school area. We avoided Ryan Street until the last minute, and then hid behind an old service station at East Hale Street and Ryan.

One of us, Williams, I believe, was going to dash out and stand on the corner when a bus got close. Then the rest of us were going to run out and jump on board as soon as the bus stopped.

Carl and someone else got on the bus, but suddenly a car horn started blowing loudly. Those of us who hadn't gotten on the bus feared the worst, and that's exactly what it was.

There in his car behind that bus was none other than Mr. Verret. As bad luck would have it, he was driving to a funeral service at Hixson's on Broad Street.

For some unexplained reason, Carl, who hadn't been seen by Mr. Verret, got off the bus anyway.

Mr. Verret took us back to school and said he would deal with us later.

You can imagine our anxiety as we awaited his return.

Mr. Verret's standard punishment was well known by everyone who attended LaGrange. And we got our medicine when our turn came.

"Three licks or three days?" he asked each of us.

The alternatives were three licks with a broom as you bent over and held your knees or being expelled for three days.

It was an easy decision. In those days, getting expelled could bring punishment at home that was much more severe than anything Mr. Verret could hand out.

That broom stung quite a bit, but we lived to tell about it.

Although I had had some minor scrapes with Mr. Verret before, this was by far the most frightening. And I compounded the problem. I told Louise Cox, a reporter for the school newspaper, I'd never get caught playing hooky again, and my words ended up in print.

Mr. Verret had a field day with that comment. He was notorious for using the public address system, which was connected to each room, and my quotes were all he needed. Being president of the student body didn't help, either. You're supposed to be above such things.

"The Student Council president didn't say he won't play hooky again," Mr. Verret said for hundreds of students to hear. "He said he won't get caught again. What kind of example is that?"

No one can imagine the terrible embarrassment of that moment. It's one of those memories etched on my brain.

After total humiliation, I turned to Miss Linnie Lacy, who was sponsor of the Student Council.

"Try not to let it get you down," she said. "The embarrassment will pass."

Miss Lacy was right, of course. I needed her encouragement at that particular time in my life more than she ever knew.

I also learned an important lesson that day. Be careful what you say around news reporters. It can get into print and get you into a world of trouble.

Those incidents may not seem serious at a time in our lives when schools are trying to cope with drugs, guns and tremendous discipline problems. But we felt they were, and the stern way those situations were handled made better people out of most of us who were involved.

It was definitely the last time I skipped school.

Thank God for those memories. Like Mr. Verret in his time, they remind each of us that we are responsible for our own actions.

Dec. 31, 1992

It began with late paper

Like some of our readers, I can become an awfully unpleasant character when the morning newspaper isn't in my driveway at 6 a.m. Ask my wife if you have any doubts about how horrible I have been on occasion.

Jo Ann told me the paper wasn't there last Sunday, but I went outside to make sure. That was a mistake.

I didn't find the paper, but I did notice that the right front tire on her car was flat. Thinking I would solve that problem later in the day, I forgot to say anything when I went back inside.

Have you ever tried to figure out what to do when you don't have a paper to read with that first cup of coffee?

I opened some mail that had been laying around for a few days, but that wasn't too exciting. The weekly magazine was there on a table, but I had read everything in it that aroused my interest.

I killed some time by setting up television programs on the VCR, and then ate breakfast.

The paper finally arrived about 8 a.m.

Let me make it perfectly clear at this point that it wasn't late because of our carrier. She's the most dependable and considerate person in the world.

Deliveries are always difficult this time of year because of the large number of advertising inserts. It's a Herculean task that brings a lot of undeserved criticism to our circulation department. The people who deliver our papers have spoiled us with early arrivals most of the time.

After spending nearly two hours digesting the news, it was time to get ready for church. I was going downtown to hear a sermon on riverboat gambling. My wife was headed in another direction to our church. She said something about stopping at the store.

I was on my way out the door about 20 minutes later when it

suddenly hit me. I had forgotten to tell Jo Ann about the flat tire on her car.

Good grief, I thought to myself as I opened the door, her car's gone!

Panic was beginning to set in, but I tried to keep my cool. I could envision her stopped along the road somewhere, and tried to follow the route she might have taken.

She was nowhere to be seen and several laps around the store's parking lot convinced me she wasn't there. I headed back home to regroup.

Could she have gone by her office at McNeese? I took off again.

Her car wasn't in the parking lot there either, but I did see it leaning hard to the right on my second trip to the store.

When I walked inside, there she was in the express line waiting her turn to check out. She didn't appear to have a care in the world.

"Didn't you notice your car had a flat tire?" I asked.

"It pulled to the right some, but I didn't know it was a flat tire," she replied.

With people standing around, I resisted the temptation to blow my top. Besides, I knew I had to share some of the blame because I had forgotten to say anything about that flat tire earlier.

I went outside to cool down a bit.

We left the car there and headed for home. I gave her my car and jumped in the old '70 VW and headed downtown.

Things pretty much returned to normal after church and lunch. But that's when I made another fatal mistake. I decided to watch the New Orleans Saints play the Los Angeles Rams.

Why I punish myself so, I'll never know. By game's end, the Saints had blown another one, so I was fit to be tied a second time in one day.

My wife is an avid Saints fan, but she's smarter than I am. About three weeks ago she decided she wasn't going to watch them play anymore. She said she hasn't missed it, and doesn't get twisted in knots over the new ways they find to lose.

Oh, well, it wasn't worth fretting over too long. I moved on to happier things. I got our Christmas tree out of the attic and was delighted to see we had left the lights on last year. There's nothing I hate worse than stringing lights.

Sharon, a close friend of my daughter Jamie, is good at that job. She does it so the electric wires are completely out of sight.

We plugged the lights in, but only half of them burned. Jamie and I figured some of the light sections weren't plugged together. However, locating the plugs was virtually impossible in that sea of green.

I eventually realized there was only one solution, and it was drastic. The lights had to be taken off the tree to pinpoint the problem.

It took over an hour to strip the tree. I had cuts all over my hands from the wires on the tree branches to prove how difficult a job it was.

I was tempted on more than one occasion to do like Roseanne Arnold did on her show Tuesday night. She picked up a pair of scissors and cut the wires on a tangled mass of Christmas tree lights her husband was holding.

Once the lights were off my tree, I solved the puzzle. The longest string just flat wouldn't light up.

Having had no Sunday afternoon nap, I was awfully touchy by 5 p.m. Unfortunately, the misery would continue. Jo Ann's car was still in that store parking lot, and the flat tire had to be changed.

As she drove me there, I told her I was sorry for behaving like Scrooge. However, I explained that circumstances throughout the day had stretched my patience to the limit.

A late newspaper had set a chain of personal disasters in motion, and I wasn't sure if I would ever recover.

By nightfall, I was in anything but a holiday mood. If Christmas wanted to pass me by, that was perfectly all right with me.

Monday went smoother. Jessica came over and she wasn't aware of her grandfather's deplorable Sunday. She insisted that we decorate the tree that evening. She's the only human being on the face of this earth that could have made me get anywhere close to that tree.

I put the good light strings back on, and she and her grandmother she calls her Joey added the other decorations. Jessica and I finished the job when we climbed a ladder and topped the tree with an angel.

We had a grand time, and I found out once again why God gives us little children.

Dec. 16, 1993

How are you cutting grass?

What does it say about someone when he spends three years trying to pick out a new lawn mower? After all that time, I still don't know whether I want to ride or walk, push or pull.

The grass doesn't wait, so every spring I get out the old Sears mower in hopes it will do the job one more time.

I always install a new spark plug, check the oil and fill it with gasoline. Then comes the hard part, pulling the starter rope 40 or 50 times while hoping it will eventually crank over.

For about three years now, that old mower has come through like a champ. And it isn't as hard to start the next time around. Even so, I'm definitely mowing on borrowed time.

Checking what others are using doesn't help much. Lawn mowers are as individual as their owners. You seldom see two of the same kind in the neighborhood.

Smitty, the fellow next door, has the luxury mower on our block. It's a riding model with a grass catcher on the back. Wayne, who lives across the street, also has a riding mower.

Jess, my other next-door neighbor, has one of those rear wheel push jobs, I think. I've never really seen it up close.

Gary, my son-in-law who lives down the road, has a Yazoo, the mower that made those big rear wheels famous. He had a riding mower at one time, and I gave it a whirl. However, like so many mowers these days, those new safety features required your hands and feet to be doing too many functions at one time.

I inherited a riding mower from my dad some years ago. It was one of those old Snapper models. It was a breeze to operate, and I used my Sears mower to trim around bushes and up next to the house.

Unfortunately, the old red mower wasn't always easy to start. The last time the engine refused to turn over, I gave it to friends of my late brother, David.

Shortly after giving it away, David asked me what had been wrong with it. I told him I didn't know, but it just wouldn't start.

I'll never forget what he said next.

"That's funny," he said. "It started the minute we unloaded it in Westlake, and it's been running fine since then."

Oh, well, I didn't have any regrets. It was time to move on to a better mower. Unfortunately, I didn't know at the time that it would take me so long to decide.

I asked Robert, a lifelong friend who helps me watch over the newsroom on Saturdays, where he got his mower.

"Oh, I just went out and bought one of those cheap Sears jobs," he said.

It was obvious from his quick response that lawn mower selection isn't a high priority with Robert.

What's my problem?

OK, do you spring for a riding mower or stick with a self-propelled model you walk behind? Anything that doesn't either pull or push itself is out of the question.

My wife says I'm being foolish not to get a riding mower, and maybe she's right. However, being tight-fisted and exercise-conscious, that's a decision I find hard to accept. So I'll probably end up with something you walk behind.

That takes us to the next dilemma. Which works best, a self-propelled mower that pushes or one that pulls?

Although I've had pretty good luck with my front-wheel drive model, I still have to do too much pushing to suit my fancy.

Environmental concerns have also compounded my problems. They have had a major impact on lawn care.

The trend used to be to bag grass. Then it was decided your lawn benefited when you left the cut grass on the ground. Someone perfected that by coming up with a mulch model.

With that in mind, do you get a mower that throws grass out the side, into a bag in back or pick one that mulches? You can get a combination model that allows you to do any of those three, but does that complicate maintenance and upkeep?

Price is another puzzler. Do you spend a couple hundred bucks for a lawn mower or move into the $500 and $600 class?

The higher-priced models are well recommended, but are they really necessary? I find it awfully difficult to spend more than $250 or $300.

Then there's the question of brands.

Frank, my Thursday coffee-drinking buddy, said I should stay away from Sears mowers. "Get something with a Briggs & Stratton engine," he said. "They are easier to repair, and almost anyone can fix them."

Since he's been cutting grass longer than I have, I figured that was sound advice. However, I realized I already had a Sears model and it had been unusually dependable. So I went downtown three or four times to look over the latest models.

There were still some lingering doubts, so I checked the mowers at Lowe's. They have rear-wheel drive models, and Consumer Reports says they generally do a better job moving the mower. Still, I wasn't convinced.

I found out about another factor to consider from Consumer Reports magazine. It suggested not buying a mower that has safety features that cut off the engine every time you run into some tough grass.

Something tells me they've taken this safety business much too far.

By the way, don't ever say anything about Consumer Reports to a sales person when you're looking at a product the magazine doesn't recommend. They can get awfully testy at the mere mention of the name.

Now, maybe you can understand why I'm beside myself in trying to figure out what to do about this lawn mower business. I've considered so many options I'm totally confused.

Despite the urgency, I'm still finding it difficult to make up my mind. Which brings us back to the original question. What does my indecision say about me?

It has to be one of two things. I've either elevated procrastination to new heights, or it's really true that a little knowledge can sometimes be a dangerous thing.

April 24, 1994

Jim Beams party with Booker

Thanks to a congenial Kentucky gentleman named Booker Noe, I was a major player last week in a once-in-a-lifetime event. I joined 120 other people named Jim Beam in Clermont, Ky., to help celebrate the 200th birthday of Jim Beam Bourbon.

Noe is the grandson of James "Jim" Beauregard Beam, the fourth-generation Beam who made his family's bourbon a household name and a worldwide favorite.

The 121 Jim Beams who made it to Clermont by 11 a.m. Friday, Oct. 13, a lucky day for them, shared in a $100,000 "inheritance" put up by Noe. It was the big prize in the "Search for Jim Beam" contest conceived by Noe as his way of celebrating "with the people who, through their names, help to keep my grandfather's spirit of adventure and tradition alive."

The Jim Beam distillery is a 20-minute drive south from Louisville and about eight miles from Hardin's Creek, the place where Jacob Beam made his first barrel of whiskey in 1795.

A roadblock near the distillery gave my wife and me a few anxious moments, but we made it with time to spare. However, one Jim Beam cut it awfully close. He didn't sign up until 10:56 a.m., four minutes before the 11 a.m. deadline.

Although I spent most of my $826.45 share of the inheritance getting to Clermont and back, the prize has been a great conversation piece since Noe put up the money back in January.

Hill & Knowlton, the national public relations firm that handled arrangements for the Jim Beam reunion, gave us red and blue baseball caps for easy identification.

Booker Noe, a r... and fellow who is master distiller emeritus, gave us a hearty welcome after we registered. When his voice faltered, someone walked up with a glass of Jim Beam. After a quick swig and a sigh, Noe was back in the groove.

Getting acquainted with the other Jim Beams was easy. All you had to do was walk up to someone in a red or blue cap and ask him where he was from. You already knew his name.

Whenever I mentioned that Lake Charles was on the Gulf Coast, most of the Jim Beams had the same response: "Isn't that where they have a lot of storms?" they'd ask.

If nothing else, we're famous for hurricanes.

The Jim Beam from Waverly, Iowa, perked up when my wife mentioned that McNeese State University was located in Lake Charles.

"Oh, we know McNeese," the man's wife said. "Northern Iowa played McNeese in football."

Jim Beams from Alabama and Ohio said they were truckers and noted that Louisiana was one of the toughest states to drive through because it is strict about the regulations of the road. Both of them had been through Lake Charles.

The Jim Beam from Prescott Valley, Ariz., had moved out West from New Orleans after he retired as a divisional vice president of the D.H. Holmes department store. He brought along a family-tree chart to search for relatives.

When I met the Baton Rouge Jim Beam, he also pulled out a family tree and gave me a quick rundown. The only other Louisianian was from Haughton, which is near Shreveport.

The Omaha, Neb., Jim Beam said when he was featured in a newspaper story back home, the governor of Nebraska — Ben Nelson — decided he wasn't going to let Booker Noe steal all the thunder. Nelson invited everyone named Ben Nelson to the mansion for a celebration of his own.

Jim Beam of Lakeland, Fla., said he knew two Jim Beams — a nephew and a friend — who had qualified for the reunion but died before it convened.

My dad's family traces its roots to North Carolina, but I wasn't able to make contact with any potential relatives from that area.

As you might expect, Texas had the most Jim Beams at the festivities (15). Then came North Carolina and Kentucky, 11 each; California, Ohio and Pennsylvania, 9 each; Florida, 8; Illinois, Indiana and Tennessee, 6 each.

Three generations of a Jim Beam family showed up from the Louisville area, and two of the three generations of a California family also attended. The father of that group doesn't like to fly, so he stayed home. The grandson was 7, the youngest Jim Beam there.

A Jim Beam from Switzerland had the distinction of being the only registrant from outside the United States.

After photographs and a Friday picnic on the shaded distillery grounds, we rested up for a gigantic celebration on Saturday. Noe didn't exaggerate when he called it "the biggest party this area has ever seen."

Opening ceremonies included a brief skit in which individuals in period dress portrayed the key figures of the Beam generations — Jacob, David, David M., Jim and T. Jeremiah Beam. Noe didn't need a stand-in.

T. Jeremiah Beam had no children, so he brought Noe, his sister's son, into the business. He could see that Noe shared the family passion for bourbon making.

A Dixieland band led the 1,800 guests from around the world on a tour of the grounds, which ended at a circus-like setting. There were huge tents to house food, drinks and carnival games and entertainment by country music performers.

Noe circulated among the crowd all afternoon and evening, signing autographs, posing for pictures and chatting with the "kinfolk" he had invited to the unique celebration.

Like other Americans, Jim Beams come in all shapes, ages and personalities. They are ordinary folks who are proud of their heritage, and it was a real treat to break bread with them for a couple of days.

Jo Ann and I left Kentucky Sunday morning, knowing we had been part of something rare and special. Every time I see a billboard or a bottle label promoting Jim Beam Bourbon, it will bring back some mighty fond memories.

Thanks, Booker.

Oct. 22, 1995

Is my body wearing out?

Wouldn't it be nice if we could take our bodies in for a complete overhaul? The endless repair trips I've been making to one doctor or another are getting to be a pain in the neck I don't need.

None of us ever thinks our riotous living will ever catch up with us, but time eventually takes its toll.

I've been to four different doctors this year, and there are at least four more to go.

What is particularly frustrating is the fact that I've tried to do most of the right things — at least in recent years. Obviously, it hasn't helped that much.

The first big break I gave my chances for good health came in 1980 when I quit smoking. Ending a 30-year bad habit was definitely a milestone and a demonstration of tremendous will power of which I'm especially proud.

Former smokers still face health risks, but they do improve their longevity odds.

High blood pressure continues to be a problem, but medication keeps it under control. I am also taking an aspirin every other day to help improve blood circulation.

About six years ago, I started an exercise regimen that is designed to lead to better health. My daughter and I began a regular program of fast walking (15-minute miles). We tried to make 2 1/2 to 3 miles a day three or four days a week.

When the cholesterol scare surfaced, I started monitoring my levels and never had a reading higher than 184. However, overall numbers can be deceiving, and I was laboring under a false sense of security.

I have a low level of HDL (high-density lipoprotein). Cardiologists will tell you men should have a minimum level of 35, and mine hovered around 26. Still, I wasn't convinced there was any cause for alarm and declined to take any medication.

The cardiologist did put me on a low-fat diet, told me to start lifting weights, to take fish oil tablets and use a teaspoon of olive oil on salad once a day. Those are four of only a few ways to increase the levels of HDL, which helps flush out the arteries.

The doctor also told me to take a multi-vitamin, vitamins C and E and beta-carotene.

Since heart trouble runs in my family, I decided last September to take a PET scan of my coronary arteries. That was all the proof the doctor and I needed. There was definitely plaque buildup, and he said I might have even had a blood clot that dissolved itself.

That's about as close as you can come to having a heart attack, and it was all the motivation I needed to start taking cholesterol medication.

Adding niacin to my existing lineup boosted me to eight tablets or pills in the morning, one at noon and five at night.

My granddaughter can't get over the number of pills stacked near my plate at mealtime.

I lost weight and it appeared I was doing all the right things and well on my way to better health than ever before. Well, guess again.

I started having lower back pain that the orthopedist diagnosed as arthritic inflammation. He helped me get that under control.

Walking was good for back trouble, he said, so I was convinced everything was still going to be OK.

Then, sometime in late-January, I started having problems with my right heel. I fought it for over a month, but decided it was time to see the orthopedist again.

It turned out to be heel spur, a common form of heel pain. I had read that the pain could last as long as 11 months, and mentioned that to the doctor. He was anything but encouraging.

"The condition can last two years," he said.

Others I spoke with who had a similar problem said nothing helped much.

Determined to overcome the odds, I started a foot-stretching program the doctor recommended and it may be helping. However, I'm going back this week to get a professional opinion.

Meanwhile, my back pain continues, and I'm unable to resume my walking program until the heel spur gets better. I'm doing a knee-bending exercise instead of walking, stretching my foot muscles in bed when I wake up every morning and then twice a day for 10 minutes while leaning against a wall.

I'm also doing some back exercises because something I'm doing is keeping my back in bad shape.

When I started hearing a roar in my right ear a few weeks ago, the ear doctor told me it was nerve damage and there wasn't anything he could do about it.

I've had my eyes checked again, and have appointments scheduled with my dentist and urologist. I'm trying to save my teeth and monitor that troublesome prostate that often affects men my age.

The skin doctor will have his turn before long, and I'll need a complete examination sometime this summer from my internist.

Maybe now you can understand why I'd love to be able to take my body in for a complete overhaul.

That isn't possible, of course, so I'll keep trying to cope with conditions as they arise.

A colleague of mine, who retired 10 years ago, may have given me the most accurate diagnosis yet. And it didn't cost me a dime.

"Jim, we're getting old," he said.

Thanks, Wayne, but on top of all my other problems, I didn't need to be reminded.

March 17, 1996

Is it aging or changing times?

Does advancing age have anything to do with impatience? I find myself less willing as I get older to accept things the way they are instead of the way I think they ought to be.

When a retired colleague of mine heard me griping a month or two ago, he said it sounded like it was time for me to hang it up. Let me tell you about some of the things that bug me and see if you agree.

We're going to vote on Sept. 21, but I only get to ballot in one out of three races for 14th Judicial District judge. Shouldn't all of us be able to vote for the judges who make decisions that affect us all?

Calcasieu Parish was sliced up into three judicial districts a few years ago in order to create a district for two minority judges. Only the voters who live in each of those districts can vote for people running in those areas. The candidates, however, can run in any of the three districts.

The state and U.S. Justice Department should have created two minority judgeships in Calcasieu Parish and let us vote on all the judges, including those running for minority seats.

Residency rules also make me see red, wherever they exist. Why should people be required to live in cities or parishes where they work? Isn't this still a free country?

New Orleans goes further than most cities. Ordinances there require that all new employees must live in the city and that workers already on the payroll who live outside the city must move into the city to be eligible for promotion.

The superintendent of police in New Orleans says he can't fill 200 vacant positions in his department. They've even called in State Police and the criminal sheriff's office to patrol the French Quarter.

Councilwoman Peggy Wilson said the city should repeal its residency rule so the police department could rehire officers who have quit rather than leave their homes in the suburbs.

The New Orleans City Council shot that idea down with a 5-1 vote. Meanwhile, other law enforcement people have to carry the load. It isn't fair. In fact, it's un-American.

I get upset anytime I read about public officials who are engaged in questionable activities, particularly those who are sworn to uphold the law.

We've been bombarded recently with stories questioning candidates who are using campaign funds for private and personal purposes. Those under the gun claim it's all legal, and maybe it is. However, why do they have to push campaign spending to its ethical limits?

If there is any doubt about what they're doing, they shouldn't do it.

Then there was the story out of Lafayette about an appeal court judge who has a bad habit of parking in the wrong places.

The (Baton Rouge) Advocate reported that Judge Sylvia Cooks of Lafayette, who serves on the 3rd Circuit Court of Appeal headquartered in Lake Charles, has received 47 parking tickets since 1989.

She paid 34 of those tickets and eight were overturned on appeal. That left five still undecided, which caused her vehicle to be immobilized Aug. 16.

Former Mayor Kenny Bowen of Lafayette had given Cooks and others the privilege of free parking without getting ticketed, but the favor was withdrawn.

"She's famous for not obeying parking laws," Bowen said.

Why does Judge Cooks park on the street when she has a parking space in a bank garage?

"There are occasions when I park in the street when I'm in a hurry to get some place," she said.

Did you park where you weren't supposed to the last time you were in a hurry? Shouldn't judges set an example for the rest of us?

An experience at the video store caused my latest flare-up.

When it comes to following the rules, I'm at the head of the class. If you doubt that, ask my wife. She came to my defense last week.

I checked out two movies on a Sunday, and they had to be back by 11 p.m. Monday. I watched one movie Sunday and the second Monday. Then I slipped on a jumpsuit at 10 p.m., took both movies back and handed them to a young man behind the counter.

You can imagine my shock when I tried to check out another movie Thursday and was told I owed over $10 in late charges. The clerk insisted one movie was a day late and the other was four days late.

After additional checking, she admitted the one they said was four days late was found on a counter. However, she and two others insisted I had returned the second movie around 7 p.m. Tuesday, a time when my wife and I were celebrating our 42nd anniversary at a local restaurant and theater.

One of the three, a supervisor, said I owed $2.70 and had to pay it to clear the computer. I paid the fee but was spitting fire by the time I left the store. Jo Ann went back later and quietly insisted they had made a mistake.

They refunded the $2.70, agreeing we were good customers. However, they wouldn't admit I took the movie back on time.

There might be some people who try to beat video stores out of rental charges, but I'm not one of them. I find it extremely insulting to think that video store clerks believe I would compromise my honesty and integrity for $2.70.

Why can't they just as easily admit that someone working there put that returned videotape down and forgot to log it in?

Yes, I'm still angry about that incident. And you can bet I'm going to get a receipt anytime I take a videotape back anywhere.

I'm also fed up with telemarketers who bug me in the evening hours, with charities that keep sending requests for money after I've already made my annual contribution, with constant appeals for money from political parties and their candidates and with schools and other organizations that turn little children into door-to-door fund-raisers.

If that means I'm just a grumpy old man, I can live with the criticism. However, something tells me older folks aren't the only ones whose patience is often stretched to the breaking point.

Sept. 5, 1996

New year is end, beginning

My millennium has arrived. No, I'm not 1,000 years old. However, I will be 65 in 1998, and that magical age qualifies under Webster's definition.

Although we normally think of a millennium as being any period of 1,000 years, it is also defined as "any period of great happiness, peace, prosperity, etc." or an "imagined golden age."

My life measures up to that standard in most respects, so while many of you will have to wait until 2000 arrives, my celebration can begin on Oct. 7.

Whether reaching 65 is going to be my "imagined golden age" remains to be seen. A number of my friends, colleagues and acquaintances have already made that transition and insist it's a new and wonderful experience.

I have been constantly reminded that I was getting close. Over the last couple of years people have been asking me the same question over and over again: "When are you going to retire?"

Well, the time is at hand, and I'm going to have to finally come up with an answer.

If I told you it would be easy, I'd be lying. How do you write the final chapter on a working life that dates back to age 12 and that has been one heckuva run?

The only time I haven't worked over those many years was in

1954-55, the first year of a marriage that is approaching its 44th anniversary. My wife was working and helping pay the tuition for my last year at McNeese State University.

With a couple of exceptions, the half-dozen jobs I've had over a lifetime proved to be valuable experiences. However, none of them comes even close to the personal, professional and financial rewards I have enjoyed at the Lake Charles American Press.

When I realize how I happened to land this job, I consider myself to be one of the luckiest people on earth.

I was teaching school in the late 1950s and Bill McMahon, a life-long and dear friend, helped me get a part-time job in our sports department. I needed a way to supplement my teaching income.

Bill's dad, the late Lloyd McMahon, was managing editor, and he eventually offered me a full-time job as a reporter.

What an offer it was, too.

"Jim, we can pay you more a week than we've ever offered anyone as a starting reporter," McMahon said.

Talk about flying high. When I finally came back down to earth, I realized I had traded nine months of teaching for a 12-month job paying about the same money.

I knew within a year's time, though, that it was the best career change of my life. I also understood why newspaper salaries weren't all that great. If you didn't have to eat and pay bills, you would almost be willing to pay a newspaper to do this kind of work.

It didn't matter what the hours were. The late Buddy Threatt and I worked as a team all week long and most Friday and Saturday nights, and loved every minute of it.

Newspaper people are a rare breed, and I've rubbed shoulders with some of the most dedicated journalists in the world. We also knew how to have a good time — too good, in fact, to suit our wives and families. I know they were happy when we finally decided to grow up socially.

The late Wayne Owens was a great investigative reporter, and he passed along many of his techniques. Hector San Miguel, one of the best in the business in this state and elsewhere, still talks about tips he picked up from Wayne.

Others I have been close to in this business include retired editor

Don Kingery, who is still a valuable resource person, personal adviser and American Press contributor; photographer Sam Guillory, who now lives in Wisconsin; and Bruce Broussard, a retired editor who never seems to age.

Scores of colleagues have come and gone over the past 37 years, and there are others still on the job that are destined to make their mark on journalism in Southwest Louisiana. The American Press is definitely in good hands as the newspaper embarks on its second 100 years.

Against that background of professional satisfaction and camaraderie, you can understand why I have some misgivings about reaching what is my millennium.

I am also bothered by those political figures out there who get too much of a gleam in their eyes when they hear Jim Beam may be on the verge of hanging it up.

I've been writing about those rascals since my first regular, personal column appeared in 1975, and it has been perhaps my most rewarding experience among many in this business. That's because there are hundreds of everyday folks out there who have said thanks for keeping them informed about what was going on behind the political scene.

If my lifetime of luck holds out, I'll retire as editor of the American Press at the end of 1998 but still be able to write about the personalities and events that make news on the state and local political landscape.

That would definitely be the best of both worlds.

Jan. 1, 1998

I'm a legitimate senior citizen

If age were all it took to become a senior citizen, I would have earned my wings a long time ago. However, it's more than a question of time. You can't claim the title until you've been to Branson, Mo.

For those of you who haven't heard of Branson, it's an entertainment mecca that is home to 38 theaters, 70 shows and seating for 51,000 people.

My wife and I have talked about going to Branson for years, but we never quite got up a big-enough head of steam to make the necessary arrangements. Thanks to Henry Bowdon, the associate pastor at our church, who is a travel agent in his spare time, we finally made it last week.

We had a grand time, and I am happy to report to you today that I am now an official member of the "Over-the-Hill Gang."

Branson has a reputation for catering to older Americans, and that's definitely the city's bread and butter.

One of the 42 members of our group summed the situation up well when she said, "I never saw so many old people in my life — and I'm one of 'em."

Despite that reputation, Branson has much to offer people of all ages. Where else, for example, can you see eight shows in three days? And the entertainment is geared to suit a number of musical and theatrical tastes.

The city has 174 hotels with more than 15,000 rooms, more than 160 restaurants and three huge outlet shopping malls.

I do have a couple of suggestions for the chefs and restaurant owners in Branson. Less fried food, please, and stock up on some skimmed milk.

Make no mistake about it, though; the shows are the big draw in Branson. Our tour group saw Russian comedian Yakov Smirnoff, Mel

Tillis and his daughter, country music sensation Pam Tillis, singer Andy Williams, world-renown violinist Shoji Tabuchi, The Platters quartet which made musical history in the 1950s and 1960s, the Lawrence Welk Show, comedian and musician Jim Stafford and an Imax theater film, "The Ozarks, Legacy and Legend."

Jo Ann and I substituted the Mickey Gilley Show for one of the eight, and enjoyed many of the singer's No. 1 hit songs. Like his famous cousins — singer Jerry Lee Lewis and evangelist Jimmy Swaggart — Gilley is a native of Ferriday.

Branson is a full day's drive from Lake Charles, so the action didn't get started until Tuesday morning. We got an early sample of things to come when we were entertained at breakfast by Kimberly Dawn, a 13-year-old singer described as the "Angel of Branson."

Try as the 42 of us did, it was difficult to handle eggs, biscuits and bacon while listening to a live country music act. However, that's how many of the big stars worked their way to the top, so we made allowances.

When you travel by coach   don't make the mistake of calling them buses — you get extra special treatment from the stars and their associates. Groups are recognized at every performance and escorted to their choice seats.

I sat next to a member of a Richmond, Va., tour group and he told me about their coach breaking down while trying to climb a hill en route to Branson. The transmission lost some bolts, but a tour group motoring in from Florida rescued the group on the side of the road.

That's the camaraderie you experience among tour groups that have so much in common. Hal Monroe, who works for Centenary College in Shreveport, was our congenial coach driver and he negotiated the sharp curves and hilly terrain extremely well.

I heard some "coach conversation" while standing around in a theater lobby.

"Don't you rotate one side at a time?" a traveler asked someone in our group.

He was talking about getting on and off the coaches, which occurs often on tours like ours.

"No, we rotated from front to back and back to front on occasion, but never from side to side," she said.

Tour groups are also famous for rotating seats after every stop. It's done to spread the good seats around.

Audience participation is big in Branson, and people who are celebrating anniversaries and birthdays are recognized before each performance. Video and audiotaping isn't allowed, but theatergoers are encouraged to shoot still photographs at most times during the shows.

Smirnoff makes a point of visiting each coach after the performance to thank everyone for coming. Stars also stick around after their shows to shake hands and sign autographs.

To tell you the truth, I wasn't excited about some of the shows beforehand. You tend to think of Andy Williams and The Platters, for example, as performers whose days have come and gone and some of the others as stars who can't make it on the major circuit.

How wrong I was. Each show had its own unique flavor, and the Williams, Tabuchi, Welk and Stafford shows were extremely elaborate productions. Laser lighting also added a special touch.

Mel Tillis and his daughter, Pam, are major stars, and they perform in the new and beautiful Tillis Theater, which sits high on a hill in Branson.

Jim Stafford and Smirnoff made us laugh like we haven't in years, and they made us feel good about country, family and friends.

Our group left town at daybreak Friday, feeling tired but enriched by the experience. We also felt better about ourselves, our freedom to love and laugh and enjoyed a renewed sense of pride in being Americans.

Branson does that to you, and the city definitely lived up to its advanced billing. Our trip was especially enjoyable because we didn't have the two or three old grouches you usually find in a tour group our size.

Jo Ann is already talking about another trip to Branson. She has always loved the theater and live entertainment, and seeing her have such a great time made my trip even more enjoyable.

I'd also like to wish her — and all other mothers out there — a happy Mother's Day.

May 10, 1998

Retirement isn't end of work

Today marks the final day of my first year of retirement. It's been a smooth transition, and I've adapted well to the change in my lifestyle. However, there have been a few drawbacks.

People who are still working and many who have also retired asked me the same questions over and over again all year long. Here are some examples:

"I see you're still writing. I thought you retired."

"Didn't you retire? Why are you still writing?"

"When are you really going to retire?"

"Aren't you retired? Why are you still going to the office?"

"If you're an example of what retirement is like, I don't want any part of it."

Sports editor Scooter Hobbs even took some digs when I appeared on "Sound Off Live," his weekly television sports show with Rick Sarro and Kevin Guidry.

"We had seven retirement parties for Beam last year, and we see more of him now than we did back then," Hobbs said.

After hearing comments like those throughout the year, you can understand why I'm starting to feel guilty about going to the office for a few hours three days a week.

Maybe an explanation is in order.

For the last 40 years, I've had what I consider the best job in the country. There hasn't been a day in that long span that I ever regretted having to get up and go to work.

I would have worked for peanuts, and almost did in those early years.

Teachers were making about $3,600 a year when I got my first newspaper job to supplement my teaching income. I became a part-time sports writer in the late-1950s and also did some news writing.

Bill McMahon, a high school buddy and lifetime friend, helped me get on at the American Press. The late Lloyd McMahon, his dad, was managing editor and the man who gave me my first full-time newspaper job.

The pay back then was about the same as it was for teachers. However, since the job was for 12 instead of 9 months, I actually took a cut in salary.

What a pleasure it was to go to work every day during those 40 years and deal with something different and unexpected. That's the way it is in the news business, and there is seldom a dull moment.

I had opportunities to go places and do things that I would have never experienced in any other line of work.

And I met a lot of nice people along the way, both inside and outside the profession.

Yes, there were some bad times — and people — but they were the exception rather than the rule.

When I became city editor in 1965, I was responsible for hiring personnel in the newsroom. You can't imagine how many capable, qualified people I've worked with over the last 40 years.

Some of them — friends of mine — have died. Many of the others went on to bigger and better jobs either here or in other places. A shining example among those who made their marks elsewhere is Molly Moore, who covered the Persian Gulf War for the Washington Post and wrote a book about her experiences.

Molly was 15 when she first worked at the American Press. Jim Stacy, a teacher at Barbe High School who had also worked at the newspaper, was right on target when he said Molly was a talented writer.

I had an opportunity in those early years to occasionally write a personal column, and I found it extremely rewarding.

In 1975, I approached Editor Truman Stacey about writing a

column on a regular basis. After rejecting five other suggestions I made at the same time, he said OK. I suppose he didn't want me to leave his desk empty-handed.

I set two goals for myself. I wanted to write about controversial subjects that most people were reluctant to discuss publicly and to try and explain the workings of complicated issues.

I had taught American history, government and English for four years, and that experience served me well in the newspaper business.

Readers especially liked personal columns dealing with my family life. They still do, and that's because they have families, too.

You can't imagine how satisfying it is to sit down at a computer (a typewriter in the earlier years) and express your views on issues that you feel are important to your city, state and nation.

Many times, it's also a great way to air grievances and relieve anxieties about a controversial issue. You also realize there will occasionally be some out there who will disagree and take serious exception to what you say. It goes with the territory.

The Shearman family treated me as a professional by placing no restraints on what I could write about and paid me well for doing what I enjoyed.

The response of readers has been overwhelming at times from both a positive and negative standpoint. However, the fact that the vast majority who responded said they liked what I had to say made it all worthwhile. Even those who disagreed said they would continue reading.

Those are some of the many reasons why I'm still writing today, a year into my retirement. I'm doing it because the newspaper has given me that opportunity, because readers still seem to appreciate the effort and because I love to do it.

Yes, I have retired from the day-to-day duties at the American Press. Those responsibilities are now in the capable hands of others. However, I'll be a newsman as long as I live and writing as long as there's something newsworthy out there.

Dec. 31, 2000

Case of mistaken identity

BATON ROUGE — Did anyone ever tell you the story about each of us having a twin somewhere in the world? It's probably an old wives' tale, but I never paid much attention to it, whatever the source. However, maybe I should have.

After recent experiences covering the Louisiana Legislature, I'm a believer. And here's why:

While making my way to a committee meeting one morning, a woman stopped me in a hall of the state Capitol basement.

"Pardon me," she said, "Don't you work for the governor?"

"No," I replied. "I'm a newspaper man from Lake Charles."

Why, I wondered, would someone think I worked for Gov. Mike Foster?

When you're walking around the Capitol, maybe it's easy to be confused with someone else. The halls are crowded with legislators, staff members, lobbyists and tourists.

I didn't give the woman's mistaken identity a second thought. I wasn't even sure who she thought I was.

A few days later, it happened again — almost in the same area. I could hear a woman behind me calling.

"Larry, Larry, hold up a minute," she said. "I need to talk to you about a bill."

There weren't many people in the hall, so I turned around to see exactly who Larry might be. And about that time, she tapped me on the shoulder and started to tell me about her legislation.

"You must have me confused with someone else," I said, "but I'm not Larry."

As her face turned a solid red, she said, "Oh, I'm sorry, I thought you were Larry Kinlaw."

I had heard of Larry Kinlaw from local government officials who had dealings with him as head of the office that handles rural grants. He has a reputation for being a fair-minded, easy-going individual with a lot of credibility.

Kinlaw is also a special adviser to Foster. His primary responsibility at the moment is serving as legislative liaison. He keeps lawmakers up to date on legislation supported or sponsored by the governor.

Now that I knew who I must have looked somewhat like, I told the red-faced woman: "That's OK. If I'm going to be confused with anyone, it couldn't be with a nicer fellow. So don't give it a second thought."

Later that same afternoon, I was coming out of the men's restroom on the first floor when an oil and gas lobbyist shouted, "Larry, Larry."

Before I could explain, he caught his own mistake.

"Pardon me," he said. "I didn't have my glasses on."

I knew it was time to look up Kinlaw and tell him what had happened. I found him in the hallway outside the back of the House of Representatives. It's where the governor's staff talks with legislators.

After telling Kinlaw about my experiences, he told me about a couple of his own.

"I know how it happens," he said. "When I walked through an office door one morning, the person inside said, "Come on in, Jim."

On another occasion, I talked with Kinlaw, who was sitting in the back corner of the House chamber where the governor's representatives talk with legislators. He told me about his experience with Morris Bruce, the husband of state Rep. Beverly Bruce of Mansfield.

The Bruces and I stay at the same hotel, and I had seen Morris

Bruce almost every morning about 6 a.m. at breakfast. One morning, I didn't make it, and that's when Bruce ran into Kinlaw at the Capitol.

"I missed you at breakfast today, Jim," Bruce told Kinlaw.

So, you see, it was a two-way street.

After telling my wife about our experiences, she asked if the two of us really looked alike. I told her I wasn't sure.

That's when I decided to ask Sheila, a congenial photographer for the House of Representatives, if she would take a picture of Kinlaw and me when she had time.

She said it wouldn't be a problem, and I waited for an opportunity to get it done.

The clincher came last Thursday. While sitting at the side of the Senate chamber interviewing Sen. Willie Mount of Lake Charles, Sen. Ron Bean of Shreveport motored up in his wheelchair. I could see he wanted something, but he turned away.

Later, he came by again and motioned for me to meet him at the back of the chamber.

I had never formally been introduced to Sen. Bean, but I knew who he was. However, I had no idea what he might want with a reporter from Lake Charles.

"Can I help you, senator?" I asked as I leaned over the railing.

Apparently at that moment, he realized his mistake and apologized.

"I needed to talk with Larry Kinlaw," he said.

Kinlaw was in a corner at the back of the Senate and, like me, was wearing a dark gray suit. There wouldn't be a better time to take that photograph.

I trekked across the rotunda to find Sheila, and she snapped the picture just outside the Senate chamber.

"Even your glasses are the same," she said.

"Do we really look that much alike?" I asked her.

"You could be brothers," she said.

I haven't seen the photograph, so I can't tell. When I get it, I'll pass it around and get some second opinions.

Meanwhile, I wonder if I could get in to see Foster and talk about some serious legislative business before he realizes who I really am.

June 17, 2001

Accident becomes personal thing

Put a personal face on a fatal accident, and it can be unsettling. I found myself in that situation early Thursday as I scanned the obituaries in the morning paper. There in the middle of the page was a photograph of Dewey Granger, 64.

Wait a minute, I said to myself. He looks awfully familiar. And suddenly it hit me. It was Buddy Granger, my barber for the last six years.

I never knew Buddy's first name was Dewey. Neither did a lot of other people.

What happened? I wondered. Did he have a heart attack?

It wasn't until I visited the funeral home that I found out Buddy drowned Monday in a boating accident.

I had read the story in Wednesday's paper about a boating mishap on Big Lake in Cameron Parish, but the name of the man who drowned didn't ring a bell.

Buddy and a friend from Beaumont, Texas, had gone fishing Monday, but didn't make it back. Buddy's wife said she called the authorities and the Cameron Parish Sheriff's Office was notified that the two were missing.

Deputies found Buddy's friend alive on the east bank of Big Lake near Grand Bayou. He had been in the water a long time, but eventually made his way to shore. He was injured, but out of the hospital by Thursday afternoon. Granger's body was found Tuesday afternoon.

I asked Buddy's wife how the friend managed to survive so long in the water, and she said it was because he was wearing a life jacket and flowed with the tide.

The boat the men were in — for some unexplained reason — did a sudden 90-degree turn and both were thrown into the water.

Buddy's wife said his friend told Buddy to stay clear of the boat because he could have been cut by the propeller, and that was the last he saw of his fishing companion.

I first met Buddy when he, Mike Rider and Bruce Doga worked out of the Image Hair Salon on Kirkman Street. I've had some great barbers over the years, and Doga was among that group. They included people like Jerry and Bert Rodrigue and others whose names I can't remember.

The Image was a favorite gathering place for some notable figures in Lake Charles circles. Sports, fishing and hunting were always major topics of discussion.

Doga also cut my dad's hair. When my dad could no longer make it to the shop because of poor health, Bruce would go to his home and cut his hair without any extra charges.

I never forgot that kindness, and Doga had me as a lifetime customer. He was a quiet, soft-spoken man, and I never had to remind him how to cut my hair.

Bruce died unexpectedly in 1996 of a heart attack at age 54. Ryder had left the business by that time, but Buddy was still there. He had cut my hair on occasion, and I decided that's where I'd stay.

If he were here today, he'd tell you it took me quite some time to get used to saying Buddy instead of Bruce. However, it didn't bother him one bit.

When barbers started scheduling appointments, I resisted the change. I had been dropping into barber shops most of my life. However, I started calling Buddy for appointments and he was always accommodating.

The conversation usually went something like this:

"Buddy, can you take me this morning?"

"Where are you, Mister Jim?" he'd ask.

"On my way to work. I can be there in 10 minutes."

"Come on in," he'd say.

Sometimes I happened to be in the neighborhood and just dropped in. He always managed to squeeze me in somehow.

I'm not a hunter or fisherman, so there wasn't a lot for us to talk about. However, getting a haircut was always a pleasant time for me.

When the Christmas and New Year's holidays rolled around, we all got a standing invitation from Bruce and Buddy to enjoy the good spread they laid out at their shop.

It was obvious Buddy had forged some strong bonds with the people he called friends. I saw some of them at the funeral home — grown men — who were teary-eyed as the full impact of what had happened hit home.

A story out of Opelika, Ala., recently talked about old-fashioned barbershops dying out across the South, their last stronghold.

"Like much of America, old-timey barber shops are disappearing," The Associated Press story said. "They are the kinds of places with a red and white barber pole outside where old men might play checkers in a corner and the magazine racks are filled with issues of 'Field and Stream'."

Statistics quoted in that story said there were about 723,000 cosmetology jobs in the United States in 1998, but only about 54,000 of those considered themselves barbers. The rest are hair stylists, hairdressers, manicurists and shampooers.

I don't have a lot of hair left on top, but I hope there will be barbers around long enough for those of us who still appreciate getting an old-time haircut. A good barber is like a good bartender. You never have to tell them what you need.

Unfortunately, there is one less barber here than there was a week ago, and I know a lot of folks are going to miss his friendly smile and warm heart.

July 22, 2001

You get attached after 31 years

An old friend of 31 years and I parted company last week. After agonizing about the possibility for months, I finally sold my 1970 Volkswagen.

The world has changed a lot since that August morning in 1970 when Jo Ann and I bought our Beetle from Watts-Pumpelly VW Inc. at the corner of La. 14 and Prien Lake Road. However, in some ways, the times are not all that different.

Automobile prices were much lower in those days, of course. I considered myself lucky to be able to buy a fully equipped VW with air conditioning for $2,387.84. I still have the application for a certificate of title that shows total sales taxes of $94.06 and fees totaling $9.50.

You could buy a 1970 Cadillac for $5,840, an Oldsmobile 88 for $3,777, an Olds Cutlass for $3,457, and a Ford Galaxie 500 or a Pontiac Catalina for $3,195.

Better gasoline mileage was my goal, and that VW filled the bill perfectly. It held only nine gallons, so you knew extra miles to the gallon were a cinch. If I recall correctly, it got something over 30 miles per gallon.

You can't buy anything new — now or then — and expect everyone you see to tell you what a good deal you made. In fact, the first person you encounter will usually find something wrong and make you feel bad after a great high.

Jo Ann had a cousin from Rosenberg, Texas, an auto mechanic, who happened to be visiting Jo Ann's folks in Sulphur about that time.

"You're making a mistake buying a small car like that with air conditioning," he said. "It doesn't have enough power to effectively run the compressor."

I figured he was probably right, but it was information I didn't need at that moment. The air actually worked well until it went out completely some years later. However, it never performed up to par on a long trip.

Two days before we bought our Beetle, I had written a Sunday column and mentioned our two youngsters. Our daughter, Jamie, was 12 at the time, and Bryan was 7. They thought the VW was a super idea.

Speaking of trips, we made a number of them to Houston and other places, and the VW — except for the air conditioning — performed extremely well on the road. On one occasion, my brother David and his family had a difficult time keeping up with us on Interstate 10.

Jessica, our granddaughter, is 13 now, and she also fell in love with that Volkswagen. I know she could see herself driving it someday, and that's one of the reasons I couldn't decide whether to sell.

I always had visions of spending my retirement years tinkering with and restoring the Beetle in my spare time. It would become my hobby, or so I thought.

However, as things turned out, I never seem to find the time. And the VW was taking up space in my carport while one of our other vehicles had to sit out in the scorching sun. It was also costing us an insurance premium every six months.

Once I decided to sell, I started putting some finishing touches on the car. The motor had been rebuilt a couple of years ago, and the car had been repainted. I bought new tires and got the body and interior in tip-top shape.

My classified advertisement with a photograph of the VW ran only once. A young woman who works at the American Press saw the ad and was hooked. We got some other calls after she decided to buy the car, and one fellow wanted to know if she'd sell. He said he "had to have it."

Unless I miss my guess, that VW has found another Beetle lover. I saw it whipping around in the newspaper parking lot Wednesday while I was gathering material for this column. It looks great.

When you part with something you've owned that long, it's never easy. But knowing it's in the hands of someone in your "newspaper family" eases the heartache.

Earlier, I said some things haven't changed since 1970. For example, I ran across a 1970 headline while doing my research that said, "U.S. seeks to save Mideast peace."

Sound familiar?

Another scary event made worldwide news in September 1970. Arab guerrillas hijacked four airplanes and tried to commandeer a fifth. They blew up three of the aircraft — a Pan Am 747, a Swissair DC-8 and a TWA Boeing 707. All three were en route to New York from the Middle East.

The fourth hijacked plane was a British jetliner. Hundreds of passengers on those planes weren't injured, but the hijackers held some of them for weeks before being released.

The Popular Front for the Liberation of Palestine claimed responsibility for the hijackings.

Apparently there is a lot of truth about history repeating itself. Unfortunately, we have let our guard down over the last 31 years and were stunned by the deadly terrorist attacks on the World Trade Center and the Pentagon on Sept. 11.

We can only hope we've learned our lesson this time, and won't be victims of another surprise attack by terrorists.

As for our Volkswagen Beetle, my wife's only regret is that no one else in our family had an occasion to say goodbye to a fixture in our family since 1970.

"Maybe we can go out to the paper one day and say our fond farewells," she said.

Don't laugh. I can remember when our daughter kissed our 1955 Ford goodbye in 1964. People do get attached to automobiles. Some take on a life of their own.

Sept. 27, 2001

Coffee, friends great blend

"How come our coffee group didn't make the paper?" asked Bobby Borel as I walked in for our Thursday morning get-together.

I didn't have the slightest idea what he was talking about. That's not unusual where Borel is concerned. Sometimes he only gets part of a story right and the rest of us have to try and put the missing pieces together as we arrive one by one at Billy's Boudin Hut Restaurant.

U.S. Sen. Mary Landrieu, who was recently re-elected to a new six-year term, was a major topic of conversation prior to and immediately after the Dec. 7 runoff election. Borel kept calling her "Senator Landreneau."

I hadn't seen anything about a coffee group in the American Press, and it wasn't until Ewell Guidry arrived that the mystery was solved. Guidry said Borel was talking about the lead story in Lagniappe, another local publication.

The newspaper spread had some excellent pictures of various groups meeting for coffee, and I knew what was coming next.

"Since we were left out, why don't you put our picture in the American Press?" someone asked.

I promised to try, but I'm not sure there is a market out there for what looks like a "rogues' gallery."

Robert Benoit, the photographer and historian in our group, asked an accommodating customer to shoot a group picture. The young man didn't have much material to work with, but the photo didn't look all that bad.

Billy was kind enough to hang an earlier picture of our group on the wall of his restaurant.

For most of us, our ties go back to our student days at either LaGrange High School or McNeese State University. It's amazing how large our group has become since it got started a few years ago.

Abbie Higginbotham, a charter member, worked near a convenience store at the corner of Lake and McNeese streets. He drank coffee at a small table in the corner of the store.

My sister Eloise was the store manager, and I started visiting her there and ran into Gerry Firmature. Firmature is a retired union leader who stopped in to buy a copy of the American Press most Thursday mornings. He didn't want to be known as a paid subscriber. The two of us started drinking coffee with Higginbotham.

Whenever I would run into someone from either LaGrange or McNeese, I would tell him about our coffee sessions and invite him to join us. The numbers steadily grew, and we changed locations.

Billy Frank Gossett, our senior class president at LaGrange, became a regular and we consider him our leader. Borel has ties to Jimmy Friesen, who also became a full-fledged member.

One morning Hulen Landry dropped by, and now we can't get rid of him. I'm kidding, of course. Landry is a retired city fireman and we love having him around to poke fun occasionally.

Landry complains often about how poorly firemen are treated by the city. One morning I winked at Gossett and then said to Landry: "Why do you think firemen need more money? All they do is sit around eating or sleeping at the firehouse."

He almost jumped out of his chair, and he started pointing his finger in our direction while giving us an earful. We love to see him get worked up and start pointing that finger.

Roy "Toddy" Moore is the golfer in our crowd, and most mornings he sits there fidgeting while waiting to leave for his tee-off time. He and Gossett were a couple of wild ones at McNeese, and have told us some tall tales about those days.

Rabbit Manuel, former chief deputy for the Calcasieu Parish Sheriff's Department who was also sheriff for a short time, stops in for a brief coffee break now and then. One morning he walked in wearing a toupee he said he got from Ray Valdetero, and nobody recognized him at first glance.

Manuel doesn't stay too long. He's always anxious to get into a big 25-cent poker game at Mallard Cove Golf Course.

John Roberts is the youngest among us. He's a retired helicopter pilot, and we count on him for aerial expertise when we get on the subject of flying.

Judge Fred Godwin of the 14th Judicial District Court drops by occasionally, and we may see more of him now that he's retiring. John Ney spends most of his time at Toledo Bend, but he also stops in when he's in town.

As you might expect, health and politics are always major topics of discussion. Most of us signed up with the Department of Veterans Affairs for medical coverage after we started meeting for coffee. We constantly pick on Gossett for trying to grab all the benefits for himself. He doesn't miss a beat on that score.

Gossett had major surgery just over a week ago, and he said he couldn't wait to get back and show off his scars.

Anytime we get bogged down on a subject, Firmature assigns me to do research and report back to the group. I suppose once you are a newspaper reporter, it's a never-ending thing.

Meeting with these lifelong friends is the highlight of my week. We all have to miss occasionally, but we try not to schedule anything else on Thursday mornings. And if you don't clear your absence ahead of time, look for a serious grilling when you return.

I missed a Thursday once and Gossett handed me a $42 bill for everybody's breakfast on the morning I wasn't there. I didn't pay it, but I got the message.

If Borel makes it today, I hope he's happy our group finally got some recognition. However, he may have gotten more publicity than he bargained for.

Dec. 26, 2002

Chapter 4

Those Who Govern

Treen must take charge

An open letter to Louisiana Gov. Dave Treen:

Dear Gov. Treen,

Although you are not doing it intentionally, you are handing the 1983 governor's race to former Gov. Edwin Edwards on a silver platter.

Even your most loyal supporters are becoming disenchanted with what appears to be your unwillingness to take a firm grasp on the controls of state government.

Ed Steimel, director of the Louisiana Association of Business and Industry, put the situation in perspective last week when he said your iron determination to do a good job has isolated you from your supporters and has hurt you politically.

Many of your supporters agree with Steimel, who said, "There are a lot of people unhappy, a lot of his own supporters are unhappy. I'm just hoping this whole thing smoothes out because I think he is a well-intentioned person, a highly moral person."

Steimel noted that another one of your shortcomings is not consulting with legislators about appointments, as Louisiana governors have traditionally done in the past. As he said, "It is the executive right to make these appointments, but to break from that tradition of always involving them (legislators) suddenly, is a little drastic and in politics it doesn't always quite work that way.

While we understand your independence, you must remember that legislators are people too. Sure, be tough, but pat 'em on the back, smile, consult with them now and then and soothe their hurt egos once in a while.

The same thing is true of those people who helped put you in office. You don't owe them anything, of course. But you don't have to send them form letters and be inaccessible by telephone or when you're in their part of the state.

Make your supporters feel important. After all, they've told acquaintances they are personal friends of the governor. And that doesn't cost you anything but a little time and a few courtesies.

Folks realize that you are not a take-charge individual, and that you believe the times call for restrained government. But, Governor, that view is so new to Louisiana it's going to take time for us to get accustomed. So wean us slowly, please.

While my part of the state didn't figure heavily in your victory, you have many followers in Southwest Louisiana who wanted you in office. They were tired of the old politics of the past.

You know what I mean – that old "you scratch my back and I'll scratch yours" type of government. I've seen people in Lake Charles get rich while Edwards was in office. They were on a first-name basis with the popular governor.

Members of that crowd are already licking their chops over the prospect of Edwards winning again in 1983. Some of that crowd is still at the public watering hole, and you don't seem willing to give 'em the boot. It's time you made changes and kicked a few tails. As the song says, "They ain't' no friends of yours."

Yes, putting your own people in office is the spoils system, pure and simple, and I guess I've been opposed to that system most of my life. But, doggone it; people wanted you in the governor's office so we could make some changes. And, believe me, change would mean improvement in most cases.

I suppose what I'm trying to say is we want you to be a different type of governor than we've had in the past, but not too different. We don't believe you have to threaten justices of the Supreme Court, set your campaign contributors up in plush state jobs or reward supporters with fat state leases and contracts.

We do think, though, that you have to let the people of Louisiana know you're in the driver's seat and can handle the job.

As Steimel said, keep your political base strong. I agree that you're a moral man and possess the integrity the office of governor so desperately needs. But unless your power base is strong, we're all going to lose in 1983.

The prospect of a return in 1983 to the politics of yesteryear scares me to death. For goodness sake, don't let it happen without a fight.

March 15, 1981

Editor's Note: The open letter to Treen got two quick responses. John H. Cade Jr., a longtime friend and supporter of the governor, said Treen was doing the things necessary to change state government. Edwards was incensed over the column and fired off a blistering reply. "I hope your letter gets you a raise, or at least, a pat on the back from your publisher, since I assure you it doesn't merit any accolades in the field of political advice or any accurate analysis of the political situation," he said.

Ex-King Edwin holds court

King Edwin is alive and well! Hail to the mighty Edwards of yore!

It was a grand sight as the knights of his roundtable greeted their exiled monarch Tuesday night. Jubilance reigned supreme.

Over a thousand of the king's followers enjoyed pressing the flesh again. How satisfying it was as they dreamed of the grandeur of yesteryear and anticipated a return to power when the king retakes his throne.

They are the chosen few whose hearts have ached for the power suddenly snatched from them so unexpectedly by King Dave.

Tuesday was a sweet moment for those who have suffered the pain and agony of being on the outside looking in over the past two years. But no more, as they jump aboard the wagon in which their charismatic leader will take them to glory once again.

Even those who have sworn no close kinship with King Edwin were openly professing their allegiance Tuesday night.

Among them was the Little Admiral of the Port of Lake Charles. He and his merry band are anticipating the fruits of victory to come with King Edwin's return. King Dave, you see, has disowned the Admiral and his court for openly defying their Republican ruler.

And there, too, was Kingmaker Bob. He was late for Tuesday's gala, but made his presence felt nevertheless. Sir Bob owes much to the former king. You might say he has over 200,000 reasons to rejoice.

Even though Sir Bob is not a favorite in King Dave's court, he has managed to hold his own under the current ruler. Like a cork, Sir Bob has the strange ability to bobble up to the top every time he's pushed underwater.

The biggest surprise of all Tuesday was the appearance of the knight from the Ketchup Kingdom. Was this the same fellow whose only confessed ties to King Edwin were malt drinking sessions in the soda shop of the king's Crowley residence?

Yes, it was without question the Ketchup Man, and there was a photograph with the Little Admiral to prove it. Since he has professed no strong political ties to King Edwin, what do you suppose the Ketchup Man was doing there with Big Fred, a partner from the hamburger law firm?

Perhaps no one at Tuesday's affair had more compassion for King Edwin than Sir Bill. He, too, wanders in exile. But even though Sir Bill has lost a city, he searches for another kingdom. You might say he's looking for a home with many mansions.

Prince Michael rounds out this tight-knit group of King Edwin's closest advisors. He is the barrister being groomed for his place in the kingdom. The prince knows that diligence to the code of his elders will reap its reward and someday he will be called Sir Mike.

They were all there, of course, and as we leave the Faithful Five of King Edwin's roundtable we touch upon other knights-in-waiting.

Sir Cliff presided over court ceremonies in his never-ending pursuit of that great political victory in the sky.

Sparkling fellow, Sir Cliff, but he was not the only maker of laws in attendance. Sir Mike represented the kingdom east of the Calcasieu and Sir Burt the western area.

Lest I tempt fate, I dare not mention the knights from the bench at King Edwin's party. It is in their courts that I often must play. But I can say the list of those who attended and those who didn't was interesting.

The biggest puzzle for many was the appearance of Smilin' Jack, the lord of Big M. Is it possible that Smilin' Jack, the man who must win the favor of King Dave for two more years, is really a knight of the realm for King Edwin? The educational peasants of Big M were scratching their heads over that one.

It was indeed a festive occasion, but for the trained observer it was more. "EWE in '83" offered a glimpse of the political kingdom and insight into the continuing pursuit of mankind for position and power.

Yes, King Edwin, your knights await your triumphant return. You need only ask, and they will give. And they will ask and you will give. That is the American way.

Long live the king!

Oct. 25, 1981

Editor's Note: Gov. Dave Treen was King Dave; Jim Sudduth, director of the Port of Lake Charles, was the Little Admiral; attorney Bob McHale was Kingmaker Bob; attorney E.C. Hunt was the Ketchup Man; attorney Fred Godwin was Big Fred; Bill Boyer, former Lake Charles mayor, was Sir Bill, and he later became known as High Rise Billy when he was named Lake Charles Housing Authority director; attorney Michael Dees was Prince Michael; attorney Cliff Newman was Sir Cliff; state Rep. Mike Hogan was Sir Mike; state Rep. Burt Andrepont was Sir Burt; Jack Doland, president of McNeese State University was Smilin' Jack.

Louisiana politics fascinating

A native Louisianian takes readers behind the scenes for a fascinating look at the 1983 governor's election in "The Last Hayride," released last week by Gris Gris Press of Baton Rouge.

John Maginnis, 36, who has been writing about Louisiana politics since 1972, is a talented writer who knows how to tell an intriguing story, which could be subtitled, "The Anatomy of a Louisiana Governor's Election."

The title brings to mind "Louisiana Hayride," an earlier book by Harnett Kane, which centered on the state scandals of the 1930s.

Scandals are not the major theme in this latest work, but Maginnnis does a superb job in shedding new light on the scandal over the Deferred Compensation Corp. of Louisiana (DCCL) and on what might be called near-scandals during two earlier terms of Gov. Edwin W. Edwards.

Maginnis said he believes Louisianians are showing less tolerance for corruption, so the "hayride" days are over. A New Orleans political analyst notes Marion Edwards, the governor's brother, said during the 1983 campaign that it would be the last of its kind, the last with real stump speaking and pressing of the flesh because of the electronic media.

The author joined the candidates on the campaign trail in early 1983, and readers are treated to a superb retelling of the election story from inside the political camps.

Although the book is not a biography of Gov. Edwards, the flamboyant leader definitely steals center stage. Readers get a rare close-up look at this dynamic Louisiana politician who racked up 63 percent of the vote in his bid for an unprecedented third term.

The author does a superb job in analyzing how former Gov. David Treen, who he believes had the best of intentions, lost his 1983 re-election bid. The defeat had its beginnings shortly after the Republican's historic election.

A disorganized staff, according to Maginnis, poorly served Treen. As one aide explained, "People say we didn't answer our mail. Hell, we didn't open our mail."

Maginnis sets the stage for his 354-page work in a short introduction titled, "The Pirate King." In it he calls Jean Lafitte Louisiana's first Robin Hood. "He stole treasure from the Spaniards, snuck it past Americans and sold it cheap to the French," notes Maginnis.

Louisiana would not see another economic savior until Huey Long burst upon the political scene. Calling Long a modern-day Robin Hood, Maginnis said the revered leader's populist demagoguery survived, thanks to John D. Rockefeller's Standard Oil.

"Huey Long revolutionized Louisiana politics by taking from the rich, keeping some for himself and his friends and giving more to the poor than government ever had before," writes Maginnis.

What fascination do people like Lafitte, Long and Edwards have for state voters? "Louisiana keeps electing colorful populist rogues because it can afford them, or, perhaps, can't afford to do without them," answers Maginnis.

After a brief history of Edwards' family, the author begins his penetrating look at the man behind the charisma.

How has Edwards survived those almost constant federal investigations into alleged wrongdoing? Maginnis tells how Clyde Vidrine, a trusted aide, fell out with Edwards and how the governor discredited his former confidant. And he gives his explanation of how Edwards has avoided possible indictments: "In a showdown of one person's word against Edwards, the governor's practice of only dealing with people shadier than himself paid off."

Edwards' pursuit of the fairer sex again makes for interesting reading, as it did in Vidrine's book "Just Takin' Orders."

"The Last Hayride" is filled with anecdotes like the story about how Edwards's forces showcased a $100,000 contribution from New Orleans supporters. The money was bid on a life-sized oil painting of Edwards. The former governor let old friend George Fischer sweat out his bid of $96,000 for a few seconds.

Then there is Scott Welch, the Treen statistician who was nicknamed "Captain Fact."

When Mayor Dutch Morial of New Orleans said he would make a great running mate as lieutenant governor on a ticket with Edwards, the latter replied, "That's a great idea, Dutch. That way no one will want to shoot me."

Area readers will be interested in the part played by Darrell Hunt in the Edwards campaign. Maginnis describes him as, "The son of high-powered attorney and lobbyist E.C. Hunt of Lake Charles."

The Edwards and Treen methods of handling the press and the Legislature also say much about why one succeeded while the other failed. Maginnis said Edwards' special oratorical gift is "not what he says, but how he says it, (which) makes him the star of the TV news."

Some may find lesser election campaigns discussed by Maginnis as digression by the author. However, they, too, help to tell the engrossing story of Louisiana politics.

A chapter titled, "With a Little Help for My Friends," makes these observations about Edwards' early terms:

"Instead of 'Union, Confidence and Justice,' the state seal should be emblazoned with the motto "When all else is equal, take care of your friends."

"The friends of Edwin Edwards, and his relatives, did quite well the first two times around. Charity and friendship begin at home.

"Of all the favors Edwin Edwards has done for all his friends, none stands out more than what he tried to do for Jules LeBlanc."

Although the retelling of these stories might be considered damaging to Edwards, the man emerges unscarred and he manages to come across as Louisiana's main hope for the future.

Maginnis believes Louisiana voters will see a different Edwin Edwards during his current term. The man who masterfully directed his own election campaign is now in charge of the state's future, according to the author. Maginnis says the job won't be easy because, "Our free and easy, banana republic, oil sheikdom days are numbered…"

"The healer is coming" was a major theme of the Edwards campaign, and the voters bought it. As the Rev. Clarence Bates said after praising voters for turning out during Edwards' 64- parish tour late in the campaign, "It shows that you've got but three friends in this world: Sears and Roebuck, Jesus Christ and Edwin Edwards!"

"The Last Hayride" is entertaining reading and it joins the list of other great works on Louisiana politics. Maginnis is a colorful storyteller. It's 1983 all over again, and as Walter Cronkite used to say, "You are there."

Don't miss it.

Aug. 12, 1984

Huey Long stops in Lafayette

Huey P. Long got a standing ovation after a recent appearance in Lafayette.

Or was the applause for actor John McConnell, who was masquerading as the late Kingfish?

McConnell looked, dressed and talked so much like Long it was difficult to tell.

The members of the audience eventually came back to reality, however, and knew there was no way they would ever see the real Huey Long in person. But they had definitely been treated to the next best thing.

For those who had never heard Long on the stump, it was a rare treat indeed.

McConnell is the one-man show entitled "The Kingfish: The Life and Times of Huey P. Long." Larry L. King and Ben Z. Grant wrote the play.

"Spud" McConnell, a native of Gonzales, said it takes him five hours to mentally prepare for the 90-minute performance. Whatever he does works to perfection.

The actor received his Bachelor of Arts degree in theater from Nicholls State University and a Master of Arts degree in acting from LSU in 1985. He did stand-up comedy in clubs around the country before beginning his tour with the now-famous "Kingfish" in 1988.

McConnell performs in three areas on stage from a rocking chair when Long is talking about his roots, at a podium when delivering some of Huey's fiery speeches and sitting behind a desk when carrying out his governor's duties or berating brother Earl K. Long.

A slide show of 1920s scenes warms up the audience, along with Randy Newman's rendition of "The Kingfish."

Writers King and Grant said they tried to show the many sides of Huey Long, "but we make no claim to the whole truth." They put some words in his mouth, they said, to make it possible for the Kingfish to comment on current politicians and events. It's a nice touch.

Those who want nothing but the facts should consult "Huey Long," by T. Harry Williams, recognized as the definitive biography of the populist governor.

For the play, however, the writers had a motive in putting words in Huey's mouth.

"We have permitted him to re-live and discuss his own assassination," they said.

"I'm back," McConnell says as the audience gets its first look at what appears to be Huey himself. He's standing at center stage wearing a white suit with red suspenders. Familiar curls protrude from beneath a straw hat.

"We had something going, me and the people, then that young doctor went and forgot his Hippocratic oath," Long said. He was referring to Dr. Carl Weiss of Baton Rouge, son-in-law of an anti-Long judge.

"Damn fellow shot me," he said. "A stranger got me. And with all those enemies out to get me."

Huey talked about those now-familiar assassination theories. Did his own guards shoot him, he wondered, or was it a conspiracy by the oilmen or Franklin Delano Roosevelt, who feared Long wanted to be president?

When he got elected railroad commissioner, his first major political office, Long said "then the fox was in the henhouse."

Long talked about the sorry condition of Louisiana when he ran for governor. "The roads were so bad even the weather couldn't get across the state," he said.

Admitting he'd say whatever it took to get elected, Long would play up to the crowds. It wasn't always easy in a Catholic group, he said, because bingo and rhythm were the only two Catholic words he knew.

The oil companies financed Long's road, bridge, textbook and free lunch programs for Louisiana. He said all politicians needed something "to whip up on," and Standard Oil fit his needs perfectly.

Defending his methods, Long said, "The Kingfish did more with what he had than Jesus did with those loaves of bread."

Long was LSU's No. 1 football fan, and he'd do anything to drum up a full house at Tiger games. McConnell shows that side of the Kingfish when he threatens to make Barnum & Bailey dip all of its show animals because a circus performance is competing with LSU's homecoming game.

When businessmen are solicited for campaign contributions, Long explains his formula for giving. Those who contribute immediately get the biggest piece of the spoils. Those who give just before the election get what's left. And those who wait until after the election get "good government."

Being governor was difficult, he said. "As Billy Shakespeare put it, 'Uneasy is the head that wears the crown.'"

Long said he had a difficult time preparing for impeachment proceedings the Legislature planned against him. "I don't know what to wear to an impeachment," he said.

He told all of his close advisers they should try to look as saintly as possible before the impeachment process got under way. Then looking at his brother, he said, "Earl, you'll have to stay out of sight for awhile."

One of the most dynamic speeches by McConnell was one Long delivered as a U.S. senator while helping elect a colleague, Hattie Caraway from Arkansas. After her husband died while a senator, Caraway became the first woman elected to the Senate.

When she ran for re-election to a full term, Long decided to give her a helping hand. He felt it would help his regional image.

Long would open his speeches the same way during a week's campaigning. "We're all here to pull a lot of potbellied politicians off a little woman's neck," he'd say.

Caraway carried 61 of 75 counties, and it was generally conceded Long had made the difference.

The Kingfish polished his speaking technique through the years, but he never used a written manuscript or notes. "Watch me vaudeville 'em," he would tell associates before addressing a rural audience.

McConnell has copied that technique so well the audience often finds itself in another day and time in Louisiana as it wraps itself up in the performance.

We don't see much of the dictatorial side of Huey Long in "Kingfish," but that's not the purpose of the play. Instead, we can enjoy the escapades of this state's most revered rascal.

Supporters and friends of Earl K. Long might find the play a bit too hard on Huey's younger brother. However, the relationship between the two men makes for numerous comic touches, so maybe Earl wouldn't take offense if he knew he was still getting laughs. Besides, as historian Williams points out, Earl was the best loved of the two Longs. "Earl was like us," his admirers would say.

"The Kingfish" was in its second run at the Heymann Performing Arts Center in Lafayette. The play came within an inch of being staged at the Lake Charles Civic Center, but the producers and local folks couldn't iron out some differences.

That's a shame, because citizens from this area who never heard Huey P. Long have missed a golden opportunity.

OK, so it wasn't the Kingfish. But with John McConnell doing the one-man show, you'd have a difficult time telling them apart.

Oct. 7, 1990

Assassination still in news

Who shot Huey P. Long?
If you believe Dr. Carl A. Weiss Sr. killed Louisiana's most famous politician, you're probably right. But there are a growing number of skeptics who don't accept the traditional story about the assassination of the Kingfish.

Scientists will try to determine how the Sept. 8, 1935, shooting happened when they open the grave of Dr. Weiss early today. However, they will be working on only half of the 56-year-old puzzle. Long's family says it won't participate in a new investigation into his death.

The team of experts which plans to do tests on Weiss' remains is headed by James E. Starrs, a forensic scientist at George Washington University in Washington, D.C. Starrs and his colleagues will try to determine whether Weiss actually fired the shot that killed Long, or whether Long's bodyguards were responsible.

Ed Reed, a public relations consultant and political analyst, looked into the Long killing while helping prepare for a 50th observance of the historic event. His research ended up in a book entitled, "Requiem for a Kingfish."

That book challenges the general assumption that Long died from a single gunshot wound from a gun fired by Weiss.

Historians have written that Weiss may have gone to the Capitol to confront Long about a racial slur against his wife's family. Or it could have been about a bill Long was backing that would have gerrymandered Judge Benjamin Henry Pavy, Weiss' father-in-law, out of office in St. Landry Parish.

Reed concluded that Weiss may have fired a .32-caliber pistol as Long stood nearby, but it didn't hit the U.S. senator and former governor. Reed said Long was hit twice by bullets fired from the weapons of two of Long's bodyguards. They shot at Weiss and hit him 61 times.

Former U.S. Sen. Russell B. Long, Huey Long's most famous son, said he doesn't accept that version of his father's death.

Russell Long said he spoke to two eyewitnesses at the time of the shooting — Murphy Roden, one of his father's bodyguards, and Louisiana Supreme Court Justice John Fournet.

The former senator said in a statement that Roden was standing close to his father when Dr. Weiss fired his gun.

"After the shot, Murphy grabbed for Dr. Weiss' pistol. He showed me a flesh wound between his thumb and forefinger where the recoil mechanism had pinched his flesh," the statement said. "Murphy said he was struggling with Dr. Weiss for possession of the gun, which Weiss was trying to fire again and that the two of them slipped and fell onto the slick marble floor....

"John Fournet told me the following: He saw Dr. Carl Weiss approach Huey Long with the gun in his hand. Justice Fournet reached out and struck at the gun, knocking the aim downward. At that point the gun went off, shooting Huey Long in the abdomen. Huey shouted, 'I'm shot' and ran from the room."

Although convinced Weiss is his father's assassin, Russell Long said he holds no ill will toward the Weiss family.

But Starrs says there are too many unanswered questions to let the matter drop. He was authorized by Carl Weiss Jr. to exhume his father's body.

"It's the one assassination that has been set apart because it's hard to find a distinctly credible motive," he said.

John Pope of the New Orleans Times-Picayune wrote back in June that no autopsies were performed on Long or Weiss.

"The confusion of the moment, the superheated political climate that prevented a credible follow-up investigation, shifting recollections over time and the assassin's character have all conspired to keep doubts smoldering for decades," Pope said.

A new development has also heightened interest in the killing. The handgun supposedly used by Weiss turned up in the hands of the daughter of the police official who investigated the shooting. Starrs would like to test-fire the weapon as part of his investigation. The test could conclude whether a bullet from the gun struck the rear of Roden's wristwatch, as he claimed. LSU has the watch.

Included with the gun are police investigative documents that have been missing since 1935. State Police have retrieved the files and started a new investigation. Meanwhile, the courts are trying to determine proper ownership of the information and whether it should be made public.

When they examine the Weiss remains, Starrs and his associates said they hope to find bullets left in his body and determine their point of entry.

Tim Talley of the Baton Rouge Morning Advocate said Starrs believes that determining the trajectory of bullets that struck Weiss could provide important evidence. It would substantiate or discredit the testimony of bodyguards who claimed that bullets they fired struck Carl Weiss Sr. in certain areas of his body.

"The more any of the bodyguards' stories are less credible, the more credible the position of Dr. Weiss becomes," Starrs said. "The more stories are made up, the less credible the storytellers become."

Pope of the Times-Picayune said the scientists would also be looking for medical clues, such as evidence of a brain tumor or mind-altering drugs that might provide a hint of a motive that Weiss might have had for the shooting.

Thomas Weiss, a brother of Dr. Weiss, said his brother was calm less than 12 hours before the incident. Blaming him "didn't make a damn bit of sense to me," Weiss said.

"I'm not so sure that someone didn't ride with him to the Capitol," Weiss told Pope.

Starrs has said he is convinced science can reconstruct the crime and clear up many doubts. But historians told Talley of the Morning Advocate they don't expect anything in the Weiss grave to rewrite history.

"It would be more logical to exhume the body of Long," said Glen

Jeansonne, a history professor at the University of Wisconsin at Milwaukee. "I doubt seriously that they're going to find anything definitive," he said. Jeansonne has written a book about Huey Long which will be published in 1993, the anniversary of Long's birth.

Any idea of exhuming the body of Long was squelched by Russell Long. "We are unalterably opposed to exhumation of our father's remains," Long said for the family.

William Hair of the Georgia College in Milledgeville, Ga., who has also written a book on Long, agrees that Weiss is guilty. "I rather doubt that this is going to exonerate Dr. Weiss from culpability," Hair said.

Estelle Williams, who helped research the book on Long by her late husband, T. Harry Williams, said, "I don't want to get into this. It's too ridiculous for words," she said.

Williams wrote what is considered the definitive history on Huey Long. Russell Long cites the investigative work by Williams as proof enough for him that Weiss was the assassin.

Although the reopened investigation may not shed any new light on the death of Huey Long, the desire of the Weiss family to probe deeper is understandable.

Remember the belief that Zachary Taylor might have been poisoned? Exhumation of the late president's body disproved that theory. So if the check of Weiss' remains only confirms the generally accepted version of how Long died, that makes it worth the effort. The results are expected in February.

Oct. 20, 1991

Editor's Note: Starrs reported in February of 1992 that Weiss' skeleton showed about 24 bullet wounds, and most of them were in the back. The remaining brain tissue showed no sign of drugs, but one researcher said that is difficult to determine after 56 years. Even with those findings, the mystery remains unsolved. State Police, who conducted their own investigation, reported in June that Weiss was the lone assassin.

Roemer bowed out with class

Looking back over the events of the last four years, Gov. Buddy Roemer was lucky he came in third in Saturday's primary. It wasn't a bad finish for a governor who has managed to offend most of the special interest groups in Louisiana.

Why did he rub so many people the wrong way?

Roemer tried to change things. That's why we elected him in 1987, but it scares folks after a while. It's particularly upsetting to groups like teachers, homeowners and politicians who are affected by those changes.

However, conditions had gotten so bad in Louisiana we wanted Roemer to shake things up when he first took office. Voters had done the same thing before when they elected governors like Sam Jones in the 1940s, Robert Kennon in the 1950s and Dave Treen in the 1980s.

Voters expect reformers to step on toes. They realize that someone has to come along occasionally to straighten out the mess left by the playboys and the demagogues.

Unfortunately for Roemer, change usually exacts a heavy toll. Those who push it eventually pay a heavy price for any progress they achieve. The voters eventually grow weary of change and throw the reformers out on their ears.

Roemer took it all in stride, however, and continued to do his thing.

And when the voters turned him out, he accepted their verdict with class.

"The people spoke and they said, 'Buddy, thanks, but you didn't do enough.' And I think that's fair," Roemer said Saturday night.

One of the first steps taken by Roemer in 1988 was to appoint an inspector general to look for wrongdoing in state government. The idea had never been tried in Louisiana, and the politicians and agencies under the gun didn't like it. Legislators tried to kill the program, but couldn't. And it worked even better than anyone expected.

In 3 1/2 years, Inspector General Bill Lynch and his staff handled 1,007 cases. Investigators completed 945 of those cases, suspended 12 and had 50 active as of the end of August.

Although the office is not primarily a criminal investigative unit, 49 persons were indicted or charged as a result of those investigations. Of that number, 34 were convicted and 12 are awaiting trial.

Anytime questionable activities were uncovered the news made headlines, and it made enemies for Roemer. Voters can now kiss the office goodbye, because neither Edwin W. Edwards nor David Duke, the runoff candidates for governor, will support such a concept.

Roemer incurred the wrath of many homeowners when he came up with a tax reform program. Part of that program called for reducing the homestead exemption. The Legislature wouldn't go along, and deleted the homestead plank.

However, it was too late to save tax reform. Homeowners were convinced Roemer was out to do them in, and they never forgave him for even suggesting a cut in the homestead exemption.

Teacher unions were the next major group to fall out with Roemer. He got them three pay raises in a row, 19 percent in all, but insisted they be evaluated. The unions fought him from the outset, and a flawed testing program spelled disaster for any hopes of weeding out bad teachers.

Reformer that he was, Roemer refused to drop his evaluation plans. So teacher unions declared war and backed Edwards in the primary.

Roemer's refusal to sign an anti-abortion law hurt him on one hand, but it helped him with the pro-choice camp. However, since anti-abortion forces probably outnumber those on the other side of the issue, the governor lost some ground.

Many legislators loyal to Edwards fought Roemer throughout his four-year term. He didn't hand out goodies in the form of special appropriations like Edwards had done as a way of gaining their support for his programs.

Even so, Roemer was effective in getting laws passed like the one that reorganized the charity hospital system and another on campaign finance reform.

I asked an adviser to the governor one time why Roemer didn't cater to legislators.

"You can't ever fill 'em up," he said. He was referring, of course, to their appetite for appointments, money for pet projects and special favors.

Blacks never gave Roemer a chance even though he appointed a number of blacks to office and has a good record on civil rights. He didn't play politics as well as Edwards, and that didn't endear him to black lawmakers. And when he became a Republican, he lost some of the black support he had always received.

Officials in New Orleans didn't like the way Roemer operated, either. They were used to rewarding their friends and supporters with government contracts, but Roemer insisted he wouldn't play by those rules.

Democratic Party officials didn't give Roemer a fair shake from the beginning because he has never been a big party man. They turned on him like mad dogs. And when Roemer switched parties the Republicans gave him the cold shoulder, which cost him votes.

Courthouse crowds were like many legislators where Roemer was concerned. He didn't make them feel more important than they are, and that deflated their egos.

Perhaps the fact Roemer didn't like to play politics in a political world was the straw that broke the camel's back. The voters of Louisiana can forgive their public officials for almost anything, but they have to love politics.

Roemer was never able to establish a personal relationship with average voters. Lacking that, they had to rely on what they heard from those who differed with him. And those messengers weren't kind.

"... While I'm not good at politics and probably take too much pride in saying that you have got to keep your oars in the political water to keep paddling the boat, and so I got that message," Roemer said Sunday.

A political analyst said it best when he concluded Roemer might have made a mistake when he urged voters not to "turn back the clock." He said that's exactly what supporters of Edwards and Duke wanted to do.

Edwards people wanted to turn the clock back to the 1970s, he said, and Duke backers wanted to turn it all the way back to the 1950s.

Let's face it. Louisiana voters can take reform only so long. Then they start longing for those days when everybody can again "let the good times roll."

Now we've worked ourselves into one helluva mess. As one newspaper columnist feared, we're now confronted with "the runoff from hell."

Before we get around to talking about the ramifications of that runoff, a few words for Gov. Roemer seem appropriate.

Thanks, Buddy, for helping us hold our heads high for four years and for leaving Louisiana better than you found it.

Oct. 24, 1991

Editor's Note: To the surprise of many, Edwards decided to retain the office of state inspector general that had been created by Roemer, even though Lynch and Edwards had been adversaries.

Huey has 100th birthday

It's going to be a big year in Winnfield. Huey Pierce Long won't be around to celebrate his 100th birthday, but the folks in his hometown plan a yearlong blowout to mark the observance.

Long, a former governor and U.S. senator, was born on Aug. 30, 1893. He was killed by an assassin in 1935, and is one of three Louisiana governors who called Winnfield home. Earl K. Long, Huey's younger brother, and O.K. Allen were the other two.

One of the highlights of the Long Centennial celebration will be a Political Hall of Fame banquet on Jan. 30. Gov. Edwin Edwards, the state's only four-term governor, will be the keynote speaker.

Edwards will also be one of the 10 initial inductees into the Political Hall of Fame. The other nine will be named any time now.

The Hall of Fame will be located in the former L&A Railroad Depot.

Citizens of Winnfield hope the Long Centennial will give their town a much-needed economic boost. Other events will include a Krewe of the Kingfish Mardi Gras Parade and Ball, Great Louisiana History Quiz Bowl, the annual Long Family Reunion and a Share the Wealth Christmas festival.

Two plays are also on tap. "The Kingfish" is scheduled for May and "All the King's Men" for November.

Actor John McConnell has played Long superbly in both those

productions.

"This is bigger than Winnfield," George Wyatt, co-chairman, said of the celebration back in August. "It is statewide, nationwide and even worldwide. We have already received calls from the world press asking what we're going to do for Huey's 100th birthday."

Claude L. O'Bryan, who gives horse-and-buggy rides through downtown, told the Monroe News-Star he studied up on Winnfield's history before starting his business.

"When I got to brushing up, I was surprised at how much history our little town's got," he said. "When I take people to tour the town and bring this to their attention, they're as amazed as I am."

The citizens of Winnfield aren't the only people who are fascinated with Huey Long. The Kingfish was in the news quite a bit during 1992 when the body of Dr. Carl Weiss, the presumed assassin of Long, was exhumed.

Long was shot in a hallway of the state capitol the night of Sept. 8, 1935, and died 30 hours later. Bullets fired by Long's bodyguards killed Weiss immediately.

It has been generally accepted that Long died from a single gunshot that entered his lower right abdomen and exited his lower back without striking any bones. The bullet was fired from less than an inch away.

James Starrs, a Washington, D.C., forensic scientist, said he found little new evidence from his exhumation to show who killed Long. But he insists that other evidence leads him to believe it wasn't Weiss.

Ed Reed, a Baton Rouge publicist and historian, thinks two of Long's bodyguards were responsible for the senator's death. Reed wrote "Requiem for a Kingfish" in 1986, which explains his theory.

Louisiana State Police did an eight-month investigation of Long's death after some of the records of the shooting and Weiss' .32-caliber semi-automatic pistol were found in New Orleans.

State Police released their report in May and concluded Weiss was the assassin.

"Nothing we found was in conflict with the original historical theory," a State Police spokesman said. He added that sooty residue on Long's coat proved the bullet had not ricocheted off a wall or passed through another body before striking Long as some people have believed.

When it comes to assassinations, there will always be conspiracy theories. And that keeps the names of famous people like President John F. Kennedy and Huey P. Long in the news.

However, even if he hadn't been assassinated there is little chance the people of Louisiana would have ever forgotten Long. He's a legend now.

And that's just fine with the citizens of Winnfield. They'd like nothing better than a prosperous 1993, and all of it thanks to the memory of the Kingfish.

Jan. 7, 1993

Take another look at '91 race

Getting backstage during a Louisiana election campaign is a rare treat for a political junkie. And that's exactly where John Maginnis takes the reader in his latest book, "Cross to Bear."

This was no ordinary election, either. It was the 1991 "Race From Hell," pitting incumbent Louisiana Gov. Buddy Roemer, the reformer, against Edwin Edwards, the state's most notorious political figure since the legendary Huey Pierce Long, and David Duke, the former leader of the Ku Klux Klan and ex-Nazi sympathizer.

Maginnis is a political columnist who has been writing about state politics since 1972. He is editor and publisher of "Louisiana Political Review," and became a national figure with his first book, "The Last Hayride." The resurrection of Edwards formed the basis for that analytical look at the 1983 gubernatorial election.

We all know that Edwards worked another miracle in 1991 when he won an unprecedented fourth term. He definitely had some unusual circumstances working in his favor, but they are only part of the reason for his phenomenal success.

That's where Maginnis makes his mark. He takes a familiar story and tells it again. However, this time it's an insider's view that puts the reader in a unique position in the backrooms of the political camps.

First, Maginnis has to get Roemer into the governor's office in

1987 in a chapter entitled, "Hamlet, Prince of Politics."

Remember the "Anyone But Edwards" movement of 1987? Maginnis said when Roemer emphasized he wouldn't endorse Edwards for governor if Roemer were eliminated from the runoff, ABE "had found its anyone." And Louisiana elected another one-term reform governor.

Reform didn't get far, unfortunately, because a series of miscues led to Roemer's downfall. Maginnis reels them off in rapid succession.

There was the debilitating defeat of tax reform, Roemer's marriage problems that eventually led to divorce, the governor's inability to work with the Legislature, which cost him leadership in the state Senate, and his general aloofness from the political trappings so cherished in Louisiana.

Maginnis said Duke then emerged on the political landscape, "a handsome young man with a nice smile, saying what other politicians wouldn't and what people wanted to hear. What they read about his past did not square with the pleasing image they saw. And seeing, not reading, is believing."

Duke's U.S. Senate campaign put him in serious contention for governor in 1991. And he, not Edwin Edwards, would become the womanizer this time around. As one of Duke's advisers said, "He just took his pick (after the rallies)."

Sam Jones, the mayor of Franklin, was the only gubernatorial candidate with the guts to take Duke on. Maginnis said Jones knew how to work a forum.

Roemer picked up some support when he vetoed the abortion bill, but Maginnis said it couldn't revive his crumbling political and personal life.

The author talks about a succession of blunders by Roemer when he managed to offend, in succession, the state's sheriffs, district attorneys and police juries.

Then there was his failure to attend the early forums. Jones said that was like a pitcher who had not been to spring training trying to come on in the seventh game of the World Series. "He got mangled."

Meanwhile, the author said Edwards was directing his own comeback and gambling on almost anything worth a wager.

Nowhere was the former governor's increasing support more

evident than during a rally in Lafayette, the site of a similar comeback gathering in 1983. Maginnis said an Atlanta newspaperman called it "the most integrated crowd I've ever seen at a political rally."

The author then takes us inside the Monteleone Hotel in New Orleans, where Edwards and his associates were working on getting the black vote he would need to make the runoff. Roemer's campaign finance law made raising money difficult, but the state Democratic Party picked up some of the slack.

A poll for Jones done by a Chicago pollster revealed for the first time that Duke had a large hidden vote. Maginnis said the poll was criticized as being unscientific, but it changed the way polling was done by other candidates.

Duke's strength got him into the runoff with Edwards, but the former governor wasn't satisfied. Edwards was denied the chance to beat Roemer, the only politician who had ever defeated Edwards. Maginnis said it was Duke who beat Roemer while Edwards only maintained his base.

The Duke camp was living in a dream world for a time, thinking it was even going to carry Calcasieu Parish.

Two media events would prove the beginning of the end of Duke. For the first time, Duke was really tested during a Louisiana Public Broadcasting forum and on "Meet the Press" on NBC.

Maginnis said Edwards and his colleagues, meanwhile, were counting their money, which was flowing in like water. "Today we just raised the three millionth dollar," said a supporter. "We've got our street money. It's in the bag."

Edwards had predicted he would win the runoff with 60 percent of the vote, and he was only one percentage point off. The final margin was 61-39 percent.

Duke was more interested in raising money than winning office, according to Maginnis, and that's why he immediately announced he would run for president. But Pat Buchanan's decision to run killed Duke's bid.

The author called Buchanan "the hard sound-biting conservative TV commentator with all of Duke's firepower and little of the baggage."

Baton Rouge political writers agree that Maginnis knows how to tell a good story and praise his lively writing. They also like his use of non-traditional and credible sources. One called his latest book "a fitting sequel to his previous work."

"Cross to Bear" is definitely all of those things and a little more. It's a personal diary (with pictures) recounting the intimate details of one of life's most fascinating events — a Louisiana political campaign.

The book is available from Darkhorse Press in Baton Rouge ($19.95). And the author will be in Lake Charles Tuesday, March 16, to address an Early Bird Breakfast of the Chamber/Southwest Louisiana.

Yes, Edwin Edwards is king again. But what are we in for during the last three years of his fourth term?

Maginnis appears to have made up his mind on that score. In a personal note in a review copy of "Cross to Bear," the author said he hopes we're not getting too old for these Last Hayrides because it "looks like there is more to come."

March 14, 1993

Politics are our bread, butter

I advise anyone who thinks he knows something about politics to go down to Louisiana and take a post-graduate course.
Texas Sen. Tom Connelly, 1927

What a fitting introduction to "Louisiana Boys: Raised on Politics," a delightful 60-minute documentary on a subject that is described as the fourth meal we eat every day.

As one observer notes in the video, politics play a big part in daily Louisiana life because so many of our citizens depend on politics for their well being.

Political consultant Raymond Strother notes that we live in a welfare state where many people look to politics as a source of income and as a provider of health care and education.

Taking care of the voters has become the main concern of Louisiana politicians at the local, state and national levels. And Gus Weill, another longtime observer, says that's why there is so much tolerance for political corruption in Louisiana.

Much of the appeal of this video comes from its rare footage of Huey and Earl Long.

Huey Long still evokes laughter with his comments about the efforts to impeach him in every political post he held. And there's a segment where he sings what became his national theme song, "Every Man a King."

The voters remembered Huey Long and got a bounty at the same time by naming their children after the Kingfish. Many of those youngsters are still around with that famous name in some form.

Earl Long had three terms in the mansion 1939-40, 1948-52 and 1956-60. He was the master of the stump speech, and that's good video footage, too.

Radio and television made stump speaking obsolete, but many of us can remember when it was the biggest event to ever hit most communities in what was then primarily a rural state.

Entertainment was a big part of those traveling political shows, and some of that intermingling continues in modern politicking.

Uncle Earl was the father of the $50 old age pension, and for many of the state's poor it was the only thing they had to keep them off the welfare rolls.

The video opens with Huey's reign as governor, which began in 1928, and takes the viewer on a whirlwind tour through the politics of 1990.

Jimmie Davis served twice — 1944-48 and 1960-64. An entertainer who gained national fame for "You Are My Sunshine," Davis is remembered for riding his horse up the capitol steps for his inauguration and for singing his farewell speech four years later.

John McKeithen came along in 1964 and had his problems with corruption. But he recaptured a place in history with construction of the Superdome and for serving two successive terms, which had previously been prohibited by law.

Although Louisiana voters have been quick to forgive political corruption, they have periods when they turn to reform. However, it doesn't last long. Weill said that's because people get bored and become disenchanted and long for the populism, which they love.

Sam Jones of Lake Charles was the first reformer of modern times (1940-44), but there have been others. They include Robert Kennon (1952-56), Dave Treen (1980-84) and Buddy Roemer (1988-92).

Edwin W. Edwards became a political force to reckon with beginning in 1971 when he was elected as the first Cajun governor. He's described in the video as "probably the most colorful politician of all."

When it comes to recognition, Edwards definitely ranks right up there with Huey Long. The experts quoted in the video — Strother, Weill, Wayne Parent and political writer John Maginnis — believe he has earned a place in the state's political history because of the impact he has made on the Louisiana political scene.

Edwards brought blacks into the political mainstream, and they have returned the favor by helping elect him to an unprecedented four terms.

The video goes past the personalities to give viewers a glimpse of political gimmickry. There's a segment on the Schwegmann supermarket chain's brown bag electioneering, some samples of creative political TV advertisements and a look at the love affair candidates and voters have with political signs.

Money plays a major role on the election scene, and we are reminded of Louisiana gubernatorial elections, which cost $20 million and $24 million. It is also noted that candidates spend more money on a New Orleans City Council race than is spent for a governor's campaign in Connecticut.

"Louisiana Boys" also talks about politics in North Louisiana and in New Orleans. The northern version is more akin to the political landscape in Arkansas, Mississippi and Texas. Shreveport is described as a suburb of Dallas.

Blacks dominate New Orleans politics and campaigning is done through a proliferation of neighborhood organizations like BOLD, SOUL, COUP and DAWN.

Whatever brand of politics various regions of the state might practice, it still gets in our blood and we love to play the game.

"We're better than our politics," Buddy Roemer said during his 1987 campaign. He said our politics involve "too much money, too much corruption and too much double-talk."

He's right, of course, but things haven't changed much over the years. As Maginnis is fond of saying, Louisiana may catch up with the 20th century before it's over, but don't bet on it.

Add this cassette to your video library. You'll get the urge now and then to relive some of those magic moments in Louisiana's political past. The tape (catalog No. 1660) is available where videocassettes are sold and rented or may be purchased for $19.95 from White Star Video (telephone 1-800-458-5887).

The program produced by filmmaker Paul Stickler has received rave reviews and was nominated for an Emmy in the documentary category. Viewers will enjoy the dozen songs that provide background music

I've been covering and observing this state's political scene for over 30 years and "Louisiana Boys: Raised on Politics" is a thoroughly entertaining one-hour capsule of those 30 years, plus 30 more.

Oct. 7, 1993

Foster turning state around

Sit down and chat with Gov. Mike Foster for an hour and a half and you can understand why the man continues to register a phenomenal voter approval rating of over 70 percent after nearly two years in office.

What you see is what you get. Foster is down to earth, and he doesn't pull any punches. His willingness to take a stand, even when you disagree with his position, is refreshing.

The governor didn't hesitate for a second last week to answer questions posed to him by a half-dozen American Press editors and staff writers. On one occasion, Marsanne Golsby, his press secretary, cautioned him that he was getting into a sensitive legal area.

Foster was a state senator when he ran for governor, and that was about all most folks knew about him. Like most voters, I found out about his political views in a series of newspaper advertisements he ran prior to the election. Foster told readers how he stood on the difficult issues, and a majority of voters bought his positions.

Although I liked what he said, I still wasn't convinced enough to vote for him in the primary. Foster had supported the New Orleans land-based casino, and that was troubling. He admitted later it was a vote he would like to have back.

Once elected, Foster began on a high note. He appointed Mark Drennen to be his commissioner of administration, the No. 2 man in state government. Drennen was well qualified for the post, and had supported many good-government issues while head of the Public

Affairs Research Council (PAR).

The naming of Bobby Jindal as secretary of the state Department of Health and Hospitals followed Drennen's appointment. Jindal has worked miracles with DHH, and rescued an ailing Medicaid program by putting it on a sound financial footing. He brought Louisiana national recognition.

John Kennedy, secretary of the state Department of Revenue and Taxation, was another first-class appointment. Kennedy told me recently that working for Foster has been as self-satisfying as anything he's done.

Foster tells you what he wants done, and he lets you do your job, Kennedy said.

Unfortunately, the great start didn't last long. Foster ended state affirmative action programs and that incurred the wrath of black leaders in the state. It took him almost a year to improve his relationship with black voters, but he gradually won the support of many of them.

Some of the governor's appointments have also turned out to be controversial. Jimmy Jenkins, secretary of the state Department of Wildlife and Fisheries, has taken actions that incurred the wrath of legislators and others. Dale Givens, secretary of the state Department of Environmental Quality, is considered to be too pro-industry to suit environmentalists.

When asked about the two men, Foster gets defensive. Actually, he's hardheaded and, like many of us, he's reluctant to admit that maybe some of the critics are right.

Foster also refuses to give in on tax reform, which legislators want to look at next year.

There's just so many ways to tax people, Foster said during a tour of north Louisiana. You can go on a crusade and mess with the homestead exemption ... you can switch taxes from businesses to individuals, and I don't think that's a good idea.

When you analyze the progress Foster has made in a relatively short period of time, it's difficult to argue with his approach.

Education and highways, two subjects of major concern to voters, number among Foster's highest priorities. Teachers have received two pay raises, more funds have gone to higher education and schools are going to be held accountable when students don't measure up.

Where highways are concerned, the major emphasis is on increased construction and maintenance.

Job training programs have been streamlined to better meet the needs of new and expanding businesses and industries.

Last week, Foster convened a three-day conference of state agency officials and asked them to improve services to the public. As the governor's chief of staff put it, agencies should be concerned about how long it takes for a contractor to get paid, how benefit checks are paid and how long it takes to get a driver's license or a license plate or to get a road fixed.

Foster is reluctant to commit himself when asked whether he will seek a second term in 1999. He said he'd make a decision in another year, and would seek re-election if the job's still fun and the people want him back.

With an approval rating in the 70s, it's obvious voters like what Foster is doing. However, there is an even more compelling reason for him to seek another term.

In case you haven't noticed, Foster's term has been characterized by the absence of cronyism. People haven't been appointed to office because of their political connections, and state contracts haven't been awarded on the basis of whether you are a friend and supporter of the governor.

Foster operates on sound moral principles and with honesty and sincerity. That all adds up to integrity, which can help this state realize its full potential.

In addition, Foster has also been able to get things done. We've had governors with integrity, but too often they have been ineffective.

The man in the mansion isn't perfect, by any means, but he's been good for Louisiana at a time when it desperately needed inspired leadership. As I told Gov. Foster last Monday, eight years of integrity and progress by his administration could set a pattern that future governors might find difficult to change.

Sept. 28, 1997

Editor's Note: Foster won a second term in the 1999 election.

Friends remember Uncle Earl

Some of the people who knew him best got together last weekend to pay tribute to the colorful and controversial Earl K. Long. The younger brother of the more famous Huey P. Long was a popular topic at a symposium held at Louisiana College in Pineville.

Known to most Louisianians as Uncle Earl, Long was a candidate for governor or lieutenant governor in every state election between 1932 and 1960, except for 1952. He became governor in 1939 when Richard Leche resigned and was elected to the state's highest office in 1948 and 1956.

B.B. "Sixty" Rayburn of Bogalusa, who was elected to the Louisiana Legislature in 1948, probably knew Long better than most. He said he spent many days on Uncle Earl's Pea Patch farm in Winnfield and said he loved the man.

"He had a heart as big as this building," Rayburn said. He was talking about the Granberry Conference Center at Louisiana College where the Department of History and Political Science held the salute to Earl Long.

What really bugs fans of Long are the stories about him being crazy, the movie "Blaze" — which they believe depicts him in an unfavorable and inaccurate light — and a book by two historians entitled, "Earl K. Long: The Saga of Uncle Earl and Louisiana Politics," which links him to organized crime.

Long launched into two tirades during a fiscal session of the Legislature in 1959, and was admitted to John Sealy Hospital in Galveston, Texas. He was subsequently committed to Southeast Louisiana Hospital at Mandeville.

Although he was diagnosed by some as being manic-depressive, his supporters — and some medical authorities — were convinced he suffered a nervous breakdown as the result of a stroke, a small stroke or a series of strokes.

"If he was crazy, he was crazy like a fox," Rayburn said as he detailed the clever way in which Long had himself discharged from the Mandeville hospital.

When the hospital superintendent refused to discharge Long, the governor manipulated the process to find someone who would. The doctor who got the job still refused, so Rayburn said a physician who was willing to do it was picked from a crowd.

Long went on a western vacation after leaving the hospital and was dogged by reporters. His antics added to the speculation that he was crazy, but observers said he didn't do anything he hadn't done for years.

Jack B. McGuire of Mandeville, author of "Uncle Earl Deserved Better," said Long — who loved horse races — wasn't on a wild tear but was actually going from one racetrack to another during his western swing.

Some of the speakers Saturday wore Long campaign buttons, which said, "I Ain't Crazy, Vote for Uncle Earl."

Some historians — to try and connect Long to organized crime — have used FBI files, but McGuire and people close to the controversial governor discredit those files. McGuire said the IRS investigated Long's sources of income and failed to turn up any illegalities.

As for the movie "Blaze," which starred Paul Newman as Uncle Earl, speakers last Saturday described it as "good entertainment but bad history."

Dr. Jerry Sanson, a historian at LSU-Alexandria, said Earl Long practiced "retail person-to-person politics," and had a sophisticated grasp of government.

Like other speakers, he talked about Long's pursuit of the common man while on his trips throughout Louisiana. He was always giving away hams, turkeys, live chickens, and loaves of bread, beer and watermelons.

Sanson said Earl often told his listeners to "vote for somebody who looks like you, thinks like you and smells like you on Saturday night."

Rayburn said no governors have been able to take away anything the Longs gave Louisiana. These include paved roads and new bridges, free textbooks and school lunches and charity hospitals and other public works projects.

Dr. Glen Jeansonne, a Louisiana native and historian teaching at the University of Wisconsin at Milwaukee, was keynote speaker at the symposium. He called the Longs "Louisiana's royal family from the sticks," and noted that they changed Louisiana politics forever.

Jeansonne said Earl Long was a better local politician than Huey Long. "He was not as astute, but he knew more people," he said.

Long's last campaign was for the 8th Congressional District seat held by U.S. Rep. Harold McSween, who also attended the tribute. Long had a heart attack at the end of the campaign on Aug. 26, 1960, his 65th birthday. It was the day before the election, and he refused to go to the hospital until the votes were counted and he knew he had won. He died in Baptist Hospital in Alexandria on Labor Day, Sept. 5, 1960.

Ray J. Ellington, who was in charge of sound trucks for Long, talked about some of the experiences of being with Uncle Earl on the campaign trail. He said he had never told anyone what Long said before entering the race against McSween.

"He (Long) said, 'Ray, I'm going to run for that congressional seat, and I'm going to beat that fella. I don't care if I die the next day, I'm going to beat him.'"

Jay Chevalier, who wrote and recorded "The Ballad of Earl K. Long" in 1958, sang it Saturday. Chevalier sold 100,000 copies of the song, which he recorded at Eddie Shuler's studio in Lake Charles. He said it made him so famous — for 24 hours, at least — he thought he was Elvis Presley.

Ellis "Easy Money" Littleton worked for Earl Long from the age of 14 until Long's death. He got emotional when recalling those days, and held up a watch Long had given him many years ago.

McGuire said the arrival of TV spelled the end of political stumping and colorful characters like Earl K. Long. He's right, of course, and the political process has lost much of its charm and appeal because of television.

For a few hours last weekend, it was great to reminisce with the people who walked and talked with one of the masters of the political process — Uncle Earl Long.

Sept. 24, 1998

Johnson impeached first

Are members of the Republican Party grabbing at straws in their effort to impeach President Bill Clinton and remove a duly elected president from office? If they are — and that's a major area of dispute — it wouldn't be the first time.

Four articles of impeachment accuse Clinton of perjury in the Paula Jones civil lawsuit, perjury before a federal grand jury, obstructing justice and abuse of power. All are related to efforts to conceal the president's extramarital affair with former intern Monica Lewinsky.

Debate on impeachment was to begin today, but was delayed upon the U.S. attack on Iraq.

The vote on impeachment — whenever it comes — will be the chamber's first presidential impeachment vote since President Andrew Johnson was impeached in 1868. Approval of just one of the four Clinton articles approved by the House Judiciary Committee could trigger a Senate trial, which is what happened to Johnson.

If you think this is a railroad job, a little history might be in order. So let's take a closer look at the Johnson impeachment.

Andrew Johnson became president after John Wilkes Booth shot Abraham Lincoln on April 14, 1865. Lincoln died the following morning.

Johnson was a Southern Democrat serving in a Republican administration. He grew up in Tennessee. When Tennessee seceded from the Union, Johnson — a U.S. senator at the time — was the most prominent Southerner to refuse to join the secessionist movement.

Republicans picked him to run for vice president with Lincoln in 1864 to broaden the party's national appeal. However, they never expected him to become president.

When Johnson did take office, he carried on the Lincoln policy of getting Southern states back into the Union as quickly as possible. And that's when he became a thorn in the side of Radical Republicans who thought Reconstruction was moving too quickly and easily.

The first thing the Radical Republicans did to counter Johnson's efforts was to pass a civil rights bill. Johnson vetoed the bill, but Congress overrode his veto.

The election of 1866 put more Radical Republicans in office, and they stepped up their attacks on Johnson. When Johnson vetoed tough Reconstruction acts, Congress simply overrode his vetoes. Those acts referred to the harsh process by which the defeated states of the Confederacy would be governed and conditions under which they could rejoin the Union.

The U.S. Supreme Court started questioning those acts, and it, too, became a target of the Radical Republicans. When the court was threatened with laws designed to curb its powers, it got the message and initiated a hands-off policy where tough Radical Republican laws were concerned.

Early in 1867, Congress began looking for ways to impeach Johnson. They knew it could only be for committing high crimes or misdemeanors in office, so they set him up.

Republicans knew Johnson wanted to get rid of Edwin M. Stanton, the secretary of war, so they passed the Tenure of Office Act. Stanton had worked with the Radical Republicans against Johnson.

The new law, which was clearly unconstitutional, said the president couldn't remove civil officials, including members of his Cabinet, without approval of the Senate. When Johnson suspended and later dismissed Stanton and key military commanders, he gave Republicans the ammunition they needed to start impeachment proceedings.

The Radicals framed and presented to the Senate 11 impeachment charges against Johnson. The first nine dealt with the president's violation of the Tenure of Office Act. The 10th and 11th charges accused Johnson of making speeches calculated to bring Congress into disrespect and said he didn't enforce the Reconstruction Acts.

Johnson's trial in the Senate lasted from March 25 to May 26, 1868. The president's lawyers said he was justified in testing the constitutionality of the Tenure of Office Act. They added that the law didn't apply to Stanton anyway since Johnson didn't appoint him.

Although Republican senators were pressured to vote to convict Johnson, seven of them joined 12 Democrats to vote for acquittal. The vote on three of the charges was identical — 35 to 19 — and one short of the required two-thirds majority. Radical Republicans then called off the proceedings, and Johnson stayed in office.

A Los Angeles Times report said the Johnson and Clinton impeachment moves are alike in some ways but different in others.

Like Clinton, Johnson was under fire from Republican hard-liners. Both presidents engaged in legal bickering with Congress over the impeachment process. Secret Service agents became an issue in both cases, and there was a media frenzy in both instances.

The reasons for impeachment are different, however. Johnson's problems grew over a policy dispute about how to deal with the defeated Confederacy, while Clinton's stem from a sex scandal.

The Times said Johnson, unlike Clinton, didn't enjoy continued strong popularity among voters because they thought he was too easy on the South. Johnson ignored the advice of his attorneys to shun public statements and worsened his public image, while Clinton has been cautious about his public statements, even to the point of being misleading at times.

After comparing the two impeachment efforts, it's obvious Congress has considerable leeway in determining what constitutes "high crimes and misdemeanors." Johnson violated the law, but it was an unconstitutional law, which never got a legitimate court test.

Clinton has been accused of perjury, obstruction of justice and abuse of power, but whether he actually violated the law has become a matter of interpretation. Republicans say he has, but Democrats insist he hasn't.

If the impeachment effort succeeds, we will have to wait for Clinton's trial in the Senate to see whose legal interpretations win out over the long haul.

Some have said getting 67 senators (two-thirds) to vote to convict Clinton is virtually impossible since there are only 55 Republicans in the 100-member Senate. However, even some Democratic senators say no one should make any hasty judgments on that score.

Whatever happens, and whenever it happens, we will witness a major historical event — and the suspense could continue even longer if impeachment moves on to the Senate.

Dec. 17, 1998

Impeachment isn't fun, games

Any way you slice up the presidential impeachment process, it still boils down to a struggle between the two major political parties. That's what happened during the impeachment of President Andrew Johnson in 1868 and nothing has changed 130 years later.

The U.S. House of Representatives voted to impeach President Bill Clinton on Dec. 19 pretty much along party lines, and it appears senators who had vowed to be non-partisan are falling into the same pattern.

Why should we expect it to be any different when the policy-making in Washington, D.C., is built around political parties? The party with the higher numbers gets to call all the shots, and many senators and representatives all too often put their party's interests above the country's best interests.

The president is no different. He, too, is wedded to his political party — with one major exception. In the case of Clinton, he puts his own interests ahead of his political party and his country.

Is it any wonder that two-thirds of the American people want this impeachment issue to go away as quickly as possible? They see it as a farce.

That's a shame, because we're talking serious business here. Although I'm not a fan of his, U.S. Sen. Robert Byrd, D-W.Va., appears to be among a handful of public officials who understand the seriousness of the impeachment process.

The House alleged in the articles of impeachment that President Clinton committed perjury and obstructed justice as part of a campaign to cover up his sexual relationship with former White House intern Monica Lewinsky. It's the Senate's job to determine whether those allegations have merit.

Byrd spelled out the Senate's task when he said, "I could go either way based on the evidence as I've seen it or heard it. And I've followed it pretty closely."

The man who is regarded as the dean of the U.S. Senate was saying the decision about whether to remove Clinton isn't cut-and-dried in either direction. He believes his colleagues should get on with the trial and then make their determination about the president's guilt or innocence.

Whether the House impeachment vote was a party decision is now water under the bridge. Clinton's been impeached and nothing is going to change that fact of his political life.

Some senators from both parties said they understood the difficult job they faced, and vowed to work together to resolve the issue. However, the spirit of cooperation didn't last long.

A number of senators now appear to be more concerned about finding the quickest route they can take to either cover their own rear ends or to embarrass members of the other political party.

The Washington Post interviewed more than 40 of the 100 senators and reported Wednesday that many of the 55 Republicans favor a full-blown trial for Clinton. Most of the Democrats favor censure, arguing it would be virtually impossible to get the 67 votes needed to remove Clinton from office.

Byrd doesn't agree with members of his own party on that score. He believes it's too early to make that judgment.

"Be careful, be careful," Byrd said in an interview with C-Span. "There's no sound and indisputable count as to votes here. And votes may shift depending on things that are unforeseen at the present. Who knows? This could conceivably end different."

The Clinton impeachment isn't unlike the impeachment of Andrew Johnson in 1868. Republicans in the House presented 11 charges against Johnson to the Senate. They were charging him with violating what was clearly an unconstitutional law, but they had the necessary numbers in the Senate to convince them Johnson could be convicted.

When it came time to vote on the charges, the first three were each rejected 35 to 19, which was one vote short of the required two-thirds majority. Seven Republicans did the unexpected and joined 12 Democrats to vote to acquit Johnson. The Republican majority then called off the trial.

Is it possible that 12 Democrats could join the 55 Republicans in the House to produce the 67-vote majority needed to convict President Clinton and remove him from office? Probably not, but it could happen.

Since senators are lining up along party lines, what might we expect?

"Taken together, the conflicting views of the Republicans and Democrats suggest that the Senate may be embarking on a protracted and messy trial with high risks for the Republican majority as well as for the impeached president," said a report in the Washington Post.

Majority Leader Trent Lott, R-Miss., and some more moderate Republicans worry that a long trial will hurt them in the 2000 elections. However, conservatives in their party insist on a full-blown Senate trial — with witnesses.

"This is obviously very serious business," Sen. John H. Chafee, R-R.I., told the Washington Post. "With no witnesses it seems to me it's quite a limitation on a very serious proceeding."

You bet this is serious business, and Clinton's arrogance throughout the process hasn't served him well. In fact, his cavalier attitude could come back to haunt him somewhere down the line.

I still have a hard time understanding how the president and some 100 Democrats could have the gall to gather on the White House lawn Dec. 19 and celebrate his impeachment with a pep rally. Talk about a slap in the face to the American people and the U.S. Constitution! Has he no shame?

A trial is expected to begin today with the swearing in of senators as jurors. Let's get on with it and give the process the serious consideration it deserves. Then, we can move on to other important matters affecting the American people.

Jan. 7, 1999

☙

Editor's Note: The Senate acquitted Clinton after a five-week trial. The vote on perjury was 55-45 against, and the vote on obstruction of justice was 50-50. Clinton declared after the trial that he was "profoundly sorry" for the behavior that led to his impeachment.

'Big John' learned from pros

When you run for governor in Louisiana, you can't win if you don't campaign among the working people of this state. Brothers Huey and Earl Long knew that better than anybody, and that's how they became political legends.

John J. McKeithen, who died Friday at 81, was a floor leader for Gov. Earl Long after his election to the state House of Representatives in 1947, and he, too, became a people campaigner.

State Sen. John J. Hainkel, R-New Orleans, Friday called McKeithen "the last great stump speaker."

Rep. Jimmy Long, D-Natchitoches, who took office during McKeithen's second term, said, "He really handled the 'country boy' image very well."

I was a young reporter when McKeithen — a member of the Public Service Commission at the time — ran for governor in 1963. I'll never forget the first time I saw the man.

DeLesseps S. Morrison, a former mayor of New Orleans, was the favorite in that Democratic gubernatorial campaign. He had been a loser in two earlier election efforts. Morrison visited the American Press and met with the publisher and editor in a private office, and then was on his way.

McKeithen also met with the top brass when he arrived, but he made a special point of circulating in the newsroom and in the back shop where printers and pressmen put the daily newspaper together.

That was a long time before modern technology had an impact on publishing, so printers worked all day with hot lead type and black ink. Every time McKeithen stuck out his hand in greeting, the printers would politely hold back because of their ink stained hands.

"Don't worry about it," McKeithen would say as he insisted on shaking their hands. And I knew the minute he left the paper that he had won over many converts.

Morrison got the newspaper's endorsement for governor, but it was

McKeithen who eventually got the votes.

Eight other candidates were also seeking the state's top job, and there were some well-known names in the crowd. Among them were U.S. Rep. Gillis Long, state Superintendent of Education Shelby Jackson and former Gov. Robert F. Kennon.

Morrison led the balloting with almost twice as many votes as McKeithen, who finished second.

McKeithen pulled out all the stops in the runoff campaign. He ran on the segregation issue, which is puzzling now in light of his constant efforts to foster racial harmony once he was elected governor.

"Won't you he'p me!" became his popular campaign slogan that most voters remember even today.

The final vote in the Jan. 11, 1963, runoff was McKeithen, 491,518, Morrison, 449,830. McKeithen went on to defeat Republican Charlton Lyons in the general election.

McKeithen's first term was extremely successful. He ran a reform administration, expanded civil service, quieted labor unrest, appointed blacks to state government posts and personally attracted over $2 billion in new business and industry to the state.

Because of his track record, McKeithen was able to convince voters to change the constitution to allow him to serve a second consecutive term. Prior to that time, governors had to sit out one term before they could run for another.

The 1967 election was a breeze for the popular governor, who became the first in this century to serve back-to-back terms.

McKeithen had five opponents, but his only serious challenger was U.S. Rep. John R. Rarick of the 6th Congressional District. Rarick was an avowed segregationist who was backed by the Ku Klux Klan.

Political consultant Gus Weill, who ran McKeithen's two campaigns for governor, said he would shift his political leanings, depending on the competition. It definitely worked in the 1967 campaign because McKeithen polled over 80 percent of the vote to win in the first primary.

McKeithen took office on May 14, 1968, and there was talk about him becoming a vice presidential candidate on a ticket with either Bobby Kennedy or Hubert Humphrey. However, it didn't happen.

Reform governors have a difficult time getting re-elected in

Louisiana, and maybe that's because of problems like those encountered by McKeithen in his second term.

Life Magazine in 1967 — just prior to the governor's re-election — wrote an article alleging that the Mafia — Carlos Marcello in particular — had influence in state government. McKeithen wasn't linked to any wrongdoing, but the magazine said he hadn't been tough enough on crime.

McKeithen denied the allegations and accepted the magazine's invitation to fly to New York and see what evidence they had. It was obvious when he returned that Life had proved its case.

The governor said Life "had hard evidence of wrongdoing in our state," and he promised an immediate crackdown on crime in Louisiana. It was a rare admission for an elected public official.

"We think we are going to put some people in the penitentiary," McKeithen said.

Life Magazine wrote another article in 1970, claiming the governor had ordered a whitewash of the 1967 investigation. McKeithen protested, but the allegation hurt him politically.

McKeithen will always be remembered for his undying support of the Superdome. It started out as a $22 million sports and convention facility and ended up costing $130 million. Even so, it is credited with giving New Orleans new life.

Sen. Hainkel said there wouldn't be any downtown New Orleans today without it.

McKeithen made one more race before returning home to Columbia in Caldwell Parish. He ran as an independent for the U.S. Senate in 1972, but came in a distant second to former U.S. Sen. J. Bennett Johnston.

"Big John" was his nickname, and it wasn't only because of his physical stature. He was a big-hearted man of the people who — like the Longs — never forgot his roots.

I'll always remember McKeithen because he came along just as I was learning the ropes about how to cover Louisiana politics. For me, the subject is just as fascinating today as it was when McKeithen burst on the state political scene 36 years ago.

June 7, 1999

Carl Weiss picks up support

Although we will never know for certain, more and more people are beginning to believe that Dr. Carl A. Weiss didn't assassinate the legendary Huey P. Long on Sept. 8, 1935.

Weiss was in the halls of the state capitol that night, and he was definitely the spark that set off a hail of gunfire that eventually killed both men. However, there is mounting evidence that Weiss wasn't there to commit premeditated murder.

Writers who have chronicled both sides of the 64-year-old mystery convened at Louisiana College in Pineville last Saturday for what turned out to be a lively — and at times heated — debate on the death of Long.

The day started off with contemporaries of Huey Long and Earl K. Long recounting their personal experiences with the brothers who made political history in this state. Most of them had humorous stories to tell, but it wasn't all fun and games.

Marian Mayer Berkett, a New Orleans attorney and prominent anti-Long student in the early 1930s, was critical of Huey Long's tactics while governor.

"I'm uncomfortable here," she said. "I'm not anti-Long, I'm anti-Huey Long.

"He was the kind of guy that if anything stood in his way — anything — he was going to knock it down," she said. "I thought it was a sign of what was to come for me."

Supporters of the man affectionately called "The Kingfish" didn't take kindly to Berkett's reference to Long's bodyguards. "Long's gestapo exceeded anything in some respects that Hitler had," she said.

The fireworks really started to fly during the afternoon session when noted forensics expert James F. Starrs of George Washington University delivered the keynote speech. It was Starrs who got the Weiss family in 1991 to agree to exhume the alleged assassin's body in an effort to determine who shot Huey Long.

Starrs was critical of the coroner's inquest following Long's death. He said it wasn't transcribed until 1949, there was no verdict assigning guilt and witnesses didn't sign the inquest. All are standard procedures at inquests, he said.

"Murphy Roden (one of Long's bodyguards) said at the inquest that he shot 10 times, but didn't know if he hit Weiss with bullets from his .38 caliber pistol," Starrs said. "That's incredible to the extreme."

Starrs said a photo of the gun Weiss reportedly used to shoot Long was fabricated. He added that those at the scene of the shooting were guilty of silence, inaction and concealment.

"They were playing fast and loose with the evidence," he said. "Clearly, the bodyguards lied. Why, we don't know."

At least two books have been written that conclude Long was accidentally shot by one of his own bodyguards.

After saying he had "grave and pervasive doubts about the guilt of Dr. Weiss," Starrs added, "Dr. Weiss did not kill Huey Long."

Capt. Donald R. Moreau of Louisiana State Police, who led the 1991 investigation of the shooting, said there was no doubt in his mind that Weiss fired the fatal shot. However, he admitted later in the discussion that there is still reasonable doubt about how things transpired that fateful evening in 1935.

Dr. Donald A. Pavy of New Iberia, whose first cousin was married to Dr. Weiss, said Weiss had no gun when he went into the capitol. Pavy is author of the recently published "Accident and Deception: The Huey Long Shooting."

Pavy said Weiss may have gone to the capitol that evening to confront Long for a number of reasons. Long was going to gerrymander Weiss' father-in-law, Judge Benjamin Henry Pavy, out of office. There was also talk that Long was going to spread the rumor that the

Pavys had Negro blood. Or Weiss may have just been there to protest Long's dictatorial tactics.

"It's more likely that, being brushed aside by Huey Long, Weiss decided to give the senator a fist to his lip," Pavy writes. "Not in his wildest dreams did he believe he would be killed with dozens of bullets for not 'minding his own business and keeping his mouth shut'...."

"Dr. Weiss had no gun, he was never convicted, he was never tried and there was no grand jury," Pavy said last week. "Dr. Weiss is innocent because he was never tried."

Dr. Joseph A. Sabatier, who was in the operating room when Huey Long was treated for a gunshot wound, quoted a nephew of bodyguard Roden.

"Uncle Murphy called the family in (just before he died) and told them he accidentally shot Long," the nephew reportedly said.

One of the most dramatic moments during the daylong symposium on the Longs came when the audience heard from Dr. Thomas E. Weiss, a retired physician and brother of Carl Weiss.

Tom Weiss painted a personal portrait of his brother and said important people were overlooked in the investigations into Long's death. It was Tom Weiss who drove his brother's car home from the capitol the night Long was shot.

No official explanation was ever offered to the family, Dr. Weiss said. He added that the only notification of his brother's death came from a Baton Rouge funeral home. Weiss said he was tailed for three months after the shooting.

"You're in for an exciting day," Long historian Michael Wynne said as we arrived for the program titled, "Huey P. Long and the Long Family Legacy."

Riveting may have been a better word. The third political symposium organized by Wynne and the Louisiana College Department of History definitely lived up to its advanced billing.

The Weiss family also has to be pleased that recent findings in the shooting of Huey Long seem to vindicate Dr. Carl Weiss. However, like all conspiracies, this one isn't over yet — and it probably won't ever be.

Nov. 25, 1999

Ron survives political process

A former broadcaster, state legislator and government reformer has combined his experience and talents in all of those areas to write an interesting and insightful book about the Louisiana political process.

"My Name Is Ron, and I'm a Recovering Legislator" was written by former state Rep. Ron Gomez of Lafayette, who served as a floor leader under three governors. They ranged from the flamboyant Edwin W. Edwards, to the unpredictable Buddy Roemer to the conservative Dave Treen.

Elected to the House three times — in 1979, 1983 and 1987 — Gomez also served as secretary of the Louisiana Department of Natural Resources from 1990 to 1992. Currently, he works with a group called Citizens Against Lawsuit Abuse.

Gomez's career in radio broadcasting served him well in helping him tell a good story. And the people he writes about are the kind of individuals many of us thought they were. That's comforting to those of us who chronicle the events in which those public officials are participants.

Take the case of Edwards, for example. Our controversial former governor, who was recently convicted in one federal trial and is soon to be tried again, isn't the man many voters think he is. As Gomez confirms, he can be mean and vindictive. Jurors heard the real Edwards in wiretapped conversations played during his riverboat corruption trial, and even the former governor felt it necessary to apologize for some of his remarks.

Gomez said Edwards could have done more than any one person — including the legendary Huey P. Long — to change the course of the state political scene because of his charisma, intelligence and communications skills. However, Gomez said Edwards squandered those assets by governing to reward his friends and political supporters.

"... He posed as a savior of the poor and needy," Gomez writes of Edwards. "Four terms and almost 30 years later, Louisiana still trails the nation in providing for and lifting its underprivileged. He initiated historic changes in some areas of state government. Still, he left the state ranked near the bottom in the nation in everything good and near the top in everything bad."

Roemer failed to make the runoff in his bid for a second term in 1991, and Edwards eventually won an unprecedented fourth term. Gomez explains why the feisty but talented little fellow from Bossier City rubbed so many people the wrong way.

Gomez describes Roemer as "one of the most intelligent, stubborn, humorous, dour, logical, unpredictable, charming, cold, challenging, distant, interesting and exasperating people I have ever known or worked with."

Holdovers from the previous Edwards administration hampered Treen's tenure. And the former governor, according to Gomez, "was never out of sight or out of mind. He still had access to high-placed appointees in various departments and the loyalty of a great number, if not the majority, of the Legislature...."

Although Gomez says most of the reporting about him was fair, he said he was disappointed many times with the lack of professionalism exhibited by some of the journalists covering the Legislature. He is particularly critical of their failure to double check quotes given to them by some lawmakers.

Gomez gives us close-up looks at current and former lawmakers like the late, colorful Carl Gunter of Pineville, James David Cain of Dry Creek, Shady Wall of West Monroe, Robert Adley of Bossier City, Jesse Guidry of Cecelia, Claude "Buddy" Leach, formerly of Leesville and now of Lake Charles, Allen Bradley of DeRidder, Sammy Nunez of Chalmette, Judge Jimmy Dimos of Monroe, Kip Holden of Baton Rouge, David Duke of Metairie, Sherman Copelin of New Orleans and a number of others.

Rep. John Alario, D-Westwego, is, according to Gomez, "an intelligent, articulate and highly effective legislator. He has a knack for making everyone feel he is their best friend...."

It's an accurate assessment of the man who is dean of the current House of Representatives and who is still a major influence in the legislative process.

Gomez takes the reader inside the decision-making aspects of that process when he writes about Roemer's efforts to reform the tax code, Edwards' attempts to pass gambling legislation, his own work on getting state support for the Cajundome at Lafayette, the state budgeting process and the handling of special interest bills.

Each chapter is introduced with a notable quote from a legislator, and there are some real gems in the lot. For example:

Rep. Thomas Wright of Jena, "I know that people in New Orleans take a keen interest in the political process. Some of them vote two or three times in the same election."

Or, Rep. Francis Thompson of Delhi, "I know you're worried about being a hypocrite for voting for this, but that's our job."

Gomez reminds us that Louisiana is still an extremely rural and poor state and that progress doesn't come easily.

Some legislators enter the political arena to enhance their personal fortunes and to help friends and associates, he said. However, he concludes that most of them he has known are honest men and women of integrity.

"The sad part is that it is very difficult in politics to tell the difference between 'the good, the bad, and the ugly' without close and constant observation," Gomez said.

That's where those of us in the news business come in. It's our job as observers to tell the straight story based on solid and reliable reporting. And judging from the Gomez version of legislative events, we haven't been too far off the mark.

For information on the Gomez book, contact Zemog Publishing in Lafayette.

I've known most of the public officials who make up the cast of characters in this insider's look at the Louisiana Legislature, and recommend the book to our readers who might want to know more about them and the work they do.

July 16, 2000

Conviction scars Edwards

We hear a lot these days about public officials who are worried about their legacies. The latest to fret over how he will be remembered is former Louisiana Gov. Edwin W. Edwards, who has been convicted in federal court of corrupting the riverboat casino licensing process.

Earlier, President Bill Clinton fretted over his legacy. In light of the Monica Lewinsky affair and his impeachment, you can understand why Clinton might be concerned.

Legacies aren't created overnight. And it's awfully late to start worrying about how you will be remembered after you've been convicted of a crime or impeached. Public officials should think about what they are leaving behind the minute they are elected to office and be aware of the importance of their image during all of their years of public service.

"If this conviction stands, it will overshadow everything that I've done in my life," Edwards said.

Yes, it will, and winning his appeal won't change things much. Edwards will never erase the blemish on his record that was of his own creation. He engaged in the questionable behavior that resulted in his indictment and conviction.

The only other former Louisiana governor to be convicted was Richard W. "Dick" Leche, and — sorry as it is — that is his legacy.

Although Leche had talked about resigning the governorship for health reasons, it was obvious that his legal troubles created by the "Louisiana Scandals" were the main motivation. He resigned June 26, 1939, and Earl Long became governor.

Here's what Harnett T. Kane, author of "Louisiana Hayride: The American Rehearsal for Dictatorship, 1928-1940," said about the scandals:

"Convicted, or awaiting trial or sentence, are the once political great of Louisiana, the near great and the little great. Two hundred and fifty indictments have broken about their heads, against the machine's governor (Leche); the president of one of the South's leading universities (LSU); legislative officials, mayors, heads of major departments; millionaire racing and gambling men, allies of Eastern gangsters; the leading contractors, architects and builders; the president of the state medical society, doctor-managers of institutions, tax experts, WPA assistants...."

Leche was convicted in federal court in Alexandria on June 11, 1940, of using the mails to defraud the state of $31,000 in a deal involving the purchase of state highway trucks. That was only one of a number of scandals involving Leche, but it was the one that netted him a 10-year prison sentence.

In a situation similar to the Edwards trial, two participants in the truck scheme pleaded guilty and testified for the government.

L.P. Abernathy, chairman of the Louisiana Highway Commission, and George Younger, an Alexandria truck dealer, received only fines at their sentencing.

Edwards said it would be almost impossible to erase the accomplishments of his unprecedented four terms as governor, and — to a large extent — he may be right. However, there may be some attempts to remove the markers that pay tribute to the former governor.

A plaque commemorating an endowed professorship named after Edwards no longer hangs in a place of honor at the LSU Law Center in Baton Rouge. Debate has already begun over a bronze bust of the former governor in Crowley, which honors him as being the first resident of Acadia Parish to be elected governor of Louisiana.

State officials in 1939-40 wasted no time removing tributes to

Leche. His name had to be chiseled off the granite at the LSU law school. The LSU board ordered that his name and photos be removed from more than 30 buildings on campus.

Earl Long announced that the state would not carry through its original plans for installing 145 additional Leche faces on bridges and along highways.

The convictions of Leche and others led to legislation banning the state from naming buildings after living persons. However, the law can be circumvented by naming parts of state buildings after those individuals.

Edwards has his plaques and tributes all over this state, and many of them will probably survive. People will also remember him for the colorful and dominant political figure that he was in this state for a generation. However, it is his indictment, trial and conviction that people won't ever forget.

"It's a shame; all of a sudden, now instead of being a golden boy, he is tarnished forever," Carolyn Phillips, director of the Louisiana Political Hall of Fame, told The Times-Picayune of New Orleans.

Edwards told the same newspaper he assumes there is justice in the next world because he didn't get it in this world.

If he didn't — and that's debatable — Edwards has no one to blame but himself. Each of us creates the legacy that we leave for future generations one day at a time, and we can't wait to polish it up when we get close to the end of the line.

Sept. 17, 2000

EWE has trouble with truth

If Edwin Edwards had shown some remorse for his crimes, he might have generated sympathy from the Louisiana residents he served for a half-century. However, our former governor steadfastly refuses to accept responsibility for the actions that sent him to federal prison Monday to serve a 10-year term.

"I'm saying I didn't do anything to justify my being here today," Edwards said outside the gates of the Federal Medical Facility, a federal prison at Fort Worth, Texas. "I'm optimistic the Supreme Court will give me a hearing.... I just want everybody to know I did not do anything wrong as governor," he said earlier.

The facts speak otherwise.

Edwards was convicted in May 2000 on 17 counts of racketeering, fraud and extortion. Six of those convictions were dismissed following a U.S. Supreme Court ruling in another case, but the 11 others were eventually upheld on appeal.

"Crimes like extortion and fraud and racketeering — those are not traffic violations," U.S. Attorney Eddie Jordan said after the guilty verdicts.

No one ever questioned Edwards' power and influence while he was governor for four unprecedented terms. But there was more.

"His popularity and personal charisma also let him wield

considerable power even while he was out of office," said The Times-Picayune of New Orleans. "Testimony and surveillance tapes from his corruption trial paint a picture of a political godfather, sought out for his advice and support, and billed by his co-conspirators as 'the boss,' the man to see in Baton Rouge for those who wanted to do business with the state."

Edwards and his co-defendants used his influence to extort payments from companies seeking riverboat casino licenses. The process began during Edwards' fourth term (1991-95) and continued after he left office.

Wiretapped conversations played during the corruption trial proved to be the most damaging evidence. Listeners heard a plotting and scheming side of Edwards they hadn't seen before. And some of his own words tripped him up, like the time he talked about how to conceal payments he and his co-defendants were getting from a former casino owner.

"The tapes definitely made the decision for me," said one of the jurors in the Edwards trial.

The woman also said she believed three government witnesses who made deals with federal prosecutors and testified about Edwards' role in extorting kickbacks from casino license applicants.

"I took the plea bargains seriously and felt they testified truthfully and honestly," she said.

Eddie DeBartolo Jr., the former owner of the San Francisco 49ers, testified he paid Edwards $400,000 for help in securing a casino license. The foreman of the Edwards jury said DeBartolo's testimony helped the prosecution's case.

"To me, DeBartolo had the least to gain by saying anything bad about Edwards," the man said. "And he had the most to lose by admitting guilt, with his team, the 49ers."

Despite the overwhelming evidence of wrongdoing, Edwards still claims the three main witnesses against him lied to save their own hides.

"That hardly can be farther from the truth," Jordan said after the guilty verdicts were returned. "This was a corruption case in which there were tons and tons of corruption...."

Jordan called the three witnesses against Edwards "extremely credible."

"They were telling the truth, and the jury believed them," he said. "And one of the reasons the jury believed those witnesses is because their testimony was corroborated by other evidence in the case. Time after time we had independent proof, independent evidence to support the testimony."

Edwards is so obsessed about his legacy, he has apparently convinced himself his crimes had nothing to do with his being governor.

"I want to reiterate that it does not have to do with me doing anything wrong as governor," he said outside the prison walls. "I hope people separate my record as governor from the events later in my life that really aren't connected."

You can't separate the two. Had Edwards not been governor, he wouldn't have had the influence and opportunity to trade favors for money.

Edwards apparently rejected a plea bargain because of concern for his legacy.

Jim Letten, an assistant U.S. attorney during the trial, said he met with Edwards in the fall of 1997 to discuss a possible plea bargain. It might have gotten Edwards two years in jail and no indictment for his son Stephen.

"Edwards said he didn't want to plead guilty to conduct that occurred while he was in office because, he said, 'I don't want to taint my legacy as governor'," Letten said.

Our former governor needs to spend some of his spare time in prison thinking about what Mark R. Johnson of Covington said in a letter to the Picayune.

"As the single most powerful person in Louisiana during the last quarter-century, no one individual is more responsible for our pitiful infrastructure, failing education system, pathetic economic state and unacceptable poverty level," Johnson said. "This puny conviction with its puny 10-year sentence in no way serves justice to the citizens of Louisiana."

That, my friends, is the real Edwards legacy.

Oct. 24, 2002

Chapter 5

Memories of Another Time

JFK anniversary still painful

Twenty-five years later, you still fight back the tears as you watch the replays of the events surrounding the assassination of President John F. Kennedy.

It is a painful reminder for many who had pinned their hopes for a changing political climate on the youthful president. Kennedy was an inspiration to a new generation of Americans who could not identify with the politics of the past.

For young idealists back in 1963, JFK represented a new age and a break from the politics of World War II, the recovery years and the Korean Conflict.

The 1960 presidential election was one you couldn't watch from the sidelines. Schoolteachers weren't supposed to politick, but you found yourself sporting a Kennedy bumper sticker on your car. When the principal said you shouldn't get carried away, you ignored his warning and continued to campaign vigorously for JFK.

When Kennedy won the presidency in 1960 in one of the nation's closest elections in history, you felt a sense of purpose and belonging. You had been part of something worthwhile that called forth the best everyone had to offer.

The new president reinforced that kinship in his memorable inaugural address on Jan. 20, 1961, when he said:

"Let the word go forth from this time and place, to friend and foe alike, that the torch has been passed to a new generation of

Americans.... Let every nation know, whether it wishes us well or ill, that we shall pay any price, bear any burden, meet any hardship, support any friend, oppose any foe to assure the survival and success of liberty...."

"And so, my fellow Americans, ask not what your country can do for you; ask what you can do for your country."

It was an inspiring message that young Americans would take seriously as they joined the Peace Corps and other voluntary movements and got involved in national, state and local politics.

Gov. Buddy Roemer, for example, has said many times that Kennedy was directly responsible for his political career. He mentions the time he heard Kennedy at Harvard and what an influence it had on his future ambitions.

But inspiration was only part of the Kennedy magic. When he and Jackie, his glamorous wife, traveled to Central America, Europe and Asia, they were loved the world over. They projected an image of competence and caring that made us proud to be Americans again.

Kennedy had his tough side, too. Nikita Khrushchev found out JFK was serious when he said in his inaugural address that this country would pay any price to protect liberty. We came dangerously close to war when the Soviets put missiles in Cuba and JFK insisted they be removed. Kennedy stood firm, and the Russians backed down in the face of the president's determination.

The United States was on a roll, no doubt about it. It was definitely the best of times, and the future looked brighter than ever.

That's why we felt so cheated when Lee Harvey Oswald, for whatever reason, fired those fatal shots that killed the president in Dallas on Nov. 22, 1963.

Kerry Childress, the Arlington National Cemetery historian, says in an Associated Press report that visitors to Kennedy's grave can't help but remember that fateful day.

"A lot of memories come back," she said. "People don't just remember Kennedy's assassination. They remember that whole period of their lives, their families, their friends. People tell me they remember smells, sounds."

My wife, the better half when it comes to recall, said we were shopping that day. We were looking for a coat for our 1-year-old son, she said. She got the first report on our car radio while I was in a watch repair shop.

By the time we got downtown, the horrible events of that day were slowly being sorted out. It was the kind of news you didn't want to accept. Only when it was confirmed did it begin to sink in, but it was a bitter pill to swallow.

Respected TV newsman Walter Cronkite recently explained how he felt about the finality of it all.

"This one really struck home," he recalled. "This was tearing the guts out.

"It was when you finally had to say the word, officially, that he was dead that it really impacted in the way it did."

Even official Washington found it difficult. Malcolm Kilduff, assistant White House press secretary at the time, told the Associated Press recently he clearly remembers the horror and tears on reporters' faces when he told them that President Kennedy was dead.

"I was half crying, with tears in my eyes, because I found it difficult to say," Kilduff said.

"It's unreal to me that 25 years have gone by," Kilduff said. "You wonder whether you said the right things. You wonder whether you said enough. You worry about that."

He needn't worry. It was more than we wanted to hear.

Not everyone was saddened by the news. Kennedy had embraced the civil rights movement and many Southerners felt betrayed. Some were extremely bitter.

Although there may have been scattered rejoicing at JFK's death, the general mood of the nation was one of irreplaceable loss. Americans mourned for four dark days that November, and the memories are no less painful.

The 25 years that have passed since JFK's death have confirmed that Kennedy was no miracle worker and no saint. However, that doesn't dim his image one bit. He offered hope and inspiration to millions of Americans, and that is one Kennedy legacy that can never be tarnished.

Nov. 24, 1988

Rejoice with East Germans

When you've been there, the realization that East Germany has opened the Berlin Wall is more than an historic event. It becomes a personal and emotional experience, particularly as you watch East and West Germans rejoice atop the once-forbidding barrier to freedom.

You remember that cold and drizzly day in November of 1985 when you crossed the wall into East Berlin with six other American journalists.

We had seen the Berlin Wall for the first time a day earlier. It was definitely an imposing structure. From a raised viewing stand, we learned for the first time that there were actually two walls. In between is a no-man's land.

It was obvious from the graffiti that covered much of the 29-mile long concrete wall within the city that West Berliners viewed it with contempt.

An artist had even painted a mural on one portion.

The wall first went up on Aug. 13, 1961, because from 1949 to 1961 some 2.6 million East Germans left their country for the West. Half of them left through Berlin.

Erich Honecker, who was recently ousted as East Germany's Communist leader, had called the wall "a great contribution to safeguarding peace."

Many outsiders scoffed at the contention of Communists that the wall was built to keep people out of East Germany. And no wonder, since 191 people are known to have died while attempting to flee to the West. Over 70 of those tried to escape over the wall.

On our visit to East Berlin in 1985, we avoided Checkpoint Charlie, the most famous crossing point for non-Germans, and took the elevated subway to Friedrichstrasse Station.

To say you're apprehensive about what might lie ahead is an understatement.

Actually, you're scared to death, but try not to show it.

You wonder what it will be like on the other side of that Berlin

Wall. Will the secret police be watching our every move? Will we have problems getting out of East Berlin? Haven't others been detained for no reason at all?

The fears turned out to be unfounded, but you didn't know that when you were getting ready to leave a lifetime of freedom behind.

It took 10 or 15 minutes to get through the East Berlin checkpoints. Once inside, the next step was an exchange of 25 West German marks for East German marks, which have no value outside the East. The exchange was a great way for the Communists to get their hands on valuable currency.

Our program coordinator and guide said if any of us got lost, we should meet back at the Friedrichstrasse Station that evening for the trip back to West Berlin. No one said it out loud, but we had every intention of sticking together like glue.

First stop was the Brandenburg Gate, the historical entry point to Berlin.

If you've been following Tom Brokaw and the other television news anchors the last few days, you've seen thousands of Germans and others celebrating at the famous gate.

Another highlight in 1985 was a visit to the Television Tower in East Berlin with its revolving, glass-enclosed Telecafe. However, when that recurring old height phobia reared its ugly head again; we had to wait in the tower lobby while everyone else had lunch hundreds of feet overhead.

Talk about a lonely American feeling forsaken in a strange and unfriendly city. We would have traded almost anything at that moment for a taste of the free life again.

When the rest of the party returned, we visited other famous tourist spots.

However, as darkness fell, the urge to head West became overpowering. We couldn't take that East German money with us, and a nearby liquor store offered the best opportunity to dispose of those worthless marks.

"Goldkorn" was the only familiar word on the label, but we weren't sure what the bottle contained.

"You have a bottle of schnapps as a souvenir of your trip to East Berlin, which you can serve your friends back home," said Gudrun

Korte, our program coordinator, as she read the label.

"Yes, but can you believe the labels on East German whiskey?" we asked.

"They may be in East Berlin, but they are still Germans," Korte said of the schnapps-makers.

That statement said it all, and that's why East Germans never lost that yearning for the freedom enjoyed by their countrymen in the West. Now they have a taste of what it's like after 28 years of oppression behind that imposing Berlin Wall.

What's it like to enjoy free travel again?

"I've waited for this day all my life. Coming here, it's like learning to walk again," Stefan Needach, a 27-year-old carpenter from East Berlin, told the Associated Press Friday.

"We've just decided to leave our jobs for a little while, have a look around and then go back over," said one young man with four friends from East Germany. "We don't know what our boss will say about that. Perhaps he's over here too."

Maybe he is, and let's hope and pray this newfound freedom for those East Germans and others will continue to spread like wildfire all across Eastern Europe.

Although our nation played no active role in the historic events taking place in East Germany and in other Communist countries, we have reason to be proud of the influence we have had.

The United States has always been a beacon to freedom-loving people everywhere. The West German foreign minister made that clear during a Friday telephone call to Secretary of State James A. Baker.

"I'm calling to express to you, and through you to the American people, our gratitude for what America has done for Germany, and particularly for what America has done for Berlin," he said.

Doesn't it make you feel good inside to be appreciated rather than scorned for those things in life like freedom that count for so much?

We found that unopened bottle of schnapps in the back of the kitchen cabinet Saturday. What better time to pop the top and wish our friends in East Germany a freer and brighter tomorrow?

Salute!

Nov. 12, 1989

D-Day only part of story

This year's anniversary of the invasion of Normandy has become almost as big a news event as D-Day was 50 years ago. It may come as a surprise, but that bothers some veterans of World War II.

"Why are you making such a fuss over the invasion of Europe?" asked one area veteran. "Those Americans who fought the Japanese in the Pacific made just as many sacrifices for their country, and they aren't getting the same recognition."

I tried to explain that the sheer size of the Normandy invasion made it a unique news event. As an example, take the air assault on German defenses along the French coast that began before midnight June 5, 1944. It has been described as "the largest airborne operation ever conducted."

By daybreak June 6, more than 4,000 ships started landing 132,000 British, Canadian and American troops on the Normandy beaches. They were protected by an air cover of 11,000 planes.

One report calls D-Day "the greatest amphibious landing ever undertaken."

The Pacific war veteran who called me wasn't buying any of those explanations.

"What's the problem? Are you afraid of offending the Japanese?" he asked.

When I tried to explain that I had little control over the international observance of D-Day, it was obvious he wasn't going to accept any excuses.

"You're the editor of the American Press, aren't you? It's the newspaper I get, and I haven't seen anything in it about the war in the Pacific," he said. "American servicemen bled and died there, too."

Yes, they did. So maybe we ought to take a few minutes out during D-Day ceremonies today and tomorrow to remember those who made sacrifices in the war against Japan.

Americans played a major role on three fronts during World War II. The first was an effort to drive the Italian and German armies out of North Africa.

There were three principal players in the North African campaign, and all of them would also make history at Normandy.

Germany's forces in North Africa were under the command of Field Marshal Erwin Rommel, known as "The Desert Fox." Gen. Bernard Montgomery was the British commander, and Gen. Dwight D. Eisenhower commanded the American forces.

In October of 1942, the British hit the Germans and Italians from the east and drove them 2,000 miles westward to Tunisia. American troops attacked the enemy in November from the west through Morocco and Algeria.

Defeat of the Axis troops at Tunis opened up the Mediterranean to Allied shipping. From Africa, Gen. George S. Patton's 7th Army launched an attack on Sicily on July 10, 1943, to begin the Italian campaign.

GIs sustained heavy losses at places like Anzio and Salerno and by the end of the war the Italian campaign had cost 70,000 American lives.

Operations in the Pacific theater, the second major front, had begun immediately after the sneak attack on Pearl Harbor by the Japanese on Dec. 7, 1941. Japan moved quickly to take over a million square miles in that area, including places like Guam, Singapore, Bataan and Corregidor.

The Battle of the Coral Sea (May 4-8, 1942) marked the first setback for the Japanese in the Pacific war. That was followed by the Battle of Midway, which stopped the Japanese advance to the east.

Americans fought long and hard — with heavy losses — to recapture the Solomon Islands, Guadalcanal, the Aleutians, the Gilbert and Marshall Islands, the Marianas, New Guinea, Leyte, Luzon, Iwo Jima, Okinawa and Burma.

Casualty lists were evidence of the fierce fighting. At Iwo Jima (Feb. 19 to March 16, 1945), the United States losses included 4,189 killed and 15,308 wounded. Japanese losses were 22,000 killed and captured.

Europe was the third major front in the war, and it began with the June 6, 1944, D-Day invasion.

D-Day, by the way, comes from "D," the first letter of day, the day on which a military attack is to take place.

Paris was liberated Aug. 25, 1944, and Allied troops touched German soil by Sept. 12. The Battle of the Bulge took place in December and in January of 1945. From there, the Allies closed in for the kill.

Hitler committed suicide after Berlin surrendered May 2. Grand Admiral Karl Doenitz, his successor, ordered Germans to lay down their arms on May 7 and they signed an unconditional surrender in Gen. Eisenhower's headquarters the next day.

May 8, 1945, became known as VE (Victory in Europe) Day. However, the war wasn't over. There was still Japan to deal with.

Franklin D. Roosevelt died April 12, 1945, and Harry Truman became president. He decided to use atomic weapons to end the Pacific conflict.

An atom bomb was dropped on Hiroshima on Aug. 6, 1945, and on Nagasaki on Aug. 9. The Japanese accepted surrender terms on Aug. 14, 1945, which became known as V-J Day.

World War II took a heavy toll on every country engaged in the conflict. Germany had 3.3 million killed in the war, and 4 million were wounded. Japanese deaths totaled 1.9 million, and 4.6 million were wounded. The United States had 16.4 million people in its armed forces during the war. American battle deaths totaled 292,131, and 115,185 GIs were killed in other situations. Over 670,000 Americans were wounded, to up the total casualty figure to over 1 million.

Of the 292,131 American battle deaths, 234,874 of those were Army personnel. The Navy lost 36,950, the Marines 19,733 and the Coast Guard 574.

We will honor the thousands of Americans who lost their lives on D-Day tomorrow, but let's not forget the others. They answered the call in North Africa, in Europe and in the Pacific theater. Nearly a half-million of them didn't make it back.

I want that veteran of the Pacific war who called me last week to know that we remember the sacrifices that he and so many others made in those island jungles 50 years ago.

Let all veterans know during this D-Day observance that what they did for the rest of us — wherever that may have been — won't ever be forgotten.

June 5, 1994

It was proud day for Press

President Clinton came to Lake Charles Thursday, and we covered him like a blanket. Actually, I mostly sat back and watched a finely tuned news organization turn in a masterful performance.

Forget the political aspects of Clinton's visit. This was a sitting president visiting Lake Charles for the first time. More than 20,000 people went to great lengths to be part of the historic event.

The Citizens of Southwest Louisiana were gracious hosts. Many of them had a difficult time getting to the Chennault Industrial Airpark because of the tremendous crowd jamming Interstate 210 and Legion Street, but they showed extreme patience.

When they could move no longer, many abandoned their vehicles and walked miles to get to Chennault and Northrop Grumman, site of the president's political rally.

Once inside the park, they stood for hours waiting for the president to make his appearance. You had to be in the middle of that tremendous throng of people to appreciate how well behaved they were. Law enforcement officers reported no problems and no arrests.

I watched mothers and fathers lifting their young children time and time again to catch a glimpse of the story unfolding out of their direct eyesight. You had to admire the obstacles they overcame to make certain their sons and daughters got to see the president.

Once some of those youngsters were airborne, they were given the difficult task of trying to take photographs of President Clinton. I'm not sure how those photos turned out, but give them all an "A" for effort.

Prior to Clinton's arrival, there was a luncheon in a nearby hangar honoring retiring U.S. Sen. Bennett Johnston, who has done so much to make Chennault a thriving aircraft maintenance facility.

The city and Calcasieu Parish Police Jury renamed Legion Street at Northrop Grumman in Johnston's honor. It was a fitting tribute to the man who can take credit for helping bring 1,400 jobs to this community.

Once we left that luncheon, most of us joined the masses outside that hangar to wait for the president. Like many people, I felt it was important to be part of history being made in my hometown.

While I waited and watched the events unfold, my colleagues were spread out everywhere, recording the event for today's readers and future generations.

It was definitely a team effort. Everyone who works in our newsroom had a hand in the final product which each of you saw Friday morning, and some of them went the extra mile.

Brett Downer, our dayside managing editor, planned the coverage of Clinton's visit and it went off without a hitch. Bobby Dower, our nightside managing editor, and Downer coordinated the production effort once the reporters and photographers returned from Chennault.

Burl Vincent, a veteran photographer who has covered many area stories of national significance, turned in another stellar performance. We also got great pictures from staffer John David Phelps. The two of them were responsible for most of the photo coverage, with additional contributions from Jamie Gates, Sunny Brown and Sonny Marks. Linda Young, our photo and state editor, helped with picture selection and caption information.

The reporters who brought our readers the inside story from every possible angle were Hector San Miguel, Edward Gately, Sunny Brown, Stephaan Harris, Wendy Juneau, Sonny Marks, Molly Benoit and Mary Jones.

San Miguel, one of the most aggressive and productive investigative reporters in this part of the country, pursued Clinton in hopes there would be a presidential press conference. When that didn't happen, San Miguel interviewed veteran ABC White House correspondent Brit Hume, who was traveling with the president.

Brown told us the heart-warming story of how Jami Lowe, a Northrop Grumman employee, was selected by President Clinton to introduce him at the rally.

Harris interviewed a mother and daughter who walked three miles to hear the president. He also talked with Adam Dautriel of Westlake, who went to Chennault with a portrait he had drawn of Clinton after his 1992 campaign swing through Lake Charles. The president signed

Dautriel's portrait Thursday.

Marks, who has a flair for feature stories, wrote about the vendors who follow the president from city to city to sell their political wares.

Juneau covered the pro-life protesters outside the gates so readers would get a well-rounded view of the Chennault scene.

Benoit covered security preparations and traffic problems that cropped up prior to the president's arrival.

Jones interviewed two Prien Lake Elementary fourth-grade reporters who were given press credentials so they could videotape the president's appearance.

Once all of that legwork was completed, photographs and stories came together on pages laid out by Joe Conway, Pamela Fontenot, Charles McPhate and Gail Norris.

Also involved in the coverage were James Richardson, Barbara Kingery and Robert Hankins, along with proofreaders Linda Hudson and Denise Spencer. Other members of our staff were covering stories unrelated to the presidential visit.

Gately and Downer were responsible for the Thursday editorial that welcomed Clinton to Lake Charles and from which the president quoted during his speech. The editorial talked about this area's economic growth and the improved self-image of its people.

I've participated in the coverage of many major news events over the last 35 years, but this one had a special flavor. When Clinton read from that American Press editorial Thursday and I saw our coverage in pictures and stories Friday morning, I've never been prouder to be a part of this great news organization.

The young people of Southwest Louisiana who turned out by the thousands to see their president Thursday and those who covered the story for our newspaper demonstrated that the future of this community and this country is in good hands.

You and I aren't the only beneficiaries of the super example and effort turned in by all of them during the president's visit. It has been recorded in this newspaper for the benefit of generations yet unborn.

History was made here Thursday, and the people of this community deserve special credit for making it a truly memorable occasion.

Oct. 27, 1996

Old Ironsides in LC in '32

When the USS Constitution set sail off Marblehead, Mass., on July 21 to mark its 200th birthday, many of us were not aware that the most famous ship in the U.S. Navy had docked at the Port of Lake Charles back in 1932.

News reports in the American Press from 1932 said the ship, which is more affectionately known as Old Ironsides, arrived here March 19. By the time she departed four days later, 37,546 persons, the largest crowd ever known for three consecutive days in Lake Charles, had visited the frigate.

Since that was over a year and a half before my time, I had no knowledge of the historic occasion. Now, thanks to two men who do remember, we can relive a bit of local history.

Pat Ford, who was a longtime mathematics professor at McNeese State University, called over a week ago to say he remembered boarding the ship as a child. He said it was in the early 1930s, but didn't remember the exact date.

I made a note of Ford's call, but was stumped about where to turn next for details. Call it luck, fate or whatever, but I got the missing information during a long-distance telephone call Friday from Ray Dietz of Penngrove, Calif.

Dietz is a native of DeQuincy who also visited the Constitution when it was here in 1932. Dietz joined the Navy in 1941 just before the Japanese bombed Pearl Harbor and retired in 1971 after a 30-year career.

A history buff, Dietz contacted Jerry Wise, a friend of mine who is publisher of The DeQuincy News, seeking additional information. Wise didn't have any press clippings, so he referred Dietz to me.

How did Dietz know that Old Ironsides had been here March 19-22, 1932? He did what I should have done. He called the curator of the ship's museum in Boston.

The Constitution was on a national tour as a way of saying thanks to hundreds of thousands of school children that had contributed pennies to finance the ship's reconstruction. It has been refurbished at least a half-dozen times since it was launched in 1797.

Once I had the dates, finding information was easy. Here is some of what I found in Lake Charles American Press files:

Old Ironsides entered the Calcasieu Ship Channel at 8:35 a.m. March 19, 1932, after leaving Orange, Texas. It was accompanied by her official tug, the US Minesweeper Grebe. She passed Ellender's Ferry at 11:20 a.m. on her way up the channel.

Escort boats met the frigate at Prien Lake and served as a convoy for the remaining distance to Lake Charles.

Louis J. Gulliver, commander of the Constitution, and his crew were welcomed at city hall by Mayor Leon Locke, other area mayors, members of the Lake Charles Dock Board, court officials, Calcasieu police jurors, city commissioners, officers of civic and patriotic organizations and members of the Association of Commerce.

The Reserve Officers Association entertained the ship's staff at a dinner and ball that evening in the Majestic Hotel. Meanwhile, members of the crew and those on the Grebe were entertained free of charge at the Arcade and Paramount theaters.

Saturday afternoon, 5,000 people toured the vessel. Sunday was the big day when 17,546 went on board. The Monday turnout totaled 15,000.

The Southern Pacific Lines railroad brought 700 passengers to Lake Charles Monday aboard what was called the Lafayette Special. They came from Lafayette, Rayne, Crowley, Welsh, Jennings and other intermediate points.

Local youngsters visited the ship on Saturday and Sunday. Two special buses ran on the Shell Beach line, leaving from Broad and

Ryan streets every 30 minutes on the hour and half hour. The fare to the port was 15 cents for adults and 6 cents for school children.

Out-of-town students were given a special treat. Here's how it was described in an American Press story:

Many neighboring parishes have declared a school holiday Monday and trains and buses and private autos will bring thousands of boys and girls into town to pay their respects to the historic old ship.

Boy Scouts in uniform assisted in directing and entertaining visitors at the docks. The drum and bugle corps of W.B. Williamson Post 1, American Legion, also performed.

A first aid station was set up at the port for the duration of the Constitution's visit. Miss Maude Reid, public school nurse, who was assisted by graduate nurses, manned it.

The Association of Commerce accepted a large amount of mail to be taken aboard Old Ironsides and mailed from there with the ship's stamp.

The Rotary and Kiwanis clubs were hosts for a banquet in honor of the officers of the Constitution at noon Monday in the Majestic. Louisiana Gov. Alvin O. King, who called Lake Charles his home, was an honored guest among a crowd of 350.

Old Ironsides, towed by the Grebe, departed Lake Charles at 6:15 a.m. Tuesday, March 22, 1932, and headed to Gulfport, Miss. Commander Gulliver had to be driven here from a Beaumont hospital where he was undergoing treatment for a slight attack of flu.

The Constitution called at 90 U.S. ports on both coasts in 1931-34 and was visited by more than 4.5 million people.

A special thanks to Ford and Dietz for calling our attention to a time when Lake Charles was part of a celebration honoring a naval vessel that has served this nation with distinction. Their assistance has helped us recapture some of the glory of a proud moment in this country — and this area's — history.

Aug. 3, 1997

First story said Titanic was OK

"All passengers are safe and the Titanic was taken in tow by the Virginian," said an April 15, 1912, report in the Lake Charles Daily American-Press.

"Steamer Titanic hits an iceberg," said the one-column headline, and a sub headline noted that 2,000 passengers were in lifeboats.

The world learned a day later that the early report was way off base and that hundreds lost their lives when the Titanic sank.

News dribbled in for a week following the disaster, and the fatality counts changed daily. However, it was obvious on the second day that only a third of the passengers survived.

A reader brought in a copy of our front page from April 15, 1912, and it piqued my interest in reading about the disaster as it was reported 86 years ago this week.

"Titanic at Ocean's Bottom," said a five-column headline on April 16, 1912. Another added, "The 866 on Board the Carpathia All that Were Saved of 2,200 Passengers and Crew; Hope Vanishes as Fuller Details are Received by Wireless."

The Titanic hit an iceberg in the North Atlantic at 10:30 p.m. Sunday, April 14, 1912, and went down at 2:20 a.m. Monday.

"The collision occurred when most of the passengers were in bed, the shock sending many to the decks scantily clad," the story said. "When they took their places in the lifeboats, not having time to return to their staterooms for additional clothes, the air was biting cold and they huddled close together for warmth."

The Carpathia — the first ship to reach the scene — found only wreckage and lifeboats filled with survivors.

Almost every news story regarding the sinking made mention of prominent people like millionaire John Jacob Astor being among the Titanic's passengers.

The 1,503 death count made the Titanic sinking the greatest marine disaster up to that point. The previous high was the loss of 1,450 lives when the Sultana, a Mississippi River steamer, blew up near Memphis, Tenn., on April 27, 1865.

Family members and friends of passengers on the Titanic kept hoping vessels in the area had picked up other survivors — the Virginia, Parisian, Californian and the Baltic — but it didn't happen.

Alexander Carlisle, who designed the Titanic and the Olympic, its sister ship, said he thought the Titanic would reach port even though it was reported to be sinking.

"The fact that she sank within four hours after the impact with the ice indicates that her side was torn out," Carlisle said.

"Two-Thirds Were Destined to Die," said the headline on a story about insufficient lifeboats. The news report noted that the Titanic's sister ship, the Olympic, had 16 lifeboats and four rafts calculated to accommodate 1,171 people, only about one-third of its passengers and crew.

As an indication of how often information changed, an April 17, 1912, story said only 710 had been saved from the Titanic.

Capt. E.J. Smith, commander, had spent 43 years at sea. He had a spotless record until the previous September when he commanded the Olympic, which crashed into the Hawke, a British cruiser. The Olympic also struck a submerged wreck in February.

The Carpathia wasn't expected to dock at New York with Titanic survivors until Friday, April 19, 1912, but the U.S. Senate started its inquiry into the disaster a day earlier.

After survivors reached New York, readers got first-hand information about the disaster.

When crewmen started to enter the lifeboats, for example, Capt. Smith urged them to step back for the passengers. "Be British, my men," he commanded by megaphone from the bridge.

"The command was obeyed," the story said. "Like martyrs, the sailors hurried the passengers into the boats, then they stepped back to die."

Col. Archibald Gracie told how he jumped from the topmast deck of the Titanic as she sank.

"The interval between the collision and the sinking of the ship was two hours and twenty-two minutes," he said. "After sinking with the ship, it appeared to me as if it were propelled by some great force through the water. Explosions under water might have occasioned this. I recall that I was most fearful of being boiled to death....

"I reached the surface after a time that seemed unending. There was nothing in sight save the ice, and a large field of wreckage. There were dying men and women all about me."

Gracie was saved by a life raft, and later transferred to a lifeboat.

Mrs. Alexander T. Compton of New Orleans and her daughter, Alice Compton, were among the survivors. Alexander, Mrs. Compton's son, went down with the ship.

Mrs. Lena Rogers of Boston talked about an officer who drew a revolver on men who were trying to jump into their lifeboat. "Too much praise cannot be given the officer for his work," she said.

Thomas Whitely, a waiter in the saloon of the Titanic, survived on an overturned lifeboat.

"I was not more than 60 feet from the Titanic when she went down," he said. "Her big stern rose up in the air and she went down bow first. I saw all the machinery drop out of her....

"It was a black 'berg we struck, and though the night was perfectly clear, it was impossible to see that color. I saw another like it when we were drifting on the overturned boat."

Most of the testimony given during the Senate inquiry indicated the Titanic's officers had unquestioned faith in the unsinkable character of the ship. It said they steamed "full speed through fields of dangerous icebergs."

Senators said they were struck by "the remarkable calmness with which the doomed passengers faced death."

After reading those 86-year-old news stories, it's easy to see why there is so much fascination today with the story of the Titanic's sinking. The disaster had all the elements of high drama, and there may never again be anything quite like it.

April 16, 1998

What would we have done?

A woman who made her way out of one of those World Trade Center buildings Tuesday made a comment that I won't ever forget.

Workers in the 110 story structures were scrambling to get out of both blazing buildings that had been hit by terrorists flying hijacked American aircraft. While they were headed down the stairs, the woman said firemen and policemen were climbing the stairwells in an effort to reach the fires and help others who might be in trouble.

"They were all nice-looking, young men," she said.

The odds are that all of those "nice-looking, young men" were killed when the two buildings collapsed.

More than 300 New York firefighters were missing Wednesday morning, and dozens of police officers were also believed to be victims.

Can any of us even imagine what it must be like to see people running for their lives from a disaster and know that you're heading right into the inferno from which they are trying to escape?

Firemen and policemen do it because that's their job. They don't think twice about doing whatever has to be done. Those who were climbing those stairwells Tuesday were making the ultimate sacrifice in an effort to save fellow human beings.

New York Fire Commissioner Thomas Von Essen estimated that more than 300 firefighters are missing. "Many of them are gone," he said.

One of them, Ray Downey, chief of special operations command, led a team of New York firefighters to Oklahoma City in 1995 after the bombing of the Alfred P. Murrah Federal Building.

Although the final death toll may not be known for weeks, it is significant that four of the early victims were firefighters. One was a New York Fire Department chaplain who was obviously on his way to offer comfort to any who needed his counsel.

If you watched television Tuesday, as most Americans did, you couldn't help but notice how many emergency vehicles were destroyed when the two buildings crumbled to the ground. Many of the people who were manning those vehicles were apparently among the dead.

Some of them included medical personnel who were also there to render assistance.

The scope of the disaster was mirrored over and over again by those on the scene who found it difficult to describe what they found.

Firefighter Rudy Weindler, for example, spent nearly 12 hours trying to find survivors and only found four — a pregnant woman sitting on a curb and three others in the rubble of a building in the trade center complex.

"I lost count of all the dead people I saw," Weindler said. "It is absolutely worse than you could ever imagine.

"There are so many other buildings that are partially destroyed and near collapse," Weindler said. "There are a lot of fires still burning."

Weindler broke into tears and couldn't speak when asked how many of his comrades he thought had fallen.

"It is unimaginable, devastating, unspeakable carnage," firefighter Scott O'Grady said at the scene of the devastation. "To say it looks like a war zone and to tell you about bodies lying in the street and blood and steel beams blocking roads would not begin to describe what it's like. It's horrible."

Many have compared the unexpected terrorist attack to the Japanese attack on Pearl Harbor on Dec. 7, 1941. However, survivors of that fateful day almost 60 years ago say there is no comparison.

"I saw the results at Pearl Harbor, and this made that look like a high school picnic," said Harlan Hosch, 80, of Danville, Ill., who survived the 1941 attack.

You could see the horror in the faces of those at the scene of the attack that were captured on film by photographers for The Associated Press. Many of those photographs were published in Wednesday's American Press.

I was only 8 when Pearl Harbor was attacked, but I can remember the great sense of loss that Americans felt. We didn't have television to send us pictures from the war scene, but newsmen who were there gave us vivid written and broadcast accounts of the death and destruction.

A wave of patriotism swept over this country, and we mobilized for war. The nation was determined to "Remember Pearl Harbor."

Newsmen and women were there again Tuesday, many of them also placing themselves in harm's way to tell a story so horrendous we found it almost unbelievable.

I suppose the woman's story about those firefighters climbing stairwells affected me personally because of my lifelong fear of heights. I've had nightmares about falling elevators or being trapped in tall buildings with no way out.

What great courage it must take to do your job knowing you may not survive. How many of us could — or would — be willing to climb a stairwell into what could be certain death? It's a frightening thought, but those New York firemen and policemen didn't think twice.

The next time we're asked to support pay raises for firefighters and police, I hope we will remember the ultimate sacrifices made by both professions at the World Trade Center buildings on Tuesday. It's a small price to pay for men and women who are prepared to die for our protection.

We will survive this dastardly attack, but let's not ever forget the thousands who lost their lives and the families they leave behind. It's difficult to fathom how many loved ones didn't make it home from their jobs in New York City Tuesday.

Sept. 13, 2001

1952 election changed parish

The most bitterly fought election contest in Calcasieu Parish history took place 50 years ago this week. If you are a reader of the "50 Years Ago" column, you've been keeping up with the contentious 1952 campaign for Calcasieu Parish sheriff.

Illegal gambling was wide open in the parish outside the city limits at the time, and crime was rampant. When law enforcement officials failed to enforce the laws against gambling, the voters decided to take matters into their own hands.

The People's Action Group was an outgrowth of that citizen movement, and I was caught up in the struggle. I had just graduated from LaGrange High School and was attending McNeese State University.

The late Rev. William O. "Bill" Byrd, pastor of University Methodist Church, was my minister at the time. Byrd was in the thick of the citizen protest that had been ignited by an anti-gambling crusade initiated by the American Press.

My mother and I attended a PAG meeting at McNeese auditorium that was jam-packed with over 2,000 people who had decided they were fed up with inaction by public officials.

Henry A. "Ham" Reid was sheriff, and most blamed him for the failure to curb wide-open gambling being conducted in parish nightclubs, particularly those on the Texas border.

Military officials placed several establishments off limits because of gambling, prostitution and unsanitary conditions.

Citizens collected affidavits to prove that gambling was taking place, but the only people indicted were American Press officials and newsmen and three members of the PAG. The three PAG people were later dropped from the case.

The newspapermen were accused of defaming Reid, District Attorney Griffin T. Hawkins, an assistant district attorney, the 13 members of the Police Jury and one private individual.

John Flanders qualified to run for sheriff, along with Reid and two others. The American Press endorsed Flanders, saying it was more than a fight against gambling.

"If you want to add to your horror reading, go back through the files of this newspaper and add up the unsolved murders, the number of bodies found in the West Calcasieu swamps and the Sabine River — and then start hunting for the stories about arrests and convictions," the newspaper said.

"You'll hunt and hunt and hunt and, in many cases, you'll never find those latter stories."

A total of 425 absentee votes were cast, and that was considered high for a parish wide election.

When Election Day rolled around, it was characterized by "threats, violence, attempted intimidation and alleged voting irregularities."

An official poll watcher for Flanders was dragged out of his home and beaten by two men. A poll commissioner who had been active in the PAG had to have an escort of peace officers to get home from work.

A deputy sheriff resigned his commission so he could campaign for Reid, and he later attacked Sam Guillory, an American Press photographer who shot his picture.

Several people were passing out campaign literature at the polls in violation of state law.

Reports were circulating in Orange, Texas, that one of the sheriff candidates had offered Orange County residents $5 for their votes if they rode or walked across the Sabine River and $10 if they swam.

When the official votes were counted, Flanders led with 12,960 votes to 12,720 for Reid. The votes of two minor candidates kept Flanders from winning in the first primary.

A story out of Orange quoted one gambler as saying, "We carried the thing too far and the people picked this man Flanders and took out after us. I don't know for sure yet, but it looks like we're finished."

Reid had other plans, and it centered on registration of new voters.

"The greatest mass voting registration in the history of Calcasieu Parish came to an end Saturday night after four days of almost unbelievably hectic conditions in the jammed parish courthouse," the American Press reported on Jan. 20, 1952.

Deputies intimidated some who tried to register. And a deputy sheriff helping guard the voter registration area said, "It's gonna be a different story in the runoff."

During a four-day registration period, 4,283 people signed up to vote, an all-time record. The 662 who voted absentee for the Feb. 19, 1952, runoff was also considered a record. Reid won the second primary with 19,009 votes to 16,201 for Flanders, and thousands of Reid's supporters that night jammed Broad Street in front of the offices of the American Press. They carried Reid on their shoulders and yelled, hooted and honked their automobile horns. The demonstration lasted until 1 a.m.

Although citizens who fought the good fight lost the election, they had actually won the war. Reid heard their message and shut down illegal gambling and eventually gained a reputation as a tough crime fighter.

In April 1952, the newsmen who had been indicted were acquitted by a New Orleans judge brought in to hear the case. He said freedom of the press gives a newspaper a right to criticize a public official when it differs with his views.

The gambling fight waged by the American Press marked a turning point in the newspaper's history. It became an effective voice in the community, and the trend continues today.

I wasn't even considering a newspaper career in those tumultuous days. However, my ties to the PAG movement through my church helped shape my thinking from that time on. It's an experience I won't ever forget.

Jan. 17, 2002

What are lessons of Sept. 11?

"What do we take home with us today?"

A former pastor of mine always ended his Sunday sermons with that question. He then explained what he hoped we had gained from his message that would serve us well throughout the coming week.

Maybe that's what we should be asking ourselves now that the first anniversary of the terrorist attacks of Sept. 11, 2001, has come and gone. What do we take home with us?

We should never forget the lives that were lost when the terrorist attacks took place. No Sept. 11 should come and go without our first thoughts being centered on the 3,025 dead and missing.

All were innocent victims working at the World Trade Center towers, at the Pentagon in Washington, D.C., or as rescue personnel at both locations. Hundreds of them were passengers on the four commercial airliners that were used as weapons of mass destruction.

The 41 American servicemen who have died in the Afghanistan conflict and the others who will make sacrifices there and in other parts of the world also need our prayers and appreciation.

"Remember Sept. 11" should become as familiar to all of us as "Remember Pearl Harbor," an earlier time in American history when more than 2,400 of our citizens were victims of a surprise attack by the Japanese that launched our entry into World War II.

We have to accept the fact that a nation we thought was invincible is vulnerable to attack.

Thomas Friedman, a columnist for the New York Times, said the cocoon we all felt safe in has been burst and this country will never feel as secure as it once did. Friedman spoke for many of us when he said it disturbs him that his two daughters won't enjoy living in the same free and protected country the rest of us inherited.

An Associated Press poll of 1,001 adults taken in August revealed that the No. 1 concern of Americans (29 percent of those polled) is flying in commercial airliners. Second, at 14 percent, is the fear of attending public events where there are large crowds.

Security will become a fact of life. We will have to get used to having our bags, backpacks, purses and luggage thoroughly searched whenever we fly or when we attend public events where there are large numbers of people.

Citizens who work in high-rise buildings will undergo additional security checks. Many of them will have to carry ID cards. Trucks entering those buildings will be checked for hidden explosives. All of us will have to be wary and vigilant when we see unattended luggage, briefcases or automobiles that might be used as weapons.

If the experiences of the last year are a fair barometer, there is every indication most of us can accept the fact security will become an everyday part of our lives.

Americans are more aware of the world they live in these days, and it is important that they continue to keep pace with news developments here and abroad. We no longer live in isolation.

As one citizen said, "Before, we didn't hear so much talk about the news. Now that's all we talk about, and I think it's for the better."

We need to have a better understanding of how the United States is viewed by the rest of the world.

The Pew Research Center polled influential leaders in 24 countries on five continents in January of this year to determine how they felt about Americans. Although a majority continues to hold a high opinion of this country, it isn't because of the good we do around the world.

It's our technology that draws people here from other lands.

"In other words, we're loved for our labs, not our good works," said R.C. Longworth, writer for the Knight Ridder News Service. He added that people come here to study and to work. "We have skills and techniques they want to learn."

Unfortunately, we became victims of our own technology and willingness to share it with others. Now we are asking our public officials and ourselves how the terrorists who flew those airliners were allowed to attend American flight schools.

Our immigration policy that is already under scrutiny has to be restructured to ensure that it doesn't happen again. And we need to find those who don't deserve to be in this country and send them home.

The molders of our foreign policy need to be more aware that our allies may not always see things the same way we do. Experts tell us to be sensitive to their priorities and sensitivities, which might be different from our own.

We have many reasons to be optimistic about the future because of the way this country and its allies reacted and because of the lessons we learned from Sept. 11. At the same time, we have to realize the terrorist threat isn't over, so we can't be complacent about keeping our country secure.

Columnist Clarence Page said Sept. 11 forced us to slow down, work a little less and reflect a little more and get reacquainted with some of the people we too often take for granted.

Page said the victims of Sept. 11 have sent us a message that speaks to all of us: "Don't put off until tomorrow the love you should be showing to somebody today."

These are some of the things we can take home with us that will serve us well in the future.

Sept. 12, 2002

City hit by two major storms

Lake Charles has been in the path of two major hurricanes over the last century, and I missed them both. I wasn't born when the first bad one hit this area on Aug. 6, 1918, and I was in the U.S. Army at Fort Benning, Ga., when Hurricane Audrey roared ashore on June 27, 1957.

The situation will be different today as I plan to ride out Hurricane Lili, which is expected to hit this area sometime today.

Hurricanes weren't given names in 1918, but it's obvious from news reports that the storm that hit Lake Charles in 1918 was a big one.

"The storm struck here shortly after noon Tuesday and continued in violence for nearly three hours," the American Press reported the following day. "The wind was terrific and during the time of the storm heavy rain fell.

"There is scarcely a building in the city which escaped damage. Some were totally wrecked, others partially wrecked, and thousands of windowpanes were demolished.

"A conservative estimate of the damage is $1 million, but it may reach a larger sum than this when all points are heard from."

The city was cut off from the outside world, and the only light people had came from lamps and candles. Streets were almost impassable because of ruined buildings and fallen trees. The Borealis Rex sunk at the bottom of the river in front of the King residence at Prien Lake.

Fortunately, only three lives were lost. One man died when a flying brick struck him, and two women died of injuries from the storm. Another man's chest was crushed when a building collapsed, and he wasn't expected to survive.

The reporter who covered the storm damage took some editorial license when he said, "Everything considered, Lake Charles was fortunate that it was no worse. It is by far the greatest disaster that ever befell the city, but the citizens are equal to the occasion and almost before the storm abated debris was being removed and repairs being made."

I will never forget the way I found out about Hurricane Audrey hitting this area in 1957.

While serving on the short side of a two-year tour of duty at Fort Benning, I was assigned as officer of the day in late June and had to spend the night at battalion headquarters.

I got a telephone call in the middle of the night — I don't remember from whom — telling me a terrible hurricane had hit Cameron Parish and that two of my uncles and an aunt had perished in the devastating storm.

When I woke up the next morning, I wondered whether it was a just a bad dream or whether it really happened. I had to call home to verify it wasn't a nightmare after all.

The Army gave me emergency leave to return home to survey the damage and check on loved ones. My immediate family had stayed home during the storm, and escaped with some tree and roof damage. However, some of them said it was a scary time.

My mother was a native of Cameron, and many members of her family were living there when a storm surge preceding Hurricane Audrey arrived on shore earlier than expected.

Audrey was described on Wednesday, June 26, as a "big and fierce lady" that was born in the Gulf of Mexico two days earlier. It was reported to have winds of 100 mph at its center and to be some 350 miles south of the city at 4 a.m. that morning, "and headed straight this way."

The full force of the hurricane wasn't expected to hit Lake Charles until Friday morning. Tides were reported to be two to three feet above normal, but weathermen said it would take 4-foot tides to put water in the streets of Cameron.

As everyone is well aware of now, those predictions were way off base. Residents of Cameron Parish went to sleep the night of June 26 thinking they could get up the next day and head for safer ground. A gigantic storm surge caught them off guard in the middle of the night, and those who survived relived their nightmares for years.

The death toll eventually exceeded 500, and Audrey has become the storm by which all others are measured by the people who lived through it.

Communications to Cameron were lost about 7 a.m. Thursday, June 27. Damaging winds of 75 mph with gusts up to 100 mph hit Lake Charles just before noon.

Telephone and electric services were quickly disrupted. Only six telephone poles were still standing between Jennings and Welsh. All areas between Sulphur and Lafayette were without power. Many roads were closed.

Most homes and businesses had some damage, and there were hundreds of fallen trees.

The late Doug McFillen of Lake Charles flew a KAOK radio reporter over Cameron, and the two men described what they saw.

"As we came over Big Lake we first began to realize the immensity of Hurricane Audrey," they told the American Press. "The shores of Big Lake were littered with dead animals — cows, horses and all types of livestock.

"We counted six or eight houses still standing in the Big Lake community. The rest of the houses were completely demolished."

The two men flew from the western end of Cameron for 50 miles to Pecan Island. They saw 75- and 100-foot boats hundreds of yards inland. A drilling barge was resting across the highway. Only the foundations or pillars of homes remained in most places.

Bill Mertena of the American Press flew to Cameron on an Air Force helicopter and talked to survivors. He said the Mermentau River Bridge had been swept away.

Death and destruction were no more evident than on "The Ridge," a strip of land higher than the rest that runs along the Gulf Coast from the Sabine River eastward. That is where my relatives lived, and those who survived told harrowing stories about the dark night they spent in raging waters.

A huge hole in the ground was all that remained of my grandfather's two-story home, a place where we spent many enjoyable hours when we were youngsters.

Geneva Griffith, well-known Cameron journalist, said she had to wait 30 years before she could describe the nightmare. And when she did, it was a chilling account of how Hurricane Audrey changed lives forever.

Cameron Parish is nearly deserted today because of an evacuation order, as it has been anytime there is a major hurricane threat. Those who had to leave their homes and cherished possessions can only hope that what they left will be there when they return.

For those of us who will experience our first brush with a major hurricane, we are wondering whether our decision to ride it out was the right one.

Oct. 3, 2002

Editor's Note: Hurricane Lili veered east away from the Lake Charles area and lost much of its intensity before hitting landfall.

Chapter 6

Pets are People, Too

Move over, dad, Levi's coming

We have a new member of our household. Levi's his name – Levi Zendt.

It's an involved story, so I won't waste time.

For a fellow who isn't crazy about pets, I've done pretty well over the years. Two cats at one time – now down to one granny – and a dog for over a year that wasn't even mine.

The granny cat – Mrs. "C" – has lived outside for lo these many years. Except for scratching up our new cars every seven years or so, she hasn't been much trouble. She'd getting rather old and feeble, though, and wants to eat every time you open the door.

Mrs. "C's" kidneys are going bad, so we try to keep her happy in her old age by giving in to her every whim.

I can thank my son-in-law for that dog I fed and put up with for a year. And there's a scratched-up back door for proof of my sacrifices.

You have to know this son-in-law of mine to understand how I ended up keeping his dog. Actually, the dog was his and my daughter's idea. They were getting married and couldn't wait to get a pet.

"Won't you have trouble keeping a dog in your apartment until you're married?" we asked him.

We got the usual answer from that happy-go-lucky guy: "No problem."

That's his stock reply for every situation. And as it usually turns out, things really aren't a problem – for him, that is.

Wouldn't you know, the landlady found out there was a dog in his apartment? An eviction threat left only one alternative – my place.

Gary and Jamie bought the pet food until they got married. But there was no place to keep the dog at their home in Westlake. So Ginger stayed on considerably longer than expected.

Eventually, we were buying the pet food. We finally worked up enough nerve to ask why the sudden shift in expenses.

"Well, you're getting to enjoy Ginger's company, so it's more than right that you pay for the food," answered my daughter. She had already picked up that guy's way of explaining himself out of a tight situation.

The fence they needed always seem to be just around the corner. Then there was the time the dog was in heat. Someone, usually my wife, had to watch her every move lest some lecherous old dog jump the fence and get the wrong idea.

Meanwhile, my son-in-law and daughter were living in a flea-free environment.

That elusive fence was finally constructed and relief was in sight. Ginger moved to Westlake and was expecting puppies before long.

All's well that ends well, right? Wrong!

The year of dog care took its toll. My wife and son got pretty attached to Ginger, and there was talk about inheriting one of those soon-to-be-born puppies.

How did I feel about the idea? Actually, I was never consulted.

Six weeks after a litter of five was born, we became the proud owners of our own registered cocker spaniel.

A name was the first problem. Experts say dogs with two syllable names are easier to train. Alex, short for Alexander, sounded a wee bit too royal. A couple of others were also ruled out.

"How about Levi?" my son asked. "Levi Zendt."

We all sort of liked the ring of Levi. Levi Zendt was our favorite character in the long running "Centennial" TV series.

The guy had character, and we hated to part company. Now Levi will be with us for a long, long time.

I asked my wife how I was going to teach Levi that he was never supposed to mess around with the master of the house.

"That won't be any problem," she replied. "You never did anything for Ginger and she left you alone. It won't take Levi long to get the message."

A day later she asked me to bring home some extra newspaper for Levi's pen.

Ever get the feeling you have a lot in common with Rodney Dangerfield, the fellow who "don't get no respect?"

Oct. 12, 1980

It's not really man's world

Did you ever sit in your living room and get the feeling you were in the middle of a wildlife refuge?

I have, and for a fellow who isn't crazy about pets, it can be an exasperating experience.

No one in his right mind ought to allow three dogs — one of them hyperactive — and a senile cat in his living room at one time. But where pets are concerned, I'm definitely in the minority around my house.

Actually, we have only one dog. He's Levi Zendt, named after one of the stars of "Centennial," one of those early television mini-series. Levi is supposed to belong to my son, but he's become my wife's lovable cocker spaniel.

Ginger, Levi's mother, belongs to my daughter and son-in-law — he's the fellow whose favorite hobby is eating. There's nothing wrong with eating, of course, but he always does it with my food.

Levi is from Ginger's first litter. She's had offspring on two other occasions, and Jamie and Gary decided to keep one of Ginger's daughters. Her name is Noel.

That explains why there are three dogs.

Well, you can imagine the activity when Levi, Ginger and Noel get together. There's constant motion and never-ending crunching —

either on dog food, dog biscuits, and ice or on one of those fancy dog bones.

Levi and Ginger have learned through trial and error that Jim Beam is forbidden territory. They don't dare jump on my leg or lap and never nibble on my ears or at my feet. Noel, unfortunately, hasn't learned the ropes.

Noel has another fault. She has one of those rear ends that's in perpetual motion. I get nervous just watching her walk around. And you'd swear they never give her a bite to eat.

But there's more.

Levi is a male and Ginger and Noel are females. That makes it mighty nerve-wracking around my house at certain times of the year. I can't blame Levi for his sexual urges, however, and I suppose I should thank my lucky stars they don't bring the females over when they're in heat.

And if that isn't enough, there's Mrs. C, the cat who's so old we've lost count. I have to stand up when she's in the room because I'm afraid she'll jump in my lap or on top of my head if I'm lying down. A few years ago, she jumped up on my bed and my heart stopped beating.

One night recently all four of those wild animals were walking around the couch and I got the feeling I was part of an African safari.

Where do you suppose I went wrong? If you'd told me a few years ago that pets were going to rule my life, I'd have laughed in your face.

Well, it's come to that. And if you think my home is my castle, come over some Thursday evening or Sunday afternoon and I'll show you who the real kings are.

And they said it shouldn't happen to a dog.

Speaking of kings around the house, Levi definitely ranks at the head of the royal class. The best way to get in trouble at the Beam residence is to pick on Levi.

You might get away with giving my wife a hard time, but mess around with her dog and you're in big trouble, buster.

Every now and then, my wife takes Levi for a stroll around the neighborhood. Actually, Levi leads her around. They both seem to enjoy it, though, so why should I worry?

Aside from getting into a few cockleburs on occasion, the walks are usually uneventful.

It was a different story just before dark Thursday. My daughter joined the strolling duo.

They weren't gone long, and when they returned, I knew something was amiss. Jo Ann was rubbing Levi's back and said, "It feels like it's swollen." She asked my daughter to confirm her diagnosis.

I wasn't sure what was happening, but I soon got the message.

Yep, you got it. A giant collie attacked Levi.

Seems the collie was out of its yard and followed the strolling trio. Suddenly, according to my wife, the monster attacked Levi without warning.

Jamie tried to fight off the attacker, but with little success. Finally, my wife said she saved Levi's life by picking him up in her arms.

She said she knew the collie's owner. "He's a nice fellow, and I'm surprised he'd have a dog like that."

The vet (I knew she'd take Levi in) said it had something to do with a male dog protecting his territory.

"I'm never taking Levi walking again," my wife vowed.

She was still pretty upset Friday because she called the collie owner's wife and told her about the attack. Jo Ann said his wife apologized and was understanding about the incident.

But I'm still not sure my wife will walk the dog anytime soon. I suggested she take along a stick or a can of spray. I even agreed to accompany her on the next outing. Call it moral support, I suppose, because I'm not the bravest thing in the world around dogs or cats myself.

I have learned one thing from my experiences with pets, however. If anyone ever says the world has really gone to the dogs, he'll get no argument from me.

May 8, 1983

It shouldn't happen to dog

"Levi is giving me that funny look," my wife said as she completed preparations for our out-of-town trip.

"Sure," I answered, "he knows something is up. After all, dogs are people, too."

They aren't, of course, but you wouldn't know it if you had lived around one as long as I have. And that's no small sacrifice for someone who has never had any special fondness for dogs and cats and other assorted pets.

I've always been terrified of cats. I have a constant fear they are going to jump on me from out of nowhere and claw me to death. So cats are strictly taboo.

I can put up with a dog, however, but only if he knows his place. It's strictly against the rules, for example, to jump on my body when I enter a room. And no sniffing at my feet or chewing on my trouser legs. And if they expect special petting or rubbing, they will grow old in anticipation.

Goober hasn't learned that yet. He's my sister-in-law's dog. Don't get me wrong. Goober is a smart rascal. Pam has taught him all sorts of things, like rolling over, playing dead – you know some of the usual dog tricks. In fact, he's a lot smarter than Levi. But Pam hasn't impressed Goober on the proper dog etiquette where her brother-in-law is concerned.

My daughter and son-in-law have two dogs. Both (the dogs) have mastered the taboos. One is Levi's mother and the other is a half-sister. See what I mean about dogs being people, too?

It looks like a dog reunion around my house when all three get together – and that's more often than you'd imagine. Even so, Ginger and Noel know their place, and we've all managed to co-exist over a number of years.

I never ask my wife what it costs to keep Levi in food, medicine and assorted necessities. There's enough stress in my line of work without adding a dog's financial upkeep to the list. The less I know, the better.

However, while writing a check the other day in my wife's checkbook, I saw a $90 entry to our neighborhood veterinarian.

Good grief, I thought to myself. I pulled a ligament in my ankle recently and my medical care added up to only $80. That's one I couldn't ignore.

"What in the world cost $90?" I asked.

"Oh, that includes $24 worth of food, too," my wife replied. "And don't forget that Levi had to have X-rays the other day for his disc problem."

Isn't that something? And I thought only people had problems with their backs.

It seems Levi has worn out whatever it is between his discs that keeps them from rubbing together.

"I knew there was something wrong with Levi the way he was acting the other night," my wife said after his initial checkup. I must admit, she knows that dog like a book.

"Remember, now, he can't go outside without a leash," she cautioned. "And I've got to tell Gary and Jamie that he can't jump up when they come over, either. If we aren't careful, he could become paralyzed."

Then she put up a big note on the refrigerator so none of us would forget the rules.

I've been doing my best to toe the line, even in my own limited association with Levi.

And let's not forget that $24 food bill. I should note that Levi doesn't eat like most dogs. No sirree. No scraps from the table for our pooch. He dines on a special canned supplement and hard food found only at our veterinarian's office. It's for weight control.

Before you dog lovers out there get the wrong idea, I'd like to make it clear there is some compassion in my soul. I've even patted Levi on two or three occasions over the last six or seven years.

That's not all. We've also gone walking together at the McNeese track. My wife gets upset because I won't go more often. But that can be an embarrassing experience. Have you noticed that dogs have no sense of modesty whatsoever? They do their thing right out there in the open for the entire world to see.

In another departure from my usual aloofness from dogs, I agreed one time to take Levi to the vet. Have you ever had that experience? It was awful. Levi's entire body began to quiver as we sat in the waiting room. And, as you might expect, the waiting time seemed like forever.

Surely he will quit trembling, I thought, but it didn't happen. Then I remembered my first few trips to the dentist, and wondered if Levi was experiencing the same sick, faint feeling. For whatever reason, I reached down and stroked him fondly. It was completely out of character. If my family had seen it, they would have probably gone into shock.

It's one of my weaknesses. Despite misgivings about pets, there's still a soft spot in my heart for dogs. They are like kids in a way. Even though you get angry with them at times, you don't ever mistreat them, and you won't stand for anyone else doing it either.

That's why I said what I did when my wife mentioned Levi was giving her "that funny look." He knew we were leaving town, and to Levi that meant some lonely days at the vet's office while we were away.

Anyone who has ever been left alone knows the feeling. Makes you wonder if dogs really are like people.

Nov. 26, 1987

Our dogs are getting older

Dogs are people, too.

Well, not exactly, but you couldn't tell much difference around my family.

Three dogs play dominant roles in our lives, although Levi is the only permanent resident of the Beam household. Ginger, Levi's mother, and Noel, Levi's half-sister and the medical nightmare of the trio, reside with my daughter and her family.

Whenever either family goes out of town, the full herd resides with those who remain. Anyone who hasn't been around on those occasions can't fully appreciate why "herd" is the only word that adequately describes the wild trio.

All three cocker spaniels are thoroughbreds that live enchanted lives. They eat nothing but the finest foods, enjoy proper grooming and receive the best veterinary care money can buy.

Speaking of veterinary care, it's a subject we don't discuss around my house. No one tells me what those trips to the vet cost, and I don't ask. Why torment yourself, for example, when you know putting a dog to sleep to clean his teeth costs big bucks?

Although Ginger is the oldest, about 13, she is probably the healthiest of the three. She doesn't see or hear well these days, but neither do many of us who are burdened with excessive years.

Levi, who is almost 11, is named after a character in "Centennial," the first major television mini-series of a decade ago. He has epilepsy.

It's treatable with pills, of course, but something to be concerned about.

Then there's Noel, a dog who could probably keep one veterinarian busy full time. She has a terrible skin problem that requires frequent baths. The horrible smell tells you when it's time.

Noel, who must be about 9 years old, also has a cataract, which means she's blind in one eye. And although she's not quite as hyper as she was in her younger years, she still tends to get excited at sounds of any kind. It's almost impossible to take a nap when she's around. She's also overweight.

As complex as all of those ailments might sound, they still aren't the most frustrating. Eating is what really tests one's patience.

If there is a cocker spaniel on the face of this earth, that has ever eaten its fill, I'd like to see it. That would definitely be one for the record books.

I've often wondered what would happen to those three dogs of ours if you put them in a washtub full of dog food and let them eat to their heart's content?

They would probably explode before they would quit eating.

It's a tempting thought, but definitely reckless thinking.

For a fellow who really isn't crazy about pets, mine has truly been quite a dog's life. And I've become as attached to that trio as anyone in the family.

Judging from a recent news release sent along by one of our veterinarians, we've been doing all the right things to prolong the lives of our dogs.

Like people, dogs will live longer and healthier through weight control, exercise, regular examinations and tests for early disease detection.

So even though I'm not sure what our veterinary and grooming care has cost, and still don't want to know, maybe it's all been worthwhile.

Do you know, for example, when dogs begin to age? Here's the word from the American Animal Hospital Association:

If they are small, less than 20 pounds, they begin aging at 11. Medium dogs, like our three (21-50 pounds), start at 10. Ginger and Levi are already there, and Noel is close.

Large dogs (51-90 pounds) begin aging at 9 and giant dogs (90 pounds and more) at 7. Most breeds of cats begin aging between 8 and 10 years old.

How can you tell if your pets are aging?

The experts say there are physical signs like weight gain, thinning and graying coats, bad breath, behavioral changes, arthritis and hearing and vision loss.

Cancer is the No. 1 non-accidental cause of pet deaths. And like people, pets suffer from kidney failure, dental problems and heart disease.

Veterinarians say the best care you can give your dog or cat is to watch its weight. Feed them too much pet food, human food or treats and you're creating health problems. The older they get, the fewer calories they need.

Exercise also adds to life expectancy. As pets age, they are supposed to be given moderate and consistent workouts instead of strenuous walks or runs.

Older dogs and cats need soft places to sleep, and outdoor pets may need warmer places to sleep.

Dogs should be bathed with special shampoos every three or four weeks and cats need daily combing.

Heartworm disease is a constant concern of pet owners. Its prevention requires continuing medication and monitoring by veterinarians.

Pets definitely play a vital role in people's lives, and the better the care, the longer they will be around to enjoy.

Take it from a fellow who wasn't crazy about this dog business when it got started in my family a dozen years ago. Today, things wouldn't be the same without Ginger, Levi and Noel.

Even with all the headaches when the three are together occasionally, the individual maladies and those never-ending feedings, they are still a big part of our lives and deserve special consideration.

So, maybe in a way, dogs are people, too.

April 21, 1991

Levi said he wasn't ready

Levi is back home after a close brush with death. Our nearly 13-year-old cocker spaniel isn't out of the woods yet, but he's looking better every day.

I've never been big on pets, but you can't live with a dog that long and not form a close attachment. And when Levi's liver quit doing whatever it's supposed to do about two weeks ago, we thought it was all over.

Actually, Levi was supposed to be my son's dog. However, that plan didn't work out and he became my wife's charge. Since my son eventually found out he is allergic to dogs, maybe that was all for the best.

Byran and I named Levi after Levi Zendt, one of our favorite characters on "Centennial." It was one of television's first successful mini-series, which ended a long run about the time Levi was born.

Levi's mother, Ginger, and his half-sister, Noel, live down the street with more of our family —Jamie, Gary and Jessica, my daughter, son-in-law and granddaughter. We have a canine family within a people family.

Gary and Jessica are bona fide dog-lovers, and pets crave the attention they get from father and daughter. My granddaughter, who will be 5 in August, gets right down in the middle of those dogs at their eye level. And she has no hesitation about trying to make friends with dogs she doesn't know.

But where Levi is concerned, my wife has no equal.

I had heard stories about Jo Ann's close ties to a dog named Spot when she was a young girl. But nothing can compare with her attachment to Levi. And he has milked that association for all it's worth.

Gary said if there is any such thing as reincarnation, he wants to come back to earth as my wife's dog.

Meanwhile, I've tried my dead-level best to live and let live where Levi is concerned. I had a lot of practice on Mrs. C., a cat that lived with us for more than a dozen years.

Jamie reminded me Friday that Mrs. C was also named after a TV personality. That's what Richie Cunningham's friend called his mother on "Happy Days."

Once they get to know me, most pets pretty much leave me alone. I don't mess with them, and I expect the same treatment. I make sure they have plenty of water to drink, but that's about as far as it goes.

Forget the petting, although there have been one or two exceptions.

I took Levi to the vet one time and he got so nervous while we were in the waiting room, he started shaking all over. My compassion got the best of me and I reached down and stroked him once or twice.

Speaking of veterinary care, Levi gets nothing but the best. He eats special food and has medicine for whatever ails him. Levi also gets his seasonal grooming.

My wife never tells me what any of that costs, and I don't ask. It's less painful that way.

We were dog-sitting our canine family two Saturdays ago when we noticed spots of blood on the floor where Levi had been resting. After realizing it wasn't coming from an over-scratched place, it was off to the vet's office.

When word got back, it wasn't good. His blood count was down and his liver wasn't working right.

Was it old age? Had he been poisoned?

The experts said it was too early to tell, but it was bad news whatever the cause.

Writing about the moment yesterday brought back the same overwhelming sense of loss I had felt when I realized that Levi might never return from the vet's office.

Has his time run out?

Reality hit home, and it was too much, even for an old meanie who doesn't get closely attached to pets. I cried at the prospect of never again seeing Levi anxiously awaiting Jo Ann's return from work or wherever she's been.

When she's away, Levi usually sits patiently in our dining room until she gets back. If we're out of town, Jamie said he sometimes waits outside by the fence for us to return.

All of those things crossed my mind as I pondered Levi's fate.

Although it's totally out of character, I'm the pooper-scooper around my house. Maybe it's because I don't like to worry about where I step in the yard. But there I was thinking my scooping days might be over.

I also noticed my wife had put Levi's big blue dog bed out of sight in a front room. She stashed his food and water bowls out with the washer and dryer.

Then I saw that store-bought bone he chewed on occasionally that often ended up in the yard.

What do you do with personal items like that when your dog dies? Could Ginger or Noel use them, or would seeing them there bring back sad memories?

Those are some of the things you think about as you try to cope with the prospect that your pet may not come home again.

As tough as the loss of Levi would be on my wife, she was determined he shouldn't suffer. And she told the veterinarians how she felt.

They respected her wishes, but Drs. Robert Lofton, Michael Woodward and Tammy Kennedy and their associates weren't ready to throw in the towel.

"Let's give him one more day," they would say. And bless them for their determination, dedication and medical skills!

Thanks to whatever miracles they worked, Levi came home early last week. The veterinarians think his problem may have been caused by a urinary tract infection coupled with his advancing age.

Levi isn't percolating on all cylinders yet, but a Friday examination showed continued improvement. Most important of all, he's back in the best two caring hands any dog ever had.

My son-in-law offered a good explanation for Levi's recovery. He said Levi probably got a quick glimpse of dog heaven at his lowest point and decided that wasn't the place for him.

Gary said Levi probably told the head dog, "Sorry, pal, but I'm going back where the living is really easy."

And that's where he is today.

June 13, 1993

Levi leaves fond memories

When the veterinarian handed me Levi's collar and dog tags, the reality that he was gone was more than I could handle. My eyes were filled with tears by the time I got out of the car.

Pets have never been a big thing in my life, but you can't live with a dog for 14 years and not become emotionally involved. If Levi's death had affected me that much, it had to be devastating to my wife. She had been his trusted companion and protector all those years.

I was off Thursday, and Jo Ann asked me to settle Levi's account with the vet's office. She said she wasn't prepared to go back there yet. Now I understand why she felt that way.

We almost lost Levi back in June of 1993. However, Drs. Michael Woodward and Robert Lofton and their associates worked miracles to keep him alive. Thanks to their professional skills and caring attitude, we were able to enjoy Levi's companionship for another year.

Levi, a cocker spaniel, got his name from a character in "Centennial," a long-running television series. He was supposed to be my son's dog, but Bryan's been on the move for the last 10 years.

Ginger, Levi's mother, and Noel, a half-sister, reside at my daughter's house. So it's been a family within a family.

There isn't a pet alive that had better care than Levi. He ate the best dog foods available, went for occasional walks with my wife and got first-rate medical treatment and expert grooming when it was necessary.

Gary, my son-in-law, often said if there was any such thing as reincarnation, he wanted to come back to earth as my wife's dog.

Although I've never been a pet lover, I've been tolerant. I feed them and make sure they have plenty of water. However, forget the touching and petting. I leave that for others.

Levi seemed to understand our relationship. He'd often look at me with an expression that said, "You leave me alone, and I'll leave you alone."

In the late afternoons, Levi loved to sit on the patio while Jo Ann worked her crossword puzzles. He stuck to her like glue.

It was difficult for Jo Ann and me to be in the kitchen at the same time. Levi was always underfoot and right where I needed to be.

When Levi wouldn't eat early last week, Jo Ann knew something was wrong. There isn't a cocker spaniel around that wouldn't eat 24 hours a day if you'd let him.

The news from the vet's office wasn't good Wednesday. His age was hampering his recovery, but Levi was hanging on. That afternoon, I began to think about the possibility he might not be back home.

I decided to cut the grass after work, but you can't do that at my house until you canvass the back yard with a pooper-scooper.

Could this be the last time for that routine? I refused to accept that possibility, and attached a new bag.

Dr. Woodward called about 7 a.m. Thursday with the fateful news. Levi hadn't made it through the night.

Jo Ann appeared to take things calmly. However, it had jolted me, so it had to be tearing at her insides.

She went on to work, and I did my usual running around and grocery shopping. That's when I began to feel the pain of Levi's absence.

Usually when I returned home from a short trip, he'd be there at the back door waiting for a small cup of dry dog food. If I repeated that four times a day, he'd expect to eat something each time I got back.

Levi was awfully impatient after my Thursday afternoon naps. That's when it was time for his canned dog food — the prime stuff. I couldn't fix it fast enough to satisfy his hunger.

Anytime we left home, we had to be sure we closed the bathroom doors. Levi had a thing for rummaging through trashcans and eating tissue paper. I found myself closing those doors again Thursday.

When Jo Ann was away at work, Levi often sat patiently in our dining room awaiting her return. Jamie, our daughter, said he'd wait by her back fence when we were out of town.

Somehow, he always sensed when Jo Ann was about to arrive. He'd pace nervously by that back door and jump for joy when she stepped inside.

There's a dog door at the back of the house, and we never lowered the drapes on the left side all the way down. That's so Levi could go in and out with ease. I knew he wouldn't be using that door Thursday and Friday nights, but I couldn't make myself let those drapes all the way down.

Time will make all of that easier, I suppose, but what's the rush?

We didn't want to spoil our daughter and granddaughter's day at school with the bad news, so we waited until Thursday afternoon.

Jessica, our 6-year-old granddaughter, is like her dad when it comes to pets. She loves them all and is afraid of none. I've seen her roll around the floor with Ginger and Noel and shower them with affection.

How would she handle the death of Levi? Jamie gave her the news after school, and told us about Jessica's reaction.

Jamie said Jessica talked about fixing some food and bringing it over to our house. And she figured there would be some kind of funeral service.

It's obvious that youngsters are more aware of what's happening around them than we might think.

After finding out there wouldn't be a need to prepare any food or plan for a service, Jessica said she'd have to break the news to Ginger and Noel.

Jamie said Jessica got down on the floor, hugged Ginger around the neck and said, "Ginger, your son died."

She repeated the process with Noel and said, "Noel, your brother died."

Jo Ann and I laughed through our tears as the story unfolded.

Thank God for little children.

We took the cushion Levi slept on and some leftover dog food to Jamie's. I noticed Saturday morning that Jo Ann had cleared Levi's medicine and heartworm pills out of the cabinet.

It's painful to have those reminders of Levi around. That's why I wasn't certain whether I wanted to keep the dog collar and tags Dr. Woodward handed me Thursday afternoon.

I put that stuff out of sight in a kitchen drawer until Jo Ann and I could decide what to do with it. Something tells me we ought to keep the collar, tags and Levi's leash to help us remember the 14 years we spent with one of the best friends a man — and woman — ever had.

Sept. 11, 1994

Lucy everyone's best friend

We said our final goodbyes to Lucy a couple of weeks ago, but I still keep looking around for her to show up whenever I open the vanilla wafer box in the morning. Like most dogs, she could hear the rustling of the foil wrapping from a long way off.

Lucy, 6, our cocker spaniel, was a victim of cancer of the lymph glands. She had a couple of good months before the end, but the disease finally proved to be too much. We had to make the decision to let her go. The care and compassion shown by Dr. Michael Woodward, Lucy's veterinarian, and his staff were a great help throughout the illness.

Although I don't have a reputation of being a dog fancier, dogs have still been a big part of my life. My wife is a dog lover extraordinaire. If any canine is looking for the good life, Jo Ann is the answer to its prayer.

Levi, our first cocker spaniel, was with us for 14 years. Drs. Woodward and Robert Lofton, the veterinarians who cared for Levi and Lucy, helped Levi live a year after he was diagnosed with a serious illness.

The reprieve didn't surprise Gary, our son-in-law. He said Levi probably got a quick glimpse of dog heaven and told the head dog, "Sorry, pal, but I'm going back where the living is really easy."

Lucy wasn't so lucky. Steroids did give her the extra months that we cherished, but the disease finally took its devastating toll.

Jo Ann has always been careful to watch our dogs' diets and to give them the medical and nutritional care it takes to keep them healthy. However, Dr. Woodward said to give Lucy whatever she wanted near the end, and she definitely got the royal treatment.

In addition to the canned dog food she loved so much, Jo Ann would boil chicken and cut it up as an added treat. And whenever Jo Ann dished up a bowl of ice cream, Lucy also got her share.

I always wake up hungry in the mornings and nibble on a couple of vanilla wafers the minute I hit the kitchen. Lucy never bothered me about that until the one time I gave her a cookie, and from then on she was hooked.

Lucy had a great disposition. All she ever wanted were a few daily hugs. If you were willing to pat her on the head, pet her a little bit or take her for a walk, you had a friend for life. I never heard her bark or snarl at anyone. She thought everybody liked her, so she liked him or her. She would run outside now and then and bark at something she heard in the neighborhood, but that was about it.

On a couple of occasions when Jo Ann and I were out of town on vacation some of my colleagues at the American Press stayed with Lucy at our home. They always asked about her after that, and told us how much they enjoyed her company.

Whenever Gary or Jessica, our granddaughter, came over, Lucy would jump into their laps or next to them on the couch. Both are avid dog lovers, and Lucy knew it.

Like Levi, Lucy loved to sit out on the patio with Jo Ann while she worked her crossword puzzles, played her word games or studied for her Bible Study Fellowship. Seeing the two of them out there enjoying one another's presence made everything seem right with the world.

I put up a gate when we got Lucy to keep her out of the bedrooms. Levi had the run of the place, and he had a bad habit of rousting Jo Ann out of bed early in the mornings when he was hungry.

You had to raise the door of the gate to get it open, and that took some getting used to. Andrew, our 5-year-old grandson, mastered the technique.

Andrew hasn't been around dogs much, so he was fascinated with

Lucy. He loved to pet her and give her dog treats. And it wasn't easy for him to understand what had happened when she died.

The first time he was told Lucy had gone to dog heaven, Andrew wanted to know if Jo, his grandmother, was gone, too.

Even though I took that gate down, I'm still inclined to reach down and open it every time I walk down the hall.

Whenever Jo Ann left the house to go anywhere, Lucy would often lie down by the back door and await her return. The minute she heard Jo Ann's car, she jumped for joy and ran around in circles once Jo Ann opened the back door.

Sometimes when the door opened and I was there, I got a special look. I sensed that Lucy was saying something like, "Oh, it's just you."

However, Lucy occasionally got excited when I returned from an extended trip. And I don't mind telling you it felt mighty good to be welcomed home in grand fashion.

Any pet lover understands that special trusting, unconditional love that pets give us and why we miss them so much when they are gone.

Although Lucy's life was cut short, it was a happy time for her and for us. And for that we are thankful.

June 30, 2002

Chapter 7

Rounding Up the Rest

Vending machines are boss

Vending machines are taking over the world and they pose a threat to civilization, as we know it today.

Man has learned to cope with most of the dangers to society, but the mechanical dispensers of soda pop and sandwiches have boggled our brains.

I've seen mild men go mad trying to deal with the monsters. Once we put our money in the machine, we expect something in return. When it doesn't happen, it's open warfare.

How many times have you put 15 or 20 cents in a coffee machine and gotten only hot water? The next time you might get coffee, but no cup to catch it in.

I watched a woman the other night put in 20 cents for a soft drink and the paper cup dropped down into the slot and bounced on the floor. She managed to retrieve the cup in time to get syrup without carbonated water.

Feeling confident, I took my turn prepared to grab the cup. It worked perfectly. I was standing there smugly drinking my soda when a youngster walked over and told me my cup was leaking. My tie and trouser leg were drenched.

One of the fellows at work the other night had a longing for a candy bar. His coins wouldn't drop. I watched three men fishing in the money slot with paper, a paper clip and a coat hanger. It was a losing struggle, so the man's sweet tooth went begging.

Sandwich machines can really wipe you out. You drop in 50 or 60 cents and pull the door open only to find there's nothing in the rack.

Some people spend a lifetime at a cigarette machine. After two quarters and two nickels fall, the last nickel won't go down or it falls all the way through. Then they have to start inserting money all over again. When they eventually get the money falling right, they realize the machine is out of their particular brand.

Every time you think you've found a way to outfox the vending machine, it comes up with a different wrinkle you've never had to cope with before.

Most frustrating is the inability to get something once the monster takes your money. Vengeance comes in many forms.

Some people rap on the front of the machine with the back of their hand. They rap and rap and rap, and usually have only a sore hand for their effort. Others jerk furiously on the coin return lever. Timid souls have been known to give the entire machine a gentle shake. The vicious do everything but pick it up and take it home.

The other night a fellow got so upset with a newspaper rack, he got out a tire tool and twisted the lock open to get his paper.

We have been fortunate with the vending machines at the Press. If we leave the man a note reporting our losses, he makes restitution. You eventually get your money back.

On rare occasions, two or three persons have hit the jackpot on the sandwich machine. The change kept falling, and winners were elated. Anytime you beat a vending machine, there's cause for rejoicing. I must admit, though, that I don't think they left the man a note saying they owed him money.

Scattered victories still don't make up for the frustrations of dealing with vending machines. There has to be a better way to enjoy the little things in life.

We can at least hope man will someday be able to devise a vending machine that knows how to deal with vending machines.

Nov. 28, 1976

Ritz comes tumbling down

While everyone was showing so much concern for saving the Arcade Theater, another Lake Charles landmark bit the dust.

I noticed Saturday that the Ritz Theater on Ryan Street had been gutted. The only things that remain are the front and side walls and a few theater seats out front.

I'd be the first to admit that the Ritz Theater didn't compare with the Arcade where theatrical talent is concerned, but for me it holds a soft spot in my recollections of early Lake Charles.

Some of those fond memories returned Saturday as I walked down to the front of the old theater to take what will probably be my last look at the Ritz.

Two things stick in my mind.

The Ritz is where I saw "The Wizard of Oz" for the first time in 1939. Ruby Sells, my first grade teacher, took her class to the local premiere of the classic story.

I can still recall how we all lined up outside waiting to march into the theater.

Recollection No. 2 was the admission price of five cents – that's right, folks, and the lowly nickel was all it took to get inside. I can't remember what popcorn cost, but it must have been, pardon the pun, peanuts.

Yes, those were the days.

Isn't it funny how one memory brings back another?

Take Ruby Sells, for example. One thing my first grade teacher did will stick in my mind as long as I live. She's the teacher who bopped me on the top of my head with a pencil. Seems as though I went to the pencil sharpener when I wasn't supposed to.

And did it hurt! Maybe that's why I have never forgotten the incident.

Then there was the time that girl who sat in front of me couldn't get the teacher's attention when she needed to go to the bathroom. You know what happened. It's like the times you sit down in the theater and realize someone higher up spilled a soft drink on the floor.

But back to the movies.

When I was in knickers, Saturday afternoon movies at the Ritz and the Arcade were a ritual in my family. My dad had a bread truck route and always had a bountiful supply of cakes and cookies. We always carried an armload into the theater.

My parents still like to talk about my getting that chocolate all over my face.

Cowboy films were the rage those days. Gene Autry had been king of the cowboys, but lost his throne to Roy Rogers when he went into the service during World War II.

Seems like the good guys were always chasing the bad guys on horseback. They would ride, ride and even ride some more. Sometimes that's all they did for an hour and a half. The hero would always ride up alongside the villain and knock him off his horse and both would roll down the side of a hill.

Then, the fight started. Those fellows could battle it out for the longest. Eventually, the rest of the good guys would ride up and the conflict was over.

The movie always ended with the hero hugging his horse and telling the leading lady he had to be moving on. She always asked him if he would return, and got a stock answer:

"I'm sure I'll be riding through these parts again."

Then he rode off into the sunset.

Sometimes my dad would take his afternoon nap in the theater and we would see the feature a couple of times. When we got tired, we would wake him up and head for home.

You didn't dare miss a Saturday afternoon because you would lose track of the serial running at that time. Television calls them mini-series – those stories that run for successive nights. Movie serials would run for about 13 weeks at a time, a new episode every Saturday.

Yes, seeing the old Ritz fade from Ryan Street brings back many memories and gives one the feeling a part of him is disappearing as well. But as Bob Hope would say, "Thanks for the Memories."

May 21, 1978

Only the memories remain

The news cut deeply. A large chunk of my social life had been wiped out in a matter of hours.

I didn't want to believe Bobby when he called at 7 Tuesday morning with the terrible news. It's still difficult to accept.

Once at work, however, I had to come to grips with reality. There was the proof in a grim photograph – Papania's had really been destroyed by fire early Tuesday morning.

For the uninitiated, I must explain that Papania's was a popular nightspot at 2601 E. Broad St. And now it's gone – only a fond memory for those of us who found it unequalled as a place to unwind after stressful hours in the newsroom.

We'd been going there for so many years, we felt like family. Just open the front door to the lounge and Eddie would have your brand of beer on the bar before you bellied up.

Eddie is a real professional. It didn't take him long to figure out why Scooter always managed to walk through that front door slightly after Jim Beam arrived. It was a sure-fire way to get the first one on someone else. And he noticed that Scooter and his beer seldom parted company – not even for a trip to the men's room.

Yes, when it comes to bartenders, I'll put Eddie up against the best anywhere.

Once your thirst was quenched at Papania's, your thoughts would often turn to food. And Neva, Vivian, Greg, Merrick or Michelle wasted no time seeing that you got preferential treatment and a first-class meal. During those long evenings, they rarely let your glass, bottle or can run dry.

Although famous for Italian food – particularly pizza – Papania's had an unmatched reputation for Oysters Bienville. I've heard the same regret expressed at least a half-dozen times in the last three days: "If only I'd had another dozen the last time I was there."

When it came to that unique brand of music, you could always count on Jimmy and Phil. They made you feel at home with those old standards. I'm particularly going to miss "I Did It My Way," which Jimmy always dedicated to the American Press crew.

Food, fun and fellowship were all we needed, of course, for a satisfying evening. But Papania's had more. It was a certain magic that's difficult to describe.

I suppose you could say it was a neutral zone where even your severest critics respected your right to put your work behind you for a few hours of relaxation. And you returned that respect in the same manner.

Take Johnnie "Popcorn" Caldarera, for example. He and I haven't seen eye-to-eye in recent months. In fact, we've been poles apart. But we've managed to keep a line of communication open. I must admit, however, that Caldarera still does most of the talking.

I wouldn't want you to think there haven't been some tense moments in Papania's. Like the night I turned around after answering the telephone only to stare former Mayor Bill Boyer squarely in the face.

Of course, I'll never forget one night a few years back following the Jupiter labor violence. It was as close as I've ever come to fearing a physical attack at Papania's. Eddie said it was fortunate for me that the labor leader's wife cooled down. He told me about the night she had broken her arm while whacking another foe over the head.

Many a Friday night I've heard those football referees reliving their gridiron exploits for the diehard fans that wanted to go anywhere but home.

While Papania's was not what you call "a place where the elite meet" on a regular basis, the who's who of the social scene eventually put in an appearance at one time or another.

I guess we've seen everybody who's anybody in recent years. And I've gotten more news tips that I can count. It's amazing how a few drinks can open people up sometimes.

And politics! The air at Papania's was filled with it. You could size up an election days before the polls opened. And I've seen many winners toast their victories and almost as many losers drown their sorrows.

It was the kind of place you felt you had to check out before going home – whatever the hour or whatever the day. My wife said she wondered if my car could ever make it home without a trip out East Broad Street.

While inside, you shut out the rest of the world. One night there was an attempted kidnapping and shootout in the parking lot and we didn't know about it until reading the next day's paper.

Well, it's all over now, and my heart is heavy. Like Scooter, I haven't had the courage to drive by the destruction. I guess that's because seeing the burned out shell would make it all seem so final.

Will they rebuild? Only Frankie Papania can answer that question. But I doubt the place will ever hold the same charm and fascination its patrons have experienced over the past 27 years.

Life goes on, though, and we must adapt. Buddy has his feelers out, but no one knows for sure where our tensed-up bodies will unwind next.

We will, I'm sure, find another home. But, oh, those memories.

Sept. 26, 1982

'Rose by any other name'

Have nicknames suddenly become taboo?

I can remember the days when a nickname was something to be cherished. You weren't anybody unless you had one of those extra names.

Now nicknames are forbidden fruit in some quarters. I got hit from three sides recently during a question-and-answer session before a local civic club.

"All you're doing with nicknames like 'Pretty Paul from City Hall' is degrading politicians," said one club member. "And there is already too much disrespect for officeholders," his wife added.

When I answered that politicians have to earn respect, the woman said, "I told my husband on the way here that would be your answer."

I got the feeling they were gunning for me long before the meeting began.

But I make it a point to never dismiss criticism outright. You don't learn anything that way. And perhaps they had a point. So I have given their comments considerable thought since that meeting.

Is there harm in giving people nicknames?

You be the judge.

When in high school, my friends called me "Muscles." And for good reason. I didn't have any.

You wouldn't know it to see me now, but in those days I had a 28-inch waistline and a 135-pound frame. I was one of those skinny-as-a-rail things.

A two-year stint in the U.S. Army ended all that, and I don't suppose I'll ever see those figures again in my lifetime.

And, you know, I really miss that nickname, even though it wasn't flattering.

It's understandable that most mothers don't like nicknames for their offspring. My mother called me Jimmy.

However, when I got into the newspaper business, I decided Jim Beam was the perfect byline. It's short and recognizable, even among teetotalers who have never had a drink of the hard stuff by the same name.

As a young reporter, I was amazed at the number of people in Sulphur who had nicknames. And if you didn't use their nicknames in obituaries, no one would have known they had died.

One fellow said nicknames are like whippings — once you get one, it sticks.

Here's what Compton's Encyclopedia says about nicknames: "Some think the word nickname comes from nick, meaning 'to cut,' since a nickname is often a shortened nickname. Actually, the word was originally eke name and it meant 'added name'."

Most of the presidents had nicknames. William Howard Taft, a heavy man from the time he was born who weighed 350 pounds when he was president, was called "Big Lub.'"

Andrew Jackson was "Old Hickory" to his troops. John Quincy Adams was known as "Old Man Eloquent." He wasn't that great a speaker, but his talks were loaded with information.

Of course, you remember "Ike," "Honest Abe" and others.

And who can forget "Stonewall" Jackson of Civil War fame, the fellow a general said was "standing like a stone wall?" The name stuck with him the rest of his life.

A junior U.S. senator from New York named Thomas C. Platt got a rather unusual nickname when he followed the lead of New York Sen. Roscoe Conkling and resigned his post in protest. Conkling was upset when President James A. Garfield ended the spoils system. Folks started calling the junior senator "Me-too Platt."

"Boss" Tweed was another well-known nickname. It belonged to William M. Tweed, the first absolute leader of Tammany Hall, a New York City political machine.

Fiorello La Guardia, the mayor of New York City from 1934 to 1945, was nicknamed "The Little Flower" because of his first name.

What do you suppose Babe Ruth would have thought of being called George Herman Ruth all his life? And how about that legendary coach, Paul "Bear" Bryant?

The Louisiana Legislature has had its share of members with nicknames. B.B. Rayburn doesn't mean much to anybody, but call him "60" Rayburn and everyone sits up and takes notice. And there's Risley C. "Pappy" Triche, a well-known former lawmaker.

Someone told me recently that Sir Cliff, our junior senator in Baton Rouge, is called "Skate" Newman by his colleagues. I understand he got the name for being fast on his feet when it comes to changing sides on an issue.

How about "The Kingfish," the name Huey P. Long loved to be called? And there was "Uncle Earl," that other famous member of the Long family.

When Earl Long ran against Sam Jones, he called Jones "High Hat Sam," "The High Society Kid" and "The High-Kickin', High and Mighty Snide Sam, the guy that pumps perfume under his arms."

Apparently those nicknames didn't hurt much since Jones won the election.

On the local scene, I'm sure Spook Stream doesn't answer to the name Harold very often.

And some folks get downright angry when you don't give their public officials an unusual handle. A woman at the bank asked me recently when I was going to give her mayor — Dennis Sumpter of Sulphur — a nickname.

She seemed pleased when I suggested that "Dennis the Menace" might be appropriate.

To paraphrase Shakespeare, you can call a rose by any other name, but it still smells as sweet.

So taking everything into consideration, I suppose the Little Admiral, Kingmaker Bob, the Ketchup Man, High-Rise Billy and Pretty Paul from City Hall aren't out of line after all.

And who knows? One of these days those fellows might be greeted with that quotation from William Archibald Spooner: "I remember your name perfectly, but I just can't think of your face."

Feb. 13, 1983

Speaking of best-laid plans

*Double your pleasure, double your fun,
Two new floors are better than one.*

I'm sure the makers of that famous chewing gum will forgive the liberties I've taken with their tuneful television commercial. It helps to tell the kind of story you read about but seldom experience.

My wife is like most women – she is already planning your next project before the one you're working on is barely off the drawing boards.

We moved into our present home just over a year and a half ago, and she was talking remodeling and change before the dust settled.

Our bedroom came first. It was larger and there was room for another nightstand just like the one on my side of the bed. And there was also room for a chest of drawers to match the bedroom dresser.

However, don't try matching furniture you've had for years. It's impossible, and I suspect furniture makers planned it that way.

You can imagine how she solved that problem. We had to buy another room full of furniture that matched. And there was no way to avoid a new paint job, along with new pictures for the walls.

Once that project was out of the way it was on to the bathrooms. Nothing major, mind you, but changing commodes. There's a lot of brown water out in our neighborhood and the bowls had been discolored through the years.

"Just buy new bowls," George said. "You can use the tanks you already have."

George is our press foreman and he was trying to be helpful. But George had better stick to presses. He doesn't know my wife. Her brain doesn't work that way.

Nothing is that simple around my house. New commodes mean new floors, and new floors mean new wallpaper. Get the message?

Well, she looked at floor and wallpaper samples until the rest of us were blue in the face. I can't recall how many times she changed her mind. My daughter, son, son-in-law and I finally gave up and told her we loved the latest samples she showed us.

D-Day came about three weeks later. Everything was coordinated for a Thursday, my day off. Here was the plan:

The new commodes would be delivered early in the week so I would have time to study assembly instructions. I had changed a commode once before and felt fairly confident I could do it again.

My son would also take Thursday off. We would remove one commode Wednesday night and the other one early Thursday before the floor installer arrived. Once the new floor was laid down we would hook up the new commodes.

It all went like clockwork Thursday morning. The floor installer, a veteran of over 30 years, worked like an artist. I watched every step and was enthralled at how smoothly it went.

He had arrived at 8:30, taken out the old floor in two bathrooms, installed the new vinyl and departed by 10:30 a.m.

Bryan and I immediately went to work on those commodes. We didn't move as professionally and as quickly as that floor installer, but we got them set up in time to await my wife's return from work about 4:45 p.m.

It was a proud moment for my son and me.

I suppose my wife wanted to savor the first look, so she delayed her trek down the hall to the bathrooms.

"What's in that corner?" she asked.

I explained it was some excess vinyl left over from the floors.

"But that's not the pattern I ordered," she said.

"Bryan, she's got to be kidding," I said it total disbelief.

Unfortunately, she wasn't.

I couldn't hear the conversation on the other end of the telephone line when she called the store where we bought the flooring, but you can imagine the sinking feeling someone must have had. She told me later the man said something like, "Say what?"

As it turned out, the factory got the order number out of sequence and sent the wrong pattern. No one down the line, including me, thought to check out the design. Besides, I had seen so many patterns and wallpaper samples I really wasn't sure which one was correct.

It was like the time we ran the same page in the newspaper in two places the same day. An irate reader asked how that could happen. Buddy told her it took the full cooperation of six departments at the paper.

The owner of the floor company was a real prince about the whole thing. He said he would make it good, and he did.

Last Thursday, that same installer rang the doorbell. I don't mind telling you I was a wee bit embarrassed to look him in the eye.

However, he, too, took it in stride. He said he would take up the wrong pattern or lay the right one on top. It was my decision. I told him to go ahead if he thought it wouldn't hurt, and I'd have a nice, thick, new floor.

Now you understand why I couldn't pass up that chewing gum jingle.

Oh, yes, I forgot to tell you about the owner of that floor company showing up after the bathroom job was completed. He was there to measure the hall and bedrooms. It seems my wife's next project is new carpeting throughout most of the house.

I'm afraid I know the answer, but the same question keeps nagging at my insides: Will it ever end?

April 8, 1984

Sometimes deck is stacked

"Why did you do it, Elsie?"

In all the hoorah over the goings-on at the Port of Lake Charles and the last-minute politicking in the mayor's race, that question from one of our readers has been almost completely overlooked.

Elsie, of course, is none other than our longtime, friendly cow from Borden's. She's been familiar in these parts for ages.

Like the rest of us, our reader was expressing his dismay that Borden's was closing down its local ice cream parlor and milk processing plant. Here's what he said in a short note that arrived in the mail a few weeks ago:

"It came as a shock Wednesday to learn that the Borden Co. closed its ice cream parlor after nearly 50 years of service to our community. For many years my family has enjoyed their products and services. All I can say is; Why did you do it, Elsie?"

We would have gotten around to discussing this traumatic revelation much sooner, but the reader's inquiry got buried under a stack of papers. After some minor shuffling, the note surfaced again.

Perhaps the letter writer felt he spoke for all of us because he just signed his note, "I.C. Cream, Lake Charles."

A sagging economy has made life extremely trying for Lake Charles area residents over the last couple of years, and the word that Borden's was closing its ice cream emporium was particularly shattering for many.

Two stories surfaced quickly about why it happened.

"I understand Borden's wanted to rezone some land behind its plant and the city rejected the plan," said one caller.

Another said, "I heard they wanted to buy property to build a new plant somewhere, but word got out and land prices skyrocketed."

One of our reporters and city planners researched the zoning records, but no one could find any requests from Borden's that were rejected.

Even though that rumor was squelched, others contend private property owners who hoped to sell to Borden's for its expansion had requested the rezoning. We're still researching that one.

Borden general manager J.D. Robinson had said when the plant closed the decision was based strictly on economic reasons. He said the company's operations were being consolidated in Lafayette and Monroe.

The rumors were so hot and heavy we called him back. The official again denied any stories about the company being angry at Lake Charles over zoning or property prices. It was purely a matter of economics, he said.

Well, there you have it, folks, but it doesn't make the pain any more bearable.

How traumatic has the closing really been? Where the ice cream parlor is concerned, some are still reeling from shock.

An acquaintance filling a prescription in a suburban drug store recently asked me whom he could contact about reopening the ice cream operation. "I'd like to get the business going again," he said. "And I'd hire those same women who worked there before."

It's been said you can't reverse the inevitable and bring back the past, but you can't blame a fellow for trying.

"Don't let this dark day go without comment," said one caller.

She's right, of course, for more reasons than one. When, for example, are companies going to give Lake Charles a break? We're part of the Louisiana scene, too. Why can't they do some consolidating in our neighborhood?

Is it strictly a matter of geography? Are we located in the wrong place? How about our political, civic and business leaders? Are they showing enough enthusiasm and concern for local industry? Do you suppose anyone asked Borden's to reconsider its move to Lafayette?

Let's hope the Borden experience will spur someone to get answers to those questions.

Meanwhile, where are we going to get those delicious chocolate malts we love so much? No one made them quite like Borden's.

Yes, I know that sounds unfair to the other ice cream establishments in town, which have much to offer. But I know they will forgive us for recalling some glorious memories from the past.

When I was a youngster many moons ago attendants at Borden's used to frown every time my buddies and I asked for a frappe. Those extra thick, rich malts you had to eat with a spoon were mighty hard to make, but, boy, were they something to savor!

Having over 30 flavors to choose from is routine these days, but I can remember when we thought selection from a dozen versions was the treat of a lifetime. It was a decision we didn't take lightly, either. Even after we made our selection we always wondered if maybe we had chosen the wrong flavor.

And how about those banana splits? They haven't made them in recent years like they did in the late '40s and early '50s. They were unquestionably unbeatable in their heyday.

Recall, if you will, that magnificent banana split from the past. A banana sliced down the middle laid on each side of the silver serving dish, then three scoops of ice cream – vanilla, chocolate and strawberry – topped with strawberries, pineapple sauce and chocolate syrup, peaked with whipped cream, pecans and that marvelous cherry on top.

What a boatload of calories those banana splits used to be. But, brother, they couldn't be topped as the ultimate in ice cream enjoyment.

My daughter was particularly disturbed about the demise of the Goldbrick sundaes. "I don't think you'll be able to get the exact same thing anywhere else," she said dejectedly.

Everyone had his favorite dish, cone or cup at Borden's, I suppose. And it's going to take some time for most of us to adjust to the realization that a landmark that's been here since 1938 is gone.

No doubt about it, life does deal you some mighty cruel blows on occasion. You tell yourself you'll survive, but down deep in your heart you know those lazy summer Sunday afternoons will never be the same.

April 21, 1985

What happened to comics?

It was an unforgivable goof, no doubt about it. As most of our readers are aware by now, we left the comics out of Wednesday's paper.

When over 350 subscribers realized the funnies were missing that morning, they called us at work and at home to express their outrage. Thousands more were probably venting their frustrations in other ways.

Wednesday is a difficult day of the week to begin with, but without the comic strips it is unbearable.

Like most of our subscribers, I cherish my daily reading of the comics. Although they lost their fascination for me at one time, I have been a faithful fan in recent years. That's probably because mounting world, state and local problems have taken their toll, and I've needed a reason to smile in the midst of it all.

Let's face it; the comic page is the most uplifting section of the daily paper. If you're like me, it's the last page you read every day. It's a great way to help us bear the unpleasant events we might encounter over the next 24 hours – like my morning exercise routine, for example.

I got no sympathy from my wife Wednesday when I told her the comics were missing. She doesn't read the funnies. "What am I going to do for a laugh this morning?" I asked her as she munched on her oatmeal.

Without missing a spoonful, she glanced up and answered, "Go look in the mirror."

Now, that's cold, brother.

A reader from Elton who called long distance Wednesday summed up the sentiments of most of our disappointed readers: "You can mess up anything else in that paper, but don't you dare fool around with the comics," he said.

A DeRidder reader suggested that we impress upon the culprit responsible the seriousness of his dastardly deed.

You might think those of us who work for the newspaper have all the answers, but that's not the case. Like most of you, we, too, awakened to the rude realization the comics were nowhere to be found.

When I got to the next-to-last page in the paper and didn't find the comics, it threw me for a moment. After remembering that our page layout department sometimes puts them on the next-to-last page of an earlier section, I scanned back through the rest of the paper.

Still no comics. I then turned to the last resort – the Page 1 index. The "Comics" line was noticeable blank.

It was then I concluded that a printer the night before had apparently noticed the page was missing and struck out that index line. He didn't want to deceive our readers. But as we learned the next morning, it was little comfort to a host of alarmed subscribers.

When mistakes are made at a newspaper, they are handled much like they are elsewhere. You look for the guilty party, but he is nowhere to be found.

Wednesday morning someone went first to the department that lays out each day's paper to see if it had left out the comic page.

"Don't blame us, " said one defensive member of that department. "It's the back shop's fault."

The back shop is the place where printers fill up pages in the paper with advertising and news copy.

Apparently that's where the foul-up occurred. A member of that department was philosophical about it all, however. "At least it gives us a pretty good idea of how our readers feel about the comics," she said.

Her philosophical attitude vanished in a jiffy, however, when she learned the publisher had called from out of town and asked, "What the hell happened?" Considering he's our No. 1 comics fan, I'm passing it on a little nicer than he probably put it.

Everyone else asked the same question in different ways.

For starters, someone forgot to put the week's comic pages together the Saturday before, which is standard procedure.

Once that flaw was detected, the next question was: "Why didn't someone catch the mistake in time?"

That's a little tougher to explain, but here's what I heard happened:

When all the Wednesday want ad pages were filled up, the printer numbered them from back to front. Unfortunately for us all, he mistakenly picked up No. 47. That's the number, which had been destined for the comic page, the next-to-last page in the paper.

That's why the editorial department was then notified it had a full page to fill with news – right in front of the want ad section. We were so happy to get the space, we didn't ask questions.

Someone wanted to know why the engraving department, the place where printing plates are made, hadn't realized the comic page was missing. Engravers do record the times they receive each page, but their tally sheet showed that all 48 pages in the Wednesday paper were present and accounted for.

The news department has to share the blame, since we send someone to the printing plant every night to give the finished product a final check. Even so, it's impossible to catch everything that could go wrong on any given day and that's awfully late to handle a major screwup.

If all of this sounds complicated, it's because it is. And even if readers understood it all, they could care less. All they know is they want those comics, and there are no excuses.

As for who was really to blame, I recall the time we printed the same page in the paper twice. A reader called on that occasion to ask one of our editors how that happened.

"All I can tell you, sir," he said, "is that it took the full cooperation of every department at the newspaper."

The same thing can be said about the comic page foul-up last week. Even so, Allen, you'd better not let it happen again.

July 6, 1986

Who said country isn't cool?

Don't consider yourself an accomplished dancer if you haven't tried the two-step, polkas or waltz to country and western music. Attempting any of those three on the dance floor without knowing the basic C&W moves can get you trampled to death.

Master the techniques, however, and you can join a growing number of local folks who are flocking to the country and western dance scene.

My wife, who's always wanted to learn how to dance The Freeze, drew me into this newest craze. In the event you've never heard of The Freeze, it's a group dance, which is popular at weddings and other large gatherings. Women are especially good at it, and my wife was tired of sitting on the sidelines.

It doesn't take two to dance The Freeze, but it does for other country and western music. So I was trapped. However, I didn't resist because I was convinced those classes couldn't be much of a challenge for a graduate of the Dancing Gators of the late 1940s and early '50s.

Unlike many young people today who don't take advantage of opportunities to learn how to dance, students at LaGrange High School in those days jumped at the chance. A young professional dance couple, which reminded us of show business dancers Marge and Gower Champion, taught the basics after school hours.

The rest was easy, thanks to the music of the times. We perfected our techniques until rock and roll pushed the likes of Glenn Miller, Harry James and Tommy Dorsey into the background.

Some of us were able to keep our dancing shoes dusted off with The Twist and other rock and roll standards, but times were changing almost too fast to keep up.

Many of our children, meanwhile, didn't feel learning to dance was all that important. For one thing, most modern dancing during their youth didn't require coordination or cooperation between man and woman. Couples simply faced one another on the dance floor, seldom touching, and then did their own thing to music.

Ballroom dancing to Golden Oldies is different, of course. But unless you're nearly 50 or older, you probably don't participate in such ancient rituals.

Then along came this sudden interest in country and western music. If you don't believe it's big and getting bigger, you haven't been to any of Rody Broussard's classes. He's had as many as a hundred couples at his beginner sessions, and he teaches up to five classes in one evening.

Don't think country and western dancing is restricted to any age or category, either. Broussard's students range from 8 to 80 and they come from all walks of life.

Other reasons I didn't argue about trying the C&W scene were my lifelong love of dancing and the inability to resist a challenge. But it became apparent rather quickly that I had been overconfident on both counts.

The country and western two-step, which is actually four steps, was unlike any dance I had ever known. The polka, also called the Texas Swing, is a six-step dance that calls for all the endurance you can muster. When Rody says take small steps, you soon understand why.

With a few exceptions during turns, you can also forget about any belly rubbing when dancing to country and western music. It's mighty wholesome stuff when you think about it.

Then there are the trademarks of country and western dancing that set it apart from all the rest. For one thing, movement is always in a counter-clockwise direction. Think of it as skating without the skates.

Remember those old western movies when the wagon trains formed a circle to protect themselves from the marauding Indians? That's how you line up for country and western dancing, but you move around like the Indians did.

When Rody says "circle the wagons," he only has to say it once. And when the music begins, you'd better start dancing or you'll be crushed in the stampede. Those cowboy boots some of those dancers wear can wreck havoc on the back of anybody's leg that isn't keeping pace.

Unlike the two-step and polka, the waltz was an old acquaintance. But I had been dancing it differently. Surprisingly, only the jitterbug proved to be a breeze. It's much the same to any kind of music.

After The Freeze, we were introduced to the Cotton-Eyed Joe and the Shoddish. All of them are line dances requiring stamina and coordination. The faint-hearted need not apply. That's especially true for Hip-Boot Joe, which came later.

If there is anything approaching graduation from country and western dance classes, it's called Sixth Night. That's a party where the dance steps learned from six hour-long sessions are tested to music.

Although hundreds of couples are dancing to the same song, no two appear to be doing it the same way. However, everyone's coming close to the ideal and they're having fun. Maybe that's why it's the only diploma anyone needs.

And don't think that's the end of it. Most people get hooked on the lessons because they provide an enjoyable change of pace.

If my wife and I had been smart, we'd have taken the beginner class again. But we jumped right into the intermediate level and found out we were soon over our heads trying to do turns to the two-step and polka.

During last Sunday's third lesson of our second round at the intermediate level, it all started falling into place. Whether it's on from here to interface, the next level, is anybody's guess. For the extremely ambitious, there are also advanced or competition classes.

Broussard and his wife, Mona, have brought home a number of prizes after competition dancing in Houston and Dallas. And it's easy to see why after watching them perform.

I'll be satisfied if I can tell a two-step from a polka or a waltz and stay alive on the dance floor while shuffling to the music of Travis Tritt, Dwight Yoakam, Randy Travis, Hank Williams Jr. and all the rest.

The main thing my wife and I got into this country and western business for in the first place was to learn The Freeze. So anything else we picked up is icing on the cake.

The next time you're on the social scene and hear the sound of country and western music, we may be there. Just look for a couple of old smoothies making fairly decent turns while keeping in step and circling the wagons.

May 19, 1991

It's an 'Achy Breaky' summer

Forget the sorry performance of the Louisiana Legislature, the lackluster presidential campaign, or anything else that may be putting a damper on your summer fun. Join the millions of other Americans who have gone bananas over a song called "Achy Breaky Heart."

The lyrics don't make much sense. But the tune has people hanging from the rafters in country and western dance clubs. They are waiting for a chance to shuffle to the hottest music on the charts.

It's got a great beat for dancing, and I never get sick of it," Caryn Paperny, winner of an achy-breaky contest in Long Beach, Calif., told Newsweek magazine.

Katey Howard of Monroe said, "This dance gets you shaking. You can't help but enjoy it. I may look like a fool when I'm out there, but hey, I'm a fool having a good time."

A place called Honky Tonk in Monroe offers dance lessons every Wednesday night, and the owner says his place is "wall-to-wall packed."

Don't expect to dance with a partner when you hear "Achy Breaky Heart." Instead, people step, swing and sway to the music while standing in a line, side-by-side. They step forwards or backwards or to the side with their hands at their waists and with a few extra movements thrown in for good measure.

In country music circles, they call them line dances. And new ones are cropping up all the time. In fact, publicity about "Achy Breaky Heart" has revealed the existence of other popular line dances in California.

The Los Angeles Daily News quoted one dance instructor as saying the achy breaky is right up there with the tush push and the electric slide. Both have been around for about 10 years and are currently the two most popular line dances in California.

A line dance was my introduction to country and western dancing. My wife wanted to be able to dance to The Freeze at weddings and other gatherings. So we signed up for classes with Rody and Mona Broussard, the best-known C&W dance instructors in southwest Louisiana.

While waiting for the session on line dances, we worked our way through the two-step, polka, waltz and jitterbug.

Line dances were done in groups of three. They included The Freeze, the schottische and Cotton-Eyed Joe. However, it wasn't long before the complicated Hip-Boot Joe was added. Then, along came Strokin', a line dance done to a naughty tune by Clarence Carter. However, it's only naughty if you let your imagination run wild.

It takes plenty of stamina to stay up with the latest developments in line dancing. That's because new songs come along and other dances are born.

I got an early tip-off recently that something big was about to break.

"Have you heard 'Achy Breaky Heart'?" my wife asked one day.

The song is by Billy Ray Cyrus, a newcomer on the C&W scene. And it has taken the country by storm.

"Some Gave All," the album, which contains "Achy Breaky Heart," debuted at No. 1 on the country music charts. It also made it to No. 1 on Billboard magazine's list of 200 top pop albums. The single is the first country record to crack the pop-top 20 in recent memory.

Video has brought a whole new dimension to music of all kinds, and "Achy Breaky Heart" is no exception.

"It's the first line dance that has been commercially choreographed, produced and promoted," a nightclub owner told the Monroe News-Star.

Paige Roane, a writer for the Monroe paper, said, "The dance craze is as hot as a branding iron. A how-to video version features tight-jeaned cowgirls and boys kicking up their ropers and making the dance look a lot easier than it is. VCR owners will be thankful for rewind and slow motion."

That's how the line dance has become a national phenomenon, thanks to Country Music Television, which airs the videotape.

Melanie Greenwood, the former wife of country singer Lee Greenwood, choreographed the dance for the Cyrus video. She, too, says she's amazed at how popular the dance has become.

"It's just craziness," said a California country-western dance instructor. "I don't know how else to describe it. I've never seen anything like it."

And you'd better be careful what you say about "Achy Breaky Heart." Criticism isn't taken kindly.

Travis Tritt, another of the new breed of country music singers, said he didn't think the song made much of a statement.

That didn't go over well with Cyrus and his fans.

"I don't care what anybody else says. From the bottom of my 'Achy Breaky Heart' I love all of you," Cyrus told a crowd of about 60,000.

And that brings us full circle back to my wife. If there's a line dance out there she doesn't know, stand out of her way. And this is one she likes.

One night at Cowboy's, the place where we practice in the real country and western world, a small group got out on the dance floor to do its thing to "Achy Breaky Heart."

One glance at her reaction, and I knew she was hooked. The Broussards introduced their students to the intricate 32-step dance, and she took it from there.

First, she had to have the single on tape. Then she practiced during every spare moment when she wasn't working on the job or at home. And true to her usual form, she insisted on having the steps written down on paper.

You can bet my wife will be on the dance floor the next time she hears "Achy Breaky Heart." And when the tush push and the electric slide get here from California, the Broussards had better be ready to do their part to get her started.

Meanwhile, I'm still trying to get past Step. No. 9.

June 21, 1992

Playoff game was rerun of '51

History does repeat itself. It's definitely one explanation for the sinking feeling I had following LaGrange High School's heartbreaking 28-27 state playoff loss to Hahnville Friday night.

My wife and I attended the game, our first high school football contest in many years. The Gators played the 5A semifinal game at McNeese's Cowboy Stadium, which is close to home, and we had followed their progress throughout the season.

LaGrange has always had a special place in my heart because it's where I went to school and made some lifelong friendships. However, during most of my Friday nights over the last 30 seasons I've been helping our sports department cover football and haven't seen many games.

We couldn't have picked a better night. It was some of the best football action I've seen in a long time, and I've watched some big ones in college and the professional ranks.

Peter Nelson, who handles kickoffs and points-after-touchdowns (PATs) for LaGrange, is the son of friends of ours and it was our first chance to see him play. Peter is the kind of youngster any couple would be proud to call their own.

Unfortunately, Peter had an off night Friday. He missed his first PAT and the all-important last one in overtime that would have tied the game at 28-28 and kept the Gators' hopes alive.

No one but Peter — or others who have been through similar experiences — can understand the agony Peter must have felt when that last kick went wide right. I certainly don't know, but that sinking feeling I experienced at the end of the game kept me awake in the wee small hours Saturday morning.

Then it hit me. LaGrange had played a game many years ago that was almost a carbon copy of Friday night's heartbreaking loss. I had been there and went to work Saturday morning determined to track down the story.

It was Dec. 7, 1951, exactly 10 years after the Japanese sneak attack on Pearl Harbor. The LaGrange Gators were playing the Ruston Bearcats in a Class A semifinal game.

A group of us who had graduated from LaGrange in May of that year drove to Ruston for the contest. Here's how Lloyd McMahon, American Press sports editor at the time, described the outcome in his story the next day:

"RUSTON, La. — Possibly the greatest combination of football players ever assembled at LaGrange High School fought their hearts out here last night, only to lose the state semifinals playoff game by the margin of a safety.

"The 2-0 victory over LaGrange was the 12th triumph this season for the undefeated, untied Ruston Bearcats, who will play Ponchatoula, the south Louisiana finalists, for the state championship in Class A football next week."

Hahnville, this year's winner, was also undefeated coming into Friday night's game.

Val Sweeney, one of the lifelong friends I mentioned earlier, was a key player on that 1951 LaGrange team. Other members of the regular starting eleven were: Larry Guillory and Bennett Ellender, ends; Nolan Lafleur and John Reed Martin, tackles; Don Daigle and Edgar Landry, guards; Charles Hansen, center; Jimmy Manuel and Richard Breaux, halfbacks, and Chris Clark, fullback.

McMahon described how Ruston got its game-winning safety:

"A LaGrange team which played its greatest defensive game of the season had just forced the Bearcats to punt for the sixth time in the game after Ruston was able to net but a single yard on a series of downs at the LaGrange 40.

"Fullback Charley Barham's punt bounded toward the goal line, and the LaGrange quarterback and safety, Val Sweeney, moved backwards as the ball came toward him, and when he scooped up the ball, he was only inches from the goal line. Turning in an attempt to evade two tacklers bearing down on him, Sweeney was knocked from his feet in the end zone by Bill Smith, a Ruston defensive end. And that was the ball game."

Sweeney rode back to Lake Charles in our car that night, too torn up to face his teammates on their bus. The anguish he must have felt was eating at his insides. We stopped once or twice along the way to give him a few moments by himself.

If you ask him about it today, Sweeney might tell you he never completely got over the hurt he felt that night. I'm sure he'll forgive me if I tell you he cried, but who wouldn't under the weight of such a heavy burden?

I'll never forget Sweeney's devastation that night. Maybe that's why I had some sense of how Peter Nelson might have felt Friday night. It's more of a burden than any human being should have to bear.

Like Sweeney before him, Peter will have to remember that he gave the game his best and that's all we should expect of any youngster. Time will heal most of the pain.

Maybe McMahon's words of 43 years ago about Sweeney's situation will help.

"Observers in the press box, including sportswriters, coaches and scouts from several states, were all agreed that what happened to the LaGrange safety was nothing new in football. The safety, moving back to receive a punt, didn't have eyes in the back of his head, and simply didn't know that he was standing on the goal line. (As best I can remember, the field was poorly marked that night).

"These same observers were also apparently unanimous in the opinion that the Gators could easily have had three touchdowns to their credit by halftime — if their football fates had not been looking the other way."

When I told my wife Saturday morning about feeling bad for Peter Nelson, she told me to read Nick Walsh's game story. "You'll feel better," she said.

Jo Ann was right. LaGrange head coach Mike Johns put Peter's role and the game in perspective when asked why he didn't go for two points after the Gators' overtime touchdown.

"We thought about it, but Pete Nelson has won some games for us this year," Johns said. "We might not even be here if it weren't for him. It was just one of those things..."

Peter and his teammates should remember this game the way Johns would.

"It was a heckuva football game," he said. "I can't be any prouder. They played their hearts out..."

Now there's a leader of young men who has his priorities in order.

Like 43 years ago, victory wasn't in the cards Friday night. However, the LaGrange players, their families and Gator supporters can take pride in the superb effort the Gators displayed in an outstanding game.

I'm glad my wife and I decided to join the 12,000 fans that witnessed high school football during one of its finest hours.

Dec. 4, 1994

Muller's gone, not forgotten

"What was Muller's?" the reporter asked after covering a meeting of the Calcasieu Parish Police Jury.

Old-timers might be surprised at the question, but it wasn't unusual for a young journalist from Texas. In fact, there are probably a number of youngsters growing up here who don't know much about one of the most famous department stores in these parts.

Muller's was our Dillard's for a long, long time. It was the center of economic activity and social interaction in downtown Lake Charles for much of its 104-year history.

Local residents who remember Muller's will recall — and fondly – the personal feeling that came when they shopped and dined there.

Muller's was back in the news this year when its former home on the northeast corner of Ryan and Division streets was donated to the Police Jury. Muller's became another victim of a dwindling downtown and closed in 1985.

For those of us who worked at Muller's, it has special memories. If it hadn't been for Muller's, I may have been unable to purchase my first home in 1958.

I cut my teeth in retail sales at age 12 as a sacker and stock boy at Fontana's Grocery on Kirkman Street. There were no age restrictions in those days, so Fontana's became a training ground for the boys in our family who grew up just a block away.

One of the toughest jobs I had as a youngster was a summer stint in the produce department at George Theriot's Food Store on Enterprise Boulevard.

Fontana's and Theriot's are gone now, two other victims of a changing economy.

My church hired me as a janitor for three of my college years, and the $25 a week helped put me through college. Tuition at McNeese State University was $22.50 in the fall, $18.50 in the spring and $10 for summer school.

See how much times have changed?

I got married before my senior year, and my wife went to work at Sun Oil Co. That made my life easier than it had been in a long time, so I was able to coast to graduation.

After receiving a B.A. degree in education, I had a two-year commitment with the U.S. Army. However, I needed a job until I had to report for duty in November of 1955.

Muller's filled the bill perfectly, and I became a salesman for Hayes Prejean in the men's suit and slacks department. I saw a lot of customers come through those side doors on Division Street.

After my tour of duty ended, I went back to work at Muller's while waiting for a teaching job to open up at Vinton High School at the beginning of 1958.

I continued to work part-time at Muller's while teaching. The $3,600 annual teaching salary wasn't enough to live on in those days, either.

Adolph Marx, who was active in Muller's management from 1919 to 1964, had offered me a shot at becoming a buyer for one of the store's departments. I gave his offer some serious consideration, but wanted to give teaching a try.

When I applied for an FHA home loan, the bureaucrats said I didn't make enough money as a teacher to qualify to pay a $90-a-month house note. That's when the officials at Muller's signed a letter saying they would pay me $350 a month in the summertime.

I couldn't move in until the loan was approved, but that letter eventually did the trick. I never forgot the favor.

One of the most enjoyable features of working at Muller's was meeting people from all walks of life. Workers from the American Press, the telephone company and other downtown stores drank coffee and ate lunch in the Azalea restaurant on the second floor. Older residents will remember when it was appropriately called The Rendevouz restaurant.

When I quit teaching to become a newspaper reporter, Wayne

Owens and I coined our own lingo for ordering lunch. Our specialty was an "F-HOT" sandwich (fried ham on toast).

Adolph Marx's mother, Julie Muller Marx, founded the store in 1882 as a dress shop and millinery business on the southeast corner of Ryan and Division streets. The store later moved across the street to the northeast corner.

One of its major expansions came when Muller's bought out the Berdon-Campbell Furniture Store next door in the 1940s.

For many years, Muller's was the major retailer between Houston and New Orleans. It became part of the Allied Stores chain in 1929, but Marx continued to be active in Muller's management. He retired as president and managing director in 1964, but still lives here. He's either 99 — or mighty close — and a prince of a fellow.

The children of Julie Muller Marx and Mrs. Helen Marx Zander donated the Muller's building to the Police Jury this year.

Adolph Marx said, "The family felt it was appropriate to give the building to the parish as its way of repaying the people of Southwest Louisiana for their patronage for 104 years.

Marx also used the occasion to clear up a misconception that someone named Jake Muller had constructed the store's building.

"There's no such person," he said.

That often happens when reporters write about historical events. As it turned out, the fictitious Jake Muller had surfaced in a letter to the editor.

I still have a pair of Hush Puppies and two umbrellas I bought at Muller's during its closeout sale. I've worn the Hush Puppies, and one of the umbrellas is a spare at work.

I haven't opened that second umbrella and may keep it under wraps. What better way to remember Muller's, a place dear to a lot of consumer hearts and former employees?

Our young reporter probably got more than she asked for when she inquired about Muller's. However, it's been a pleasure to recall a landmark that played a key role in some of our lives.

If nothing else, maybe the Police Jury can keep the Muller's name alive. We shouldn't forget our past so soon — or so easily.

Dec. 10, 1995

McNeese enriches many lives

Support for McNeese State University's efforts to save vital degree programs that are on the cutting board has been overwhelming. Numerous arguments have been advanced, and here's one that says it all:

"Every time a program is eliminated, it diminishes us as a community," said one person responding to our Your Call phone survey. "Most of the students at McNeese commute, and can't afford to go somewhere else to school. If they're not offered what they need here, and can't afford to go elsewhere, the education level of the community is diminished."

If you doubt that, let's get personal.

McNeese has played a key role in the educational and economic development of my family for the last 45 years. My brothers and I cut our teeth in the working world at Fontana's Grocery on Kirkman Street. It was our way of helping our struggling family makes ends meet.

Attending college out of town was simply not an option. However, with low tuition at McNeese and a scholarship from the late Jesse J. Verret, my LaGrange High School principal and a state representative, I was on my way to an education that would open doors for the rest of my life.

My tuition for summer school at McNeese in 1951 was $10.50. It was $22.50 in the fall semester and $18.50 in the spring.

While that might not sound like much money today, it was a major hurdle nearly a half-century ago.

I got more than a quality B.A. degree in social studies and English education at McNeese. As a member of the ROTC, I was well trained for two years of military service.

It was also at McNeese where I met the lovely woman who was to become my wife in 1954. She worked in the ROTC office while attending classes.

After graduation, I spent two years in the U.S. Army. When I left the service in 1957, I started teaching at Vinton High School. I moved to Marion High School for the fall term in 1958, and started thinking about getting a master's degree.

Higher degrees improve the pay for teachers and give them advanced educational training that serves their students well. Unfortunately, I had to attend LSU in the summers to get that higher degree.

Teacher friends and I drove to Baton Rouge on Sundays and returned to our families after LSU classes on Fridays. Class demands made it impossible to go home on many weekends to see my wife and young daughter.

Being gone from our families during four summers was bad enough, but it was also expensive. We were spending money for tuition and room and board and missing an opportunity for summer employment to supplement our teaching pay.

Although that master's degree proved to be expensive and time-consuming, it was well worth the effort.

When our daughter reached college age, we were prepared to send her wherever she wanted. She decided she would stay at home, and enrolled at McNeese. She, too, became a teacher after college and attended McNeese whenever possible to get her master's degree. It was less expensive and more convenient than my experience.

My son is a graduate of the business program at McNeese, training which serves him well. He had to attend LSU for a master's degree in public administration and will tell you it wasn't easy financially.

McNeese provided an employment opportunity for my wife, who retired in January after 20 years in the Office of Student Services. It was an enriching experience for our whole family.

You can see why McNeese means so much to the four of us. However, ours is only one family's story. Similar experiences can be recounted by thousands of other families throughout Southwest Louisiana.

So forgive us if we get riled up when we read about outside consultants who want to eliminate vital programs at McNeese. Maybe they would have some credibility if all of them had visited the university before making their ill-conceived recommendations.

Consider the report that said McNeese' engineering program should be scratched. It's only three pages long and based on a paperwork analysis.

Elimination of master's degree programs in education will make their bachelor degrees a dead end for many teachers and other professionals in the field.

McNeese serves an isolated corner of Louisiana. If the trend of ending programs there continues, it will be only a matter of time before McNeese becomes a community or junior college.

No one disputes the fact there is too much duplication in higher education. However, it's questionable whether those outside consultants have really taken a serious look at the programs they want to eliminate.

In most cases, little money is going to be saved, and it won't come close to comparing with the increased costs for students who will have to go away for higher degrees or abandon the idea.

Those of us who attended McNeese when other educational opportunities were out of our reach have been well served. McNeese has touched our lives in ways we haven't even thought about.

Look around you. There are successful people throughout our community who owe so much to the educational experiences they had at McNeese. However, the university is more than a place of learning. It is the center of cultural and educational development for all of Southwest Louisiana.

It seems the height of folly for the regents to enhance the programs at LSU, Louisiana Tech and the University of New Orleans at the expense of universities like McNeese.

Michael Dees is our representative on the Board of Regents. Although he is only one of its members, he's in a position of influence because he's currently the chairman. Let him know how you feel about the threatened programs at McNeese.

We will publish the names, addresses, and telephone and fax numbers of all the regents. If you know any of them, send them a letter or fax or give them a call. If you know Gov. Mike Foster that would definitely help. McNeese is worth your time and effort.

I know that my family owes the university more than it can ever repay. I hope the same educational opportunities are available for our granddaughter.

April 18, 1996

Lake Charles needs links to past

Is America losing its flavor? In a story last year, The Times of Shreveport reported that chain outlets are instilling a blandness in U.S. cities — "from sea to shining sea."

"Chains and franchises have laid a carpet of uniformity on the landscape, in the process often killing downtowns," the newspaper said.

The Times called it a national good news/bad news joke.

"Wherever in this country you travel, wherever you stay or eat, the good news is there are no surprises. The bad news is ... there are no surprises."

In 1980, the top three fast food companies had 13,000 outlets. That number climbed to 36,000 in 1994. Wal Mart had 276 stores in 1979, and today there are more than 2,200.

If we accept the fact that chains and franchises are changing the landscape on their own terms, how do we retain some of the unique qualities of our cities and towns?

Some cities have architectural firms that figure out how chains and franchises can complement the area. The Times said Shreveport gets national outlets there and then figures out how they will fit in.

You can bet Shreveport isn't alone when it comes to reacting instead of laying out ground rules before chains start construction.

In addition to better planning, many cities — Lake Charles included – are turning their attention to downtowns in an effort to retain some of their local flavor. Revival of downtowns is no easy task, but the effort is seeing some progress.

The Main Street Center at the National Trust for Historic Preservation in Washington, D.C., was working with 1,200 cities last year. It was advising them on local issues of law, resources, community organizing, planning and design.

Before we can hope to succeed at reviving downtowns, we have to stop the razing of buildings, which were unique to our early history. Lake Charles has turned that corner. However, we lost numerous structures — many to make room for parking lots — before realizing how historically significant many of those buildings were.

Two recent stories in The Daily Town Talk of Alexandria demonstrated the extremes of historical preservation.

In Winnfield, a silent crowd watched as a wrecking ball destroyed the 100-year-old Winnfield Hotel. Some of the nation's most famous politicians and criminals stayed there.

The hotel was election headquarters for the late Gov. Earl K. Long and had guests like former presidents Theodore Roosevelt and Dwight D. Eisenhower. Moviemakers used the hotel when they filmed "Blaze," the story of Long's affair with a burlesque artist.

Old-timers said Bonnie Parker and Clyde Barrow, the infamous bank robbers, had eaten at the hotel's restaurant.

An effort to save the hotel in 1994 fell short of its goal. It then became the property of the Winn Parish Police Jury because the owner owed back taxes.

Lamar Tarver, president of the Police Jury, said, "It's a shame that it's gotta go. But it's gone now. It's not even safe to go into."

"History's going down," said Mrs. Betty Turner of Winnfield. "It's a sad thing when something old and historic isn't taken care of."

On the opposite extreme was the story of James Fontenot's efforts to save the Eagle Hotel in Washington, La. It was host to travelers in the 1800s when Washington was the closest steamboat port to New Orleans.

Here is how Fontenot's role was described in an Associated Press report:

"Ever since he laid eyes on the old Eagle Hotel, which has stood proudly perched since the 1820s on a high bluff overlooking the spot where Bayou Courtableau meanders under the present-day bridge in this St. Landry community, he couldn't get her out of his head," The Town Talk said.

Fontenot, an Abbeville attorney and former state senator, bought the old hotel in 1989. Many of his family and friends reportedly thought he had lost his mind. However, he is gradually bringing the building back with research, renovations and hard work.

Restoration of the Eagle is no easy task. One corner was crumbling from foundation failure, its brick complexion was weathered and cracked and the rusted tin roof was leaking badly.

Private and public agencies and individuals here are trying to restore what's left of downtown Lake Charles. Renewed interest comes too late for landmarks like the Vallery and Majestic hotels and the Paramount and Arcade theaters.

The citizens of this city believe in restoration and demonstrated their support when they approved a sales tax for renovation of the former Central School.

The Calcasieu Parish Police Jury has formed a citizens committee to find a use for the former Muller's department store building that was given to the parish by the family of the late Adolph Marx.

Renovation of old homes in the Lake Charles Charpentier Historical District has been under way for years now, and the movement is gaining momentum.

Restoration efforts do have to contend with critics who insist downtowns won't come back. They will never be like they were before, perhaps, but downtowns are vital and can be revived.

Jennings, for example, has done wonders with its downtown and the effort has paid dividends in the form of increased tourism and a sense of civic pride.

Richard Moe, president of the National Trust for Historic Preservation, explains why downtowns are significant.

"It's important because if you have a traditional downtown it means that you have an active business leadership and an active civic leadership and from that a sense of community," Moe said.

Like cities everywhere, Lake Charles is what it is because of its past and the willingness of its citizens to adapt to changing times. We can continue to grow economically and still retain the historical flavor that sets us apart from other communities.

We can be like other places, but still feel a sense of pride because we have unique qualities.

Feb. 27, 1997

5,500 left their imprint

If you make it out to Shiver Me Timbers Millennium Park anytime soon, take a close look at the screws in the Crying Eagle's Nest. That's the three-story tree house that is the dominant feature in the park.

You won't find my name on any of those screws, but that's OK. I know I drilled in a few of them, and that's all that really matters.

Like the 5,500 people who worked at the park over a 10-day period, I'm awfully glad I didn't miss an opportunity to participate in the greatest volunteer effort ever in Southwest Louisiana.

Site captains, who were the ramrods on the various park attractions, worked at least 12 hours a day.

Hector San Miguel, our investigative reporter and father to four youngsters, spent a week at the park, and he has become one of its biggest boosters. It was hard work, he said, and it gave him a newfound respect for people involved in construction.

San Miguel said Jack Clark, his site captain, wanted the work to be enjoyable. "He said over and over, 'There are no problems, only opportunities.' That became our mantra as we built the park. Whenever we had a problem, we would call Clark and say, 'We have an opportunity'."

George Rivet, another site captain, said volunteers did everything they were asked to do. He said there were no low jobs or high jobs. "There are just jobs to be done, even if it's just carrying the end of a board for somebody," Rivet said. "You've got $100,000 engineers using screwdrivers."

A woman volunteer said to San Miguel, "My kids were so excited about my coming here. That makes it worth all of the hard work to know that."

It was amazing how well people got along when you consider the number involved in the project.

"It has been nothing but smiles here," said a site captain.

You get a sense of how important the volunteer effort was when you think about what this park would have cost without it.

San Miguel said a local engineer told him if the city had hired a contractor to build the park without volunteers, the final cost could have been as high as $1.2 million.

Park organizers raised about $400,000 for the project. Leathers & Associates, the consulting firm that spent a year designing the park and organizing the effort, was paid $50,000. Out of that came their expenses of overseeing the construction phase.

Materials were purchased at "very reasonable prices," according to Kay Barnett and Jake Philmon, general coordinators for the park project. Some materials were also donated.

Barnett said one of the biggest surprises of the community effort was the number of volunteers who turned out to help. A call was put out for 3,000 volunteers, and 5,500 showed up over the 10-day period.

"To have almost double the number requested is quite a compliment to the community," Barnett said. "It just shows the attitude that's here. It was just such a wonderful feeling to see that many people in a community this size get involved in this."

Lake Charles Mayor Randy Roach said of the effort, "These are blueprints for a community of any size to do something that really pulls people together in a positive way."

Roach said he would like to see a community project like this one done every three years for other Calcasieu Parish cities like Sulphur and Westlake.

"This is the kind of thing that needs to happen on a regular basis," he said. "I was thinking about the fact that we had people from Sulphur over here. We had people from all over Southwest Louisiana participating in this project. It was truly a regional event."

When I showed up one evening, someone stuck a nametag on me that indicated I was supposed to be a skilled worker. I can handle a screwdriver and hammer with the best of weekend do-it-yourselfers, but I'm not sure I qualified as a skilled worker.

Joe, a member of Telephone Pioneers that I worked with, must have thought, "Boy, is this guy mislabeled."

However, Joe — a real craftsman — was a patient fellow and I eventually figured out how to use that power tool to drill those screws into the wood.

Whatever each of us did, we were enriched by the experience. As one site captain said of the volunteers: "They leave with a sense of confidence and pride."

Perhaps two site captains overheard by San Miguel expressed the greatest lesson learned from this gigantic volunteer effort.

"This proves that Lake Charles doesn't need a disaster to bring people together," they said.

The park will officially open at 8 a.m. today. Find some time to visit the park soon and see for yourself what a community can accomplish when everyone is pulling in the same direction.

If we're lucky, this park project is just the beginning of even bigger and better things for the future of the place that each of us calls home.

Sept. 24, 2000

Familiar item back on menu

The Dilly Dish is back at the Piccadilly Cafeteria chain, and it's a great example of why you shouldn't mess with success.

If you've never eaten at the Piccadilly — and there can't be more than a half-dozen of you out there — the Dilly Dish allows customers to select an entree, any two side dishes and a bread item for $5.29. The price may vary in some markets.

My family has a tradition of sharing evening meals at the Piccadilly on Wednesdays, and we were there about a year ago when the Dilly Dish disappeared. The combo meal took its place, and it was never fully understood — or accepted.

The men and women who work at the Piccadilly spent most of their time trying to explain the combo meal to customers. It cost a little more, but you had a wider selection with a combo meal. However, that still didn't smooth the transition.

Our weekly bill went up when the combo meal appeared, and part of that can be attributed to the confusion over trying to figure out how to get the best deal for the money.

"In spite of good intentions, we confused a lot of our customers," said Brian Dixon, Piccadilly's executive vice president of marketing.

Declining sales also played a part in the Dilly Dish's return. Sales were down 3.4 percent in the first quarter of this year and 5.7 percent during the second quarter.

Most folks, as they grow older, become creatures of habit. I've been that way all my life. We simply don't like change for the sake of change.

I remember a year or so ago when the manufacturers of Safeguard face soap decided to come out with a new bar that was curved on both sides. Promotions touted the newly designed bar as easier to grip.

Actually, it was so poorly designed it was difficult to grasp.

I lodged a written complaint with the makers of Safeguard and got one of those nice form letters in return that said the new design would go over well with customers.

As I usually do in such matters, I quit buying Safeguard in protest. I realized the loss of my few bucks wouldn't bankrupt the company, but it made me feel better.

You can't imagine how delighted I was the other day to receive a letter and some coupons from the Safeguard people. They said they were going back to the old soap bar design.

My dissatisfaction didn't turn the tide, but maybe it helped.

Zest was my choice of face soap when I split with Safeguard, but it has redesigned its bar as well. The change wasn't as drastic, but I keep asking myself why.

Now, here's a story of change closer to home.

A couple of weeks ago, I picked up Focus, our weekly television section, and learned that the layout had been changed. For some reason, the prime-time programs are published in the center of the magazine rather than on the outside edges.

I used to be able to find those listings without having to open up the section all the way. Suddenly the process is more complicated and time-consuming.

You can't imagine how unsettling these things are to someone who is as well programmed as I am.

Once in a while there is a change that makes sense, but all too often it doesn't last.

I remember when Kraft started making its mayonnaise and salad dressing jars with a wider opening. It was much easier to keep from getting salad dressing all over your fingers while trying to scoop some out of the bottom of the jar.

The change didn't last long. The company went back to the old style jars. I wrote a column about that experience and sent Kraft a copy. Unlike the Safeguard people, they didn't even have the courtesy to reply to my letter.

If you think I've exaggerated any of this, just ask my wife. She's been putting up with my programmed lifestyle for over 47 years. It's a wonder she's been able to survive.

Just the other night at bedtime, I couldn't find a house key that we keep by the back door. When I mentioned it was gone, I got the stock answer in such situations.

"I didn't use it," she said. "I know you think I did."

After throwing in the towel and realizing I wouldn't sleep well with that key missing, I headed for the bedroom. However, on the way I saw that key hanging on a nail by the front door with the other spare key.

Jo Ann didn't go out the front door all day, and I don't remember using that key there either. But I had gone out to retrieve the mail and there it was in full view. It must have been one of my rare slip-ups.

You can see why a lot of other people were happy to hear that the Dilly Dish is back. We have a difficult time coping with change, and our lives haven't been the same since it left.

The next time someone gets the bright idea to upset our daily routine, they could at least sound us out beforehand. However, if past experience is any guide, we may be the last to know.

Nov. 29, 2001

Astrodome was our place

If there is really such a thing as a home away from home, I suppose Houston would qualify for my family. We drove there again Saturday to attend an afternoon production of "Swing," a musical that is part of the Broadway Series at Jones Hall.

However, live theatre has been only a small part of our Houston experiences. Until recent years, the two main attractions have been Astroworld and the famous Astrodome next door. I can't count the number of trips we've made to both facilities.

My son wrote about those 1960s trips in "Vacation Memories," a gift to me on Father's Day in 1998.

"So, just about the time of year when the weather reached the sweltering stage, Mom, Dad, Jamie and I would load up the (station) wagon and head west for some fun away from home," Bryan said.

"As we would arrive on the outskirts of Houston, you could feel your heart beat a little faster," he said. "The traffic picked up, the speed seemed a little faster, the tall skyscrapers were coming into view, and highways stretched in every direction. It was the big city, and you could feel the excitement."

The Houston zoo was another familiar hangout with the Imax Theater next door that came later. The Galleria in the western part of the city with its ice skating rink was also popular with tourists. However, nothing compared to the Astrodome and its surroundings.

I still remember the first time we paid to take a tour through the Astrodome back in 1965 shortly after it opened. The Dome had been billed as the Eighth Wonder of the World, and it deserved the title.

Now, 37 years later, the Astrodome is being called a "has-been" among sports facilities.

Judith Graham, a Chicago Tribune writer, talked about the Dome's beginnings in a story she wrote last year, and it brought back some fond memories.

Domes are considered run-of-the-mill structures today, but not in 1965. And considering the Astrodome only cost $35 million, it was a truly remarkable achievement.

The Astrodome was the brainchild of Judge Roy Hofheinz of Houston. It was the world's first multipurpose dome sports stadium and helped attract major league baseball to Houston. It became the home of the Astros.

The Houston Oilers of the National Football League also made the Dome their home. It was quite an improvement over the games held in Rice University's football stadium that offered no protection from the elements.

Astroturf, the artificial grass, made its debut in the Astrodome.

The Ringling Brothers Barnum and Bailey Circus always drew large crowds in the Astrohall next door to the Dome.

When Astroworld opened, it became an annual vacation spot for our family. Bryan talked about our stay at the Astroworld Hotel that is now the Sheraton Astrodome.

"It was higher brow than what we were used to seeing," he said. "As evidence that we came from a small town, Jamie and I jumped up and down on the bed holding hands going in circles when we found out the room had a color TV. We were used to black and white. The elevator was also a novelty."

You knew the Astrodome's days were probably drawing to a close when the Oilers moved to Nashville, Tenn., and the Astros began playing their games at Enron Field downtown near the convention center.

Houston never gave up on getting another professional football team, and the NFL Texans will play there for the first time this summer. However, the games will be next door to the Astrodome in the new $402 million Reliant Stadium.

Reliant Energy Corp. bought the naming rights to the entire Astrodomain complex for $300 million last year. So the company name comes first.

The Astrodome doesn't have the luxury boxes, club seats and wider concourses that are a must for new indoor football stadiums.

The Houston livestock show and rodeo is also moving to the new stadium.

What happens to the Astrodome is still up in the air, but for now it's home to monster truck shows and motorcycle races.

Houston is bidding for the 2012 Summer Olympics and could use the Dome if it gets the nod. The Astrodome would be refurbished as a 70,000-seat indoor track and field facility.

If that doesn't happen, the future looks bleak. Other NFL cities are also abandoning their domes for improved stadiums.

Michael Surface, chairman of the Harris County Sports and Convention Corp. that is caretaker for the Dome, said it wouldn't be torn down.

"That's not really being considered," he said. "It has too much historic significance. It's not going to come down any time in our lifetimes."

Ramona Davis, executive director of the Houston Preservation Alliance, isn't so sure. Her group wants to get the Astrodome listed on the National Historic Register.

"Houston is a build it and tear it down city," Davis told Graham. "If it sits there unused for very long, they'll find some reason to take it down."

A Reliant Energy spokesman said, "It's a Houston landmark, but I can't say I'm in love with it."

Whatever happens, no one can take away the many enjoyable hours we've spent in and around the Astrodome and Astroworld. As Bryan put it, "It was our place, a family ritual and a dreamland where so many fond memories reside."

March 31, 2002

Saints keep dream season alive

My son and I were part of sports history Saturday. We were eyewitnesses to the New Orleans Saints winning their first-ever NFL playoff game in their 34-year history. Bryan said he was going to hang on to his ticket stub, believing it might be a collector's item someday.

You can't imagine the joy of actually seeing the Saints defeat last year's NFL champion St. Louis Rams, particularly after seeing them lose to St. Louis a week earlier, 26-21. The visiting team gave New Orleans fans some heart-stopping moments in the fourth quarter, but 31-28 is a victory no matter how you size it up. And that won't ever change.

When the Saints went up by 31-7 in the final period, a fellow sitting behind me said statistically there was no way the Rams could recover. Apparently he hasn't seen some of the Saints games many of us have witnessed over the years. If anything could go wrong during those games, it usually did. So I wasn't about to start celebrating a victory just yet.

Nevertheless, there was an awful lot to cheer about throughout the contest. And we stood up for much of the game because of the intensity of every play. I've seen the crowd get involved in games before, but nothing like this one. Whenever St. Louis had the ball, New Orleans fans roared.

The Times-Picayune used a sound (decibel) reader to check the crowd noise. It ranged from 67 decibels when the Saintsations drill team warmed up in a nearly empty Superdome to 104 decibels when New Orleans special team member Brian Milne recovered a fumbled punt by the Rams' Az-Zahir Hakim that sealed the Saints victory.

Keith Montgomery of New Orleans told the Picayune what it was like to be a New Orleans fan in the Dome last Saturday: "To be at the Superdome was definitely a thrill," Montgomery said. "It was just awesome to see the city come together. It didn't matter if you knew the person that you were sitting next to, or whether you were black or white, but the city came together. Everybody was high-fiving everybody. It just really brought everyone together ... ."

I'm not big on high-fiving, but there was no escaping it. A young man sitting behind me tapped me on the left shoulder, and I thought he was going to ask me to sit down. When I turned around, there he was with his arm raised waiting for one of those high-fives.

It was 1995 when I decided to purchase season tickets to Saints games. They weren't that expensive, and there wasn't a lot of demand. The Saints have had a few winning seasons, and they have been in the playoffs. However, they didn't win any post-season games until Saturday's thriller.

Now, they are headed to Minnesota for a divisional playoff game Saturday against the Vikings. Saints fans will remember Jan. 3, 1988, when New Orleans lost its first playoff game at the hands of the Vikings, 44-10.

First-year Saints Coach Jim Haslett, a miracle worker, is confident and so are his players. Some fans have said a win in Minnesota doesn't matter, considering how far the team has come. However, you know deep down they don't mean that and want the streak to continue.

The odd-makers have New Orleans as an 8-point underdog, and maybe that's for the best. The three touchdowns the Rams scored in just six minutes in the fourth quarter proved to the Saints that they aren't invincible.

Members of the New York media are also discounting the Saints possibilities.

"Forget the Rams. They're done," Gary Myers of the New York Daily News wrote following Saturday's game. "The road to the Super Bowl just became a lot less risky for the Giants. You can almost see straight from Giants Stadium all the way to Tampa (site of the Super

Bowl) this morning. The Rams were the only NFC team for the Giants to fear."

Like a lot of other folks in this part of the country, I certainly hope Myers is eating a lot of crow late Saturday afternoon or following the Giants-Philadelphia Eagles game Sunday.

The Saints have been described as a "team of pickups and castoffs," and the starting backfield and primary receiver aren't expected to play. The team has lost nearly a dozen key players to injuries.

"We've got quite a team in the training room," said Randy Mueller, the Saints general manager who — along with Haslett — is an architect of the spectacular turnaround this season.

Bernie Miklasz, a columnist for the St. Louis Post-Dispatch, may have paid the Saints their greatest compliment.

"In other words, the Saints were the better team," Miklasz said after his team's loss. "They were certainly the more efficient team. The smarter team. And probably the hungrier team. The true, new, undisputed champions of the NFC West."

How about this for wishful thinking? The Saints win at Minnesota, and the Eagles upset the Giants. It could happen, and that would bring the NFC championship game back to New Orleans. I just happen to have a couple of tickets for that possible matchup.

The best quote of the last 34 years came from one of the Saints radio announcers in the final minutes of last Saturday's game. After Milne recovered that muffed punt to clinch the playoff victory, he shouted, "There is a God after all."

Jan. 4, 2001